Car Safety Wars

Car Safety Wars

One Hundred Years of Technology, Politics, and Death

Michael R. Lemov

FAIRLEIGH DICKINSON UNIVERSITY PRESS
Madison • Teaneck

Published by Fairleigh Dickinson University Press
Copublished by The Rowman & Littlefield Publishing Group, Inc.
4501 Forbes Boulevard, Suite 200, Lanham, Maryland 20706
www.rowman.com

Unit A, Whitacre Mews, 26-34 Stannary Street, London SE11 4AB

British Library Cataloguing in Publication Information Available

Library of Congress Cataloging-in-Publication Data
Lemov, Michael R., 1935- author.
Car safety wars : one hundred years of technology, politics, and death / Michael R. Lemov.
p. cm.
Includes bibliographical references and index.
ISBN 978-1-61147-745-0 (cloth) -- ISBN 978-1-61147-746-7 (electronic)
1. Automobiles--Law and legislation--United States. 2. Automobiles--Safety regulations--United
States. 3. Automobiles--United States--Safety measures. I. Title.
KF2212.L46 2015
629.2'31--dc23
                                        2015005602

ISBN 978-1-6114-7747-4 (pbk:alk paper)

∞™ The paper used in this publication meets the minimum requirements of American
National Standard for Information Sciences Permanence of Paper for Printed Library
Materials, ANSI/NISO Z39.48-1992.

Printed in the United States of America

For Penny, Becky, and Doug with love

Contents

Acknowledgments

One hundred years of automotive technology, politics, and history make for a long and turbulent story. I could not have written it without a great deal of assistance from many dedicated and knowledgeable people. I am indebted to all of them for their invaluable help. Most are referred to or quoted in the book. There are a few people who deserve special thanks.

Nate Jones of George Washington University, my research assistant for two important chapters of the book, was always thorough and accurate. Louis Lombardo, who served with the National Highway Traffic Safety Administration for twenty-seven years, was a most knowledgeable fact expert. Clarence Ditlow, of the Center for Auto Safety; Carl Nash, adjunct professor of engineering at GWU; Michael Stanton, chief executive officer of the Association of Global Automakers (who was also with the Alliance of Automobile Manufacturers); and Edward Cohen of Honda and former staff counsel, Senate Commerce Committee, all offered unique perspectives. Adrian Lund, president of the Insurance Institute for Highway Safety, and Ben Kelley, formerly IIHS's senior vice president, have my special thanks for their invaluable assistance.

In particular, former Secretary of Transportation and senator Elizabeth Dole has my thanks for her willingness to furnish personal views and recollections of the auto safety struggle at the upper levels of government. And my great thanks to my friend Joan Claybrook, the former administrator of NHTSA, who furnished great insight for this book.

Zoe Davis and the staff of the U.S. Senate Library furnished unfailing and excellent research assistance. Floyd Nelson, my literary agent, consistently gave us sound and thoughtful advice. Steve Roth read the manuscript, Christine Retz copyedited it. Katrina Stirn typed the manuscript, Bonnie Becker handled photographs. And Harry Keyishian of Fairleigh Dickinson University Press has my gratitude for believing in this book and in me.

Most of all, my lasting love and deep appreciation to my brilliant wife, editor, and advisor Penny Lemov.

Any omissions or errors are my responsibility alone.

Bethesda, Maryland
September 2014

Prologue

There are more than 211 million licensed drivers in the Unites States. Every day they collectively make millions of driving decisions. Should they text a friend, or answer a telephone call? Should they exceed the posted speed—by just a couple of miles an hour? Should they run through that yellow traffic light? Should they keep driving when they feel tired, or are just a little bit tipsy?

If one of these drivers makes a single mistake, should he or she, or a friend, or a pedestrian pay for it with their lives?

Marina Keegan was a promising Yale graduate, class of 2012. She had just completed her undergraduate studies magna cum laude. On a May Saturday just after graduation, she was dozing in the passenger seat of a Lexus ES-300 driven by her boyfriend Michael. They were driving on Route 6 in Massachusetts, returning to New Haven after visiting family on Cape Cod.

A talented, idealistic writer on the staff of the *Yale Daily News*, Marina had worked summers for the *New Yorker* magazine and the *Paris News*. She was president of the college Young Democrats. Her folk musical "Independents" was scheduled to open that summer at a New York City film festival. In four days she was due to start a coveted job as an editorial assistant at the *New Yorker* in Manhattan.[1]

Marina was a striking young woman. She had long chestnut-brown hair and bright, dark eyes. She burned with literary ambition. She and Michael were on a post-graduation celebration. She was probably thinking about her future and the things she might do with her ideas and ideals. Marina and Michael were both wearing lap and shoulder belts.

She never returned to New Haven. Michael fell asleep at the wheel and lost control of the Lexus. The car veered right and struck the right-hand guardrail. The Lexus careened hard off the rail, crossed the road, and hit the opposite left-hand guardrail almost head-on. The car rolled over twice, landing on its roof directly over the passenger side. The roof of the car collapsed, killing Marina instantly. Michael survived with only minor injuries. According to the Yarmouth police department, there was no evidence of speeding or any other traffic violation.[2]

"This was a classic far-side rollover caused by a weak roof structure," said Clarence Ditlow of the Center for Auto Safety in Washington. "The driver on the near side (Michael) seldom suffers serious injuries. The far side, and its passenger (Marina), are usually the second side to impact." The car, Ditlow explained, strikes with great centrifugal force. The passenger often suffers serious or fatal injuries. That is the result of an inadequate Federal Motor Vehicle Safety Standard (FMVSS) for roof strength, which was first issued in 1971. It was not upgraded until 2009, with a phase-in period for new vehicles ranging from 2013 to 2017. "She was the victim of years of lobbying which persuaded the government to issue and retain the inadequate standard," he said. "It has lasted for almost 40 years. It has failed to save a single life. Ironically, cars made in the 1960s, before the standard took effect, had stronger roofs than those made afterward."[3]

Shortly after her death, Marina's mother Tracy Keegan recalled: "By putting her pen to paper, or her fingertips to her computer, she wanted to take things that she felt needed attention and use her amazing intellect to try to make a difference in the world."[4]

A driver error cost Marina her life. Did it have to? A safer roof design might have allowed her to survive a common type of car crash.

The year 1966 was a turning point in the history of automobile safety. Men, women, and children were being injured, some for life, in great numbers in automobile crashes. Traffic deaths, which had been rising steadily for years, hit about 51,000 that year. Many of the deaths and injuries related to the way in which American cars were designed. It is a sad part of our national history.

The rate of death in 1966 was 5.5 people for each 100 million vehicle miles driven or 50,894 people killed that year.[5] Since the advent of the automobile in 1900, over 3.5 million people have been killed in motor vehicle accidents. Currently, about ten people die each year in car crashes for each 100,000 living Americans. In addition to the yearly death toll, about 2,300,000 motorists and pedestrians are injured, some disabled for life *each* year. The economic cost of these so-called "accidents" was $50 billion a year in 1966. It had risen to $230 billion by 2000 and a staggering $871 billion by 2010, which includes the cost of deaths, injuries, lost wages, medical expenses, property damage, pain and suffering, and all the other costs of automobile crashes.[6] The numbers are so large they are almost impossible to grasp. The suffering of the families and friends, like Marina Keegan's Mom and of the others killed and injured over the decades, can hardly be imagined.

Among the multiple causes of any car crash may be a reckless, drunk, or distracted driver, or just a very bad driver decision. But all too often over the years the deaths and injuries stemmed from the design and quality of the cars sold and enthusiastically bought by Americans. As a nation we long ignored the life-saving potential of innovations such as lap and shoulder belts, air bags, anti-lock brakes, energy-absorbing steering columns and safety glass.

For decades preceding the passage of the National Motor Vehicle and Traffic Safety Act in 1966, manufacturers, government, and the "safety establishment" focused the public's attention almost exclusively on the elusive goal of making better drivers, not making better cars. Cars were mostly sold based on attractive new styling and increased horsepower, not safety. The public, the manufacturers said, would *never* pay for safer cars.

This book is not a critique of the automobile industry. Its leaders had reasons for trying to avoid a federal motor vehicle safety law and most of the resulting safety standards. They argued that safety standards would be very costly to car owners and would restrict designs which the public wanted. They also said that mandatory standards would stifle the economic growth of the automobile industry and that the goal of a "safe" car was mostly unattainable anyway.

There were exceptions. Individuals like Robert McNamara who, before he became Secretary of Defense under presidents John F. Kennedy and Lyndon Johnson and later the architect of the Vietnam War, was a safety-conscious vice president of Ford. There were some domestic manufacturers—more often foreign producers, such as Volvo and Mercedes-Benz—that offered cars with optional safety features, such as lap and shoulder belts and frontal air bags.

To be sure, industry executives were and are part of a vigorous, competitive system that produces millions of jobs and places a high premium on this year's bottom line. They must weigh the cost of sometimes unseen or unappreciated safety devices, such as stronger roofs, back-up cameras, collapsible steering columns, and padded dashboards.

Not surprisingly, part of the blame for over half a century of neglect must go to our political system. For a long time America's politicians feared the automobile industry's power, its money, and the possible effect on the economy of mandating safer automobile design. After all, as Charlie Wilson, the CEO of General Motors (and also a one-time Secretary of Defense) said, "What is good for the country is good for General Motors and vice versa."

Yet this story is ultimately the history of a triumph. It is about the individual doctors, policemen, engineers, and safety advocates who saw what was happening on the nation's roads. It is about how they changed America. By winning an unequal battle to force safer cars on a reluctant car industry, a disinterested government, and an unaware public, they sharply reduced the highway carnage and helped change the public's attitude toward safety and toward more crashworthy cars. This book is, in the end, a success story.

It has become popular in the America of today to damn the government and government regulation—and to call for less of it. Three conservative policy stars—Congressmen Paul Ryan, Eric Cantor, and Kevin McCarthy, once wrote "We are offering Americans the same choice as

Ronald Reagan did more than a quarter of a century ago, when he said: "It is not my intention to do away with government. It is rather to make it work. . . . Government can and must provide opportunity, not smother it; foster productivity, not stifle it."[7]

Yet, government's role in regulating certain industries is a fundamental duty and a means of protecting the public safety. Motor vehicle regulation offers a dramatic case in point. The mandates and incentives ultimately imposed on an unwilling industry have saved millions of lives—and done nothing to harm the industry's long-term growth over succeeding decades. If the Reagan-Ryan policy that "government is not the answer, government is the problem" is true and not merely an effort to free some business constituencies from what they view as burdensome safety, environmental, and financial regulation, a look back over a century at the life-and-death struggle between citizen-advocates and the then-largest industry in the nation may be enlightening.

By 2012, forty-five years after the enactment of the National Motor Vehicle and Traffic Safety Act and the dozens of safety standards it forced on the automobile industry, there had been a change. Americans had compelled a new direction in automobile design and manufacture. As important, there had been a cultural change, a shift in people's attitudes about the need for safer cars. The political system, in large part due to a series of stunning blunders in the 1960s by General Motors and other manufacturers, finally responded.

The number of automobile accident deaths dropped by almost half between 1966 and 2012 to about 33,600 a year. The rate of death per 100 million miles driven, a seemingly better measure of the danger, under downward pressure from dozens of new federal and state vehicle and highway safety standards—from lap and shoulder belts, to air bags, to collapsible steering columns, to safety glass—also dropped 77 percent, from 5.5 to 1.1 deaths in 2012.[8] The difference in the U.S. death rate between 1966 and 2010 adds up to an astounding 2.9 million lives that were *not* lost, the avoidance of millions of permanent injuries, and of hundreds of *billions* of dollars in economic losses that were not incurred.[9]

This remarkable progress may fade away. It may not be permanent. Periodically, it has been slowed or reversed. There continue to be major battles fought almost daily over new safety advances, such as better crash protection from rollover accidents that killed 7,400 people in 2011,[10] ineffective recalls (such as the General Motors–Chevy Cobalt ignition disaster in 2014), reducing drunk and distracted driving, and preventing ejection from a car in a crash.

The advances in automobile safety over the last sixty or so years were not solely because of federal and state safety laws and standards. Individuals often moved first. Some producers in the automobile industry broke ranks and supported new safety improvements. Thanks to a lot of federal and state money there is much less drunk driving now and wider, better-designed highways.

There are unsung heroes too: an obscure Alabama congressman who fought for federal safety standards in 1955 when politically it was very dangerous to do so; a Republican Secretary of Transportation, who ignored political pressure to move a controversial federal air bag (passive restraint) standard to final enactment. There was a senator from New York, remembered now mostly for his efforts to assist poor families, who was an early, forgotten champion of a federal motor vehicle safety law. And a there was tenacious young law school graduate who came to Washington to fight for safer automobiles. He wrote one of the most compelling social protest books of the twentieth century and went on to found the modern consumer movement.

The reader will find in these pages plenty of misguided villains, too.

But the major credit for the lives saved, the injuries avoided, and the economic losses that were *not* incurred must go to the citizen-advocates and a few political leaders who gave the nation the National Traffic and Motor Vehicle Safety Act and the state and federal safety laws and regulations that built upon it.

The credit must go to the safer automobile designs the law forced into effect and to the mostly unsung people who dedicated their lives to conceiving, enacting, and enforcing the new laws. This is their story and ours.

People will still die unnecessarily, every day, in automobile crashes. Some economists and business leaders will still argue that safety standards strangle profits and hurt the economy. The struggle for safer vehicles and for more effective government will probably never end. But what you will read in these pages is a story about an unlikely victory. About some laws and changes and the people behind them that saved millions of lives and ultimately saved what was the largest American industry. About how it happened and about what we can learn from it all.

And about whether or not we can keep it.

NOTES

1. See Marina Keegan, *The Opposite of Loneliness: Essays and Stories* (New York: Scribner, 2012), published posthumously.

2. Interview by the author with Massachusetts State Police, Yarmouth Barracks, Sergeant Timothy Whelan, June 7, 2012; Sarah Armaghan and Ehab Zahriyeh, "Cape Cod Car Crash Kills Recent Yale University Graduate," *New York Daily News,* May 27, 2012; "Wayland Woman Dies in Dennis Car Crash," *Boston Globe,* May 26, 2012.

3. Clarence Ditlow; quoted in *Huffington Post,* May 29, 2012, http://www.huffingtonpost.com/2012/05/28/yale-student-marina-keegan-dies-dead-graduation_n_1550673.html.

4. *New York Daily News,* May 27, 2012.

5. "Traffic Safety Facts," NHTSA (2012), table 2, at 18.

6. DOT HS 812 013 (May 28, 2014); see also NHTSA http://www-nrd.nhtsa.dot.gov/Pubs/811754AR.pdf, (inside cover) for 2004 estimate.

7. Eric Cantor, Paul Ryan, and Kevin McCarthy, *Young Guns* (New York: Simon & Schuster, 2010), 113.

8. See NHTSA note 5, table 2, at 18: http://www.nrd.nhtsa.dot.gov/Pubs/812832AR.pdf. There was an increase in deaths in 2012, to almost 34,000 people and in the death rate to 1.15 deaths per 100 million vehicle miles traveled. It has been attributed to distracted driving, the failure to use motorcycle helmets, and possibly causes, including an improving economy. It may, or hopefully, may not turn out to be a permanent change. "Traffic Safety Facts," National Highway Traffic Safety Administration, May 2012.

9. Interview by the author with Henry Hamburger, professor emeritus and chair, Department of Computer Science, George Mason University. The "deaths avoided" estimate was confirmed by memorandum to the author May 11, 2012.

10. NHTSA, Traffic Safety Facts, 2012 (DOT HS 812 032), table 90, at p.142, http://www-nrd.nhtsa.dot.gov/Pubs/812032.pdf.

ONE

Love and Death on the Open Road

I remember my first car. It was a bright yellow 1949 Ford convertible, with a black top and red, leather-trimmed seats. I bought it used in 1952 while I was in college. It looked hot.

My yellow Ford convertible had a shiny, red metal dash board and black tires. It had a smart-looking, pearl-handled gear shift that was mounted on the steering wheel column—not the stuffy old floor-based stick shifts of my dad's generation. On the dash there were bright silver, pointed metal buttons that I could use to work the radio, the heater, and air vents.

I was not a dangerous driver. At least I don't think so. I drove mostly around the speed limit, perhaps just a little bit faster. But, I do recall that on trips to and from school to home in New York City, when I was accompanied by gas-sharing fellow students, someone always rode in the backseat, facing backwards. They were looking out, through the often fogged-up, plastic rear window, in an attempt to avoid the state and local police. This was known as "riding shotgun."

I drove all over rural, upstate New York, with its hilly, curving, two-lane roads that were often slick and icy during the long winter months.

It seems a miracle that I survived.

My 1949 Ford did not have seat belts. Although lap and shoulder belts were already in use in military aircraft—and had been for thirty years—they were not offered on any American-made car in 1949. Lap and shoulder belts were not required in American cars, nor even offered as options, for over a decade more. I never thought about the omission.

My car's front seats folded forward, so that passengers could more easily get into the backseats. But they did not lock in place. Of course my Ford did not have air bags, known sometimes as "passive restraints." (They were not mandated by the federal government for another thirty-

1

five years.) My car did not have a padded dashboard, a collapsible steering wheel, laminated safety glass in the windshield, a five-mile-per-hour crash-resistant front bumper, or anti-lock disc brakes. It had no reinforced protection against side impact from other vehicles and, because it was a convertible, no roof strength at all. None of that equipment was available to consumers then—although its potential for making a car safer was known to many automotive engineers and to automobile industry executives as well.

Looking back now, I realize that I risked my life for freedom of the road. I survived, sometimes narrowly. Some of my classmates died that year in automobile crashes on those same roads, driving cars very much like mine.

During that same year—1952—36,088 Americans, driving similarly under-equipped automobiles, did not survive. They died in motor vehicle accidents on America's highways at the alarming rate of seven deaths per 100 million "vehicle miles traveled" (known as VMT—one of the most utilized accident death rate measures). It may seem hard to believe, but the current death rate has plunged from 7 (in 1952) to 1.3 deaths per 100 million VMT.[1] An estimated four times the number of people that die (over 100,000 per year) suffer serious or permanent injuries such as brain or spinal traumas. An estimated two million additional drivers, passengers, and pedestrians are injured less seriously in automobile crashes each year.[2] A major cause of the deaths and injuries in 1952 was the design and construction of the cars we drove; the failure of the motor vehicle industry, the government, or the public to focus on the "collision-mitigation"; or the crashworthiness potential of vehicle construction. The economic cost of automobile accidents was estimated by the National Highway Traffic Administration in the year 2000 to be $230 billion including loss of life, but without any value added for pain and suffering.[3] That was about 1,000 times the current yearly automobile safety budget of $267 million for the federal safety agency (the National Highway Traffic Safety Administration).[4]

But the real history of motor vehicle crashes, the deaths and injuries— then and now—cannot be told by statistics alone. These were and are human lives, prematurely ended, often in suffering and pain.

One Halloween night in the early 1960s four young people, two boys and two girls, were driving to a party in rural Michigan. According to authors Jeffrey O'Connell and Arthur Myers, "all the kids were in costume."[5] In the front seat of the car, Helen, a small-statured girl, was dressed as a clown. She was seventeen years old and a senior at her high school. Her escort, Bill, was twenty-one and had a reputation among the younger set in Washtenaw County, Michigan, as being a somewhat reckless driver. Directly behind Helen was Tom, a 190-pound tackle on the high school football team. They were talking and laughing, having a great time anticipating the Halloween party. Bill was driving his 1963 two-door Chevrolet a bit fast on a narrow winding road. The seventeen-year-old in the clown suit did not know it, but she had just three seconds to live.

The Chevy careened off the road, tore a track through the slippery grass, and slid violently into a utility pole. It was going only 35 miles per hour upon impact with the utility pole. Today, with good luck and adequate safety equipment, 35 miles per hour is a survivable crash speed. In fact, three of the youngsters escaped with relatively minor injuries. Helen might have escaped too, except for a couple of things. The front seat of the car, like the seat on my 1949 Ford convertible, was not built to lock in place and would fold forward with a push from behind. The instrument panel, like the red instrument panel on my Ford convertible, was unpadded and had sharp, decorative protrusions pointing directly at the occupants of the front seat.

When Bill's Chevy struck the utility pole the passengers in the backseat, including Tom the football tackle, became missiles as the car slammed into the pole and the inertial force threw Tom forward into the front seat, toward Helen. The front seat jackknifed as Tom struck it and Helen, hurling Helen forward with so much force that she hit the dashboard hard. The impact crushed her chest and ripped apart her liver. She died on the spot. Her escort, Bill, got away with a bloody cut on his arm. As he was led away by the police for treatment to stop the bleeding, Bill fought with the police officers. He pulled at his bandages. "Let me die, let me die," he cried.[6]

Bill's shock and remorse, perhaps even his youthful driving habits, might be understandable. What is less understandable is how in 1963, American cars themselves could be so deadly, even at 35 miles per hour, a survivable crash speed. Our cars were not a lot safer—although a lot faster—than those that had been produced sixty years earlier at the dawn of the automobile age.

The 1963 Chevy the kids were riding in that Halloween night had no collapsible steering column—in a crash it became a spear—and no seat belts in any seating position to prevent ejection onto the pavement or impact with the interior surfaces. It had no air bags to block head and chest impact with the front and sides of the car interiors; no dual or anti-lock brakes or electronic brake-assist to prevent brake failure and out-of-control skidding. There was no laminated safety glass[7] to prevent the knife-like slashing of a broken windshield, no padded dashboard to shield Helen's chest from the rock-like impact that crushed her. It had no locking front seats to prevent the backseat passengers from becoming missiles aimed at the kids in front.

One might ask how the federal and state governments, the automobile industry, and the driving public could be unaware of or ignore such deadly threats? How could they exist in cars and increase steadily for so many years? It is a hard question to answer.

It is over 100 years since the Duryea brothers rolled a small internal combustion engine, placed in a modified horse-drawn buggy, onto the streets of Springfield, Massachusetts. The automobile industry was a huge commercial success from its beginnings at the dawn of the twentieth century. Within a short time after its invention, the automobile became a symbol of individuality, power, and mobility for Americans. Like me, people remembered their first automobile—its color, make, model, and year. They remembered it almost as a rite of passage. Young people saw a car as an entry ticket to adulthood and romance. A car could take them where their dreams beckoned.

No industry in history started its rise to economic power and political influence amidst so favorable a climate of public opinion. Popular acceptance and a "hands-off" attitude by governments—state, local, and federal—prevailed. Deaths and injuries were apparently accepted by Americans as the price of progress. They were dealt with ineffectually, if at all, primarily at a local, traffic-enforcement level.

The number of automobiles sold each year rose sharply during the first sixty years of the century and particularly in the boom years of post–World War II economic prosperity. But the postwar years also accelerated a death spiral that had started with the commercialization of the automobile at the beginning of the twentieth century.[8] By 1966 (when the first federal safety law was passed, but not yet implemented) about 51,000 people died in automobile crashes. The number rose to about 54,000 in 1972, before the federal safety act fully took effect. For the preceding sixty years, deaths and injuries in car accidents had increased annually to more than two million people killed and injured each year, every year. Even after the federal law was enacted, the number of crash deaths continued to rise until older cars were off the roads and were replaced by newer models that met new government safety standards, such as seat belts and other safety requirements.[9] State laws and regulations, such as mandatory seat belt use laws and 21-year-old minimum drinking-age laws, followed and played a major role.

Safety was not a big concern when the automobile industry got its start. The fight was for a fair share of the transportation market—against the horse, railroads, boats, and even the trolley car. There were some people, however, who had a vision of the horseless carriage's potential and its dominant future.

At the turn of the twentieth century, Colonel Albert A. Pope, then the largest bicycle dealer in America, predicted that "inside of ten years there will be more automobiles in use in the large cities of the United States than there are now horses in those cities." Pope added, somewhat proudly, that his 15,000 bicycle agents throughout the nation "were fairly howling" for automobiles "to meet an enormous demand."[10] When the Ford Motor Company was started in 1903, one of its original financial investors happily exclaimed "Now the demand for automobiles is a perfect craze . . . and it is all spot cash on delivery, and no guarantee or strings attached of any kind."[11]

Horseless Age, one of the growing number of newspapers and magazines devoted exclusively to the surging popularity of all things automotive, was pleased to report:

> Fanatical opposition to the automobile is on the whole very rare in this country. The metropolitan dailies occasionally print strong editorials denouncing speed excesses and careless driving, but the whole press is practically unanimous in recognizing the automobile as a legitimate pleasure vehicle and destined to a great future in the commercial world."[12]

The automobile industry easily fulfilled the predictions of Colonel Pope and the automotive press. Cars replaced the horse, streetcars, railroads, bicycles, and even human feet as the primary means of transportation by the time the twentieth century was a decade or two old. By the time Henry Ford's Model T, introduced in 1908, was withdrawn from production in 1927, this single, mass-produced, low-priced model had sold an amazing fifteen million cars. During that decade, the ratio of cars to people in the United States exceeded that of any country in the world. There was one car in America for every five people. Canada and New Zealand tied for second, with one car for every ten people. England and France were tied for sixth place with a car for every forty-four people.[13]

The industry's growth continued, with a brief pause for the World War II years. By 2013, U.S. motor vehicle dealers sold more than fifteen million cars and light trucks annually. Today there are over 265 million motor vehicles registered in the United States—almost as many cars, vans, and light trucks as America's 314 million people.

I did not realize it when I bought my Ford convertible in 1952, but my initiation into America's love affair with the automobile came at a gruesome time. When I bought my car, the number of deaths had risen by 25 percent since the end of the war in 1945 and the subsequent surge in car-buying frenzy.[14]

The best thinking at that time was that the death and injury rate from car accidents was mostly due to "driver error." It was a theme adopted early and repeated often. Government and the private sector appeared largely blinded in their attempt to staunch the flow of blood through driver education and public safety appeals. This was particularly evident every July 4th weekend, when annual predictions of the number of people who would die over the coming holiday weekend were given major press attention. An enthralled public seemed to accept the explanation of driver error and tolerated the carnage.

Within a few decades, the automobile industry became the largest manufacturing sector in the nation and the world. It now employs over four million people worldwide.[15] It invests hundreds of billions of dollars in the manufacture and sale of automobiles, vans, and trucks in America and worldwide. One author noted in 1995 that jammed bumper-to-bumper on a six-lane highway, the earth's 350 million cars would stretch for 200,000 miles, or eight times around the world and two-thirds of the way to the moon. It was graphic symbolism of the continuing indispensability of the automobile to American and world commerce.[16]

Bruce Barton, a mid-twentieth-century advertising legend (of Batten, Barton, Durstine & Osborn fame—Madison Avenue's famous BBDO) who is credited with naming General Motors, attempted to describe the personal and emotional significance of the American automobile by recalling the remarks of one oil company executive:

> Friends, it is the juice of the fountain of eternal youth that you are selling. It is health. It is comfort. It is success. And you have sold merely a bad smelling liquid at so many cents per gallon. . . .You must put yourself in the place of men and women in whose lives your gasoline has worked miracles.[17]

The United States became a nation on wheels. The popularity of the automobile literally drove the American economy into the twentieth century. The automobile industry, by most measures still one of the nation's largest,[18] supported the growth of many other industries, including gasoline production and sale, hotels and shopping malls, automotive parts, and road construction. Automobiles promoted the development and continued growth of the nation's suburbs, as well as the traffic jams and air pollution that go with them. It cannot be said, even if anyone had foreseen all of this, that the automobile has been an unmixed blessing.

There was no great outcry over what a few doctors began calling an "epidemic" on the highways. The public did not react, nor did government, with the exception of largely inadequate state traffic-control and registration laws. Most of all, motor vehicle manufacturers, then almost exclusively General Motors, Ford, and Chrysler, did not react. For decades they pretty much ignored the problem.

"Collision avoidance" was the predominant safety principle during the first sixty years of the century.[19] The safety establishment argued that three factors made up the driving environment: the driver, the road, and the vehicle. Many organizations worked hard to make these three components work the way they were supposed to. Manufacturers assumed the duty of designing automobiles that had reliable brakes and steering and did not have mechanical malfunctions. Safety-related design flaws were another matter entirely. The road-construction industry and government agencies created methods for building straighter, smoother, more durable roads, culminating in the authorization and federal funding of the interstate highway system in 1956 during the administration of president Dwight Eisenhower. Many safety organizations, automobile clubs, insurance companies, local governments, and the motor vehicle manufacturers focused on teaching motorists to drive without crashing. "Rules of the road" defined what the driver's responsibilities were by legislating speed limits and driver registration. Intense educational efforts, financed in large part by automobile manufacturers and designed to encourage drivers to drive "safely," were led by groups like the National Safety Council and the American Automobile Association. The automobile "safety establishment" came to believe that while roads and vehicles might be contributing causes to accidents, the primary factor was almost always the driver's recklessness or error. Little attention was paid to automobile design.

Before 1965, the "safety establishment" included the automobile companies, the insurance industry, the National Safety Council, the American Automobile Association, similar drivers' organizations, and state safety officials. Predictably, they focused on driver education and tougher traffic-law enforcement as the antidote to the growing epidemic of death and injury on the highways. When it came to marketing their product, automobile manufacturers agreed that safety did not sell. In fact, industry leaders at times pressed competitors to steer clear of the safety issue.

In 1956 Ford Motor Company, facing stiff competition from new Chevrolet models from GM, broke industry ranks and offered a "Lifeguard Safety Package" as an option on some of its its1956 cars.[20] Based on crash results during Ford's own tests and testing by Cornell University's automotive crash-injury program, Ford offered two standard features and three safety options on its 1956 Fairlane and Crown Victoria models. The standard features were a "deep center" steering wheel to prevent occupant impalement by the steering column and "double grip" door latches to prevent occupant ejection during a crash. The options were front and rear lap-only seat belts, a padded dash board with recessed instruments, and a safety glass rear-view mirror. Led by its young "whiz kid" Ford vice president Robert McNamara, it mounted a major advertising campaign to push its safety package.

GM did not like Ford's campaign. It pressured Ford to recognize that emphasizing safety could harm sales by all car companies. GM, much larger than Ford, threatened a price cut in its competing Chevy models if the safety campaign was not discontinued. McNamara took a long vacation for "health reasons" and the Ford safety campaign ended within a year. The belief that "safety does not sell" became accepted wisdom.

There is, however, persuasive evidence from Ford's own records that it actually sold an additional 200,000 cars *because* of its Lifeguard safety features and that consumers wanted to buy them (even as extra-cost options). The myth that "Ford sold safety while General Motors sold cars" became the industry's Holy Grail.[21] The automobile makers (with a rare exception here and there such as Ford and Volvo offering optional seat belts in the 1950s) persisted and the industry returned to business as usual. That tended to shift public and government focus away from crashworthiness of the car and back to the actions of the driver.

Ralph Nader, then an unknown young lawyer, fueled a change in American attitudes toward safety with his 1965 book *Unsafe at Any Speed*. He offered a different explanation for the public's apparent reluctance to demand crashworthiness in cars:

> A principle reason why the automobile has remained the only transportation vehicle to escape being called to meaningful public account is that the public has not been sufficiently supplied with the information nor offered the quality of competition to enable it to make effective demands . . . for a safe, non-polluting and efficient automobile. . . . The consumer's expectations regarding automotive innovations have been deliberately held low and mostly oriented to . . . annual style changes.[22]

It is more than 110 years since the first automobile fatality occurred. In 1898—just a year after the first internal combustion engine was placed in a modified horse-drawn buggy—a courteous gentleman was killed instantly by a car while assisting a female passenger stepping off a trolley car in New York City. But for the first six decades of the twentieth century the risks of automobile travel to drivers, occupants, and pedestrians were largely hidden by the scattered location of car crashes and the lack of a centralized place for collecting national information on deaths, injuries, and economic losses. There were a few doctors, researchers, and others who noted the increasing numbers of accidents and attempted to refocus the discussion. Because of the decentralized impact of car accidents and the public's almost insatiable desire for cars, the safety of the overwhelmingly popular new machine was delegated to the states and localities.

The motor vehicle industry was at first doubtful about leaving regulation to the states and localities. During the first decades of the 1900s, leading American trade journals and automotive organizations actually endorsed the idea of federal government standards, at least for driver qualification and vehicle registration, as a way of standardizing and simplifying the driving and marketing of cars and, of course, improving the prospect of increased sales. The National Association of Automobile Manufacturers petitioned both the United States House and Senate in 1902 for the enactment of legislation providing for a uniform national automobile license and later initiated a campaign to secure a national motor vehicle registration law.

Horseless Age, a trade journal of the time, went further. It called for government standards as a way of keeping "unsafely built" motor vehicles off the highways.[23] Several bills were introduced in 1907, during the 59th Congress, calling for federal regulation of speed, identification and registration of vehicles, licensing of drivers and, most significantly, the establishment of a Federal Motor Vehicle Bureau, presumably to collect injury data. In 1908, the *New York Times* reported that the National Grange had endorsed a proposal by the American Automobile Association for enactment of a federal registration law to promote uniformity among state laws in dealing with vehicle "equipment, lights, brakes, horns etc.," as well as motor vehicle registration.[24]

No proposal for a national approach to highway safety got much attention from the Congress. The legislators appeared concerned that regulation of the safety and operation of motor cars was primarily a matter for the states and localities and not within the legal responsibility of the federal government. Despite the authority of Congress later established by the Supreme Court[25] to regulate virtually anything "affecting" interstate commerce, questions were raised about the constitutionality of a federal law affecting motor vehicles and their operators.

Nonetheless the motor vehicle industry forged ahead. It sponsored a National Legislative Convention in Washington in 1910 to push for federal driver and vehicle safety laws. The effort was unsuccessful in getting any attention from Congress.[26] Not until fifty-six years later did Congress act—and then it was not at the request of the industry.

The states responded to concerns about confusing and different driver licensing and registration laws. State laws became more uniform and states began to recognize each other's licensing and registration laws. But the states did not do much of anything about vehicle design safety, nor could they, given the growing national scope and power of the automobile industry and its effect on interstate commerce. The trend toward uniformity of state motor vehicle registration and policing laws soon ended any effort by the motor vehicle industry and its organized supporters to obtain a national motor vehicle safety law.[27] Regardless of the rising death and injury toll in the succeeding six decades, federal vehicle safety regulation was never again requested, much less endorsed, by any motor vehicle manufacturer or industry organization. Federal vehicle safety laws remained far in the future.

The failure of the first and only effort of the automotive industry and its safety establishment allies to obtain federal legislation—to some extent addressing safety concerns—did not deter them from seeking growing sums of federal money for road construction. Congress passed the first federal highway legislation in 1916. It authorized $75 million in state aid over the next five years for the improvement and construction of highways.[28] The financial support of the federal government for building roads rose steadily to billions of dollars, ultimately resulting in funding and building the largest public works project in American history, the interstate highway system.[29] Federal support for road building never wavered.[30] No comparable effort was made to obtain federal or state vehicle safety legislation or any vehicle safety regulation at all.

Since 1900 more than 3.5 million Americans have been killed and more than three hundred million injured in motor vehicle accidents.[31]

That is three times the number of Americans killed and two hundred times the number wounded in all the wars our nation has fought in since the Revolution.[32] Most were injured or killed on the same roads the federal government was paying to build and maintain.[33]

The history of the growth of the automobile in America and of automobile safety regulation, or rather the lack of it, raises a question. How could the nation go from a handful of jalopies on small rural and urban roads to millions of vehicles sold annually and over two million injuries a year (2012)[34] without doing something drastic to reduce the toll? Why did it take us so long to learn that focusing on the "nut behind the wheel" to the virtual exclusion of the vehicle was not a productive approach? One barrier, in addition to the lack of good accident data, was that there was little money or interest in examining how people actually died in car accidents. There was minimal understanding of what happens to the human body inside a car when it hits another vehicle or some fixed object.

The rare exception to the lack of interest in what happened during automobile crashes was triggered not by car manufacturers but by outsiders like the Indiana State Police. The department was one of the first organizations to recognize the importance of detailed traffic fatality investigations in 1948.

An Indiana state trooper, Corporal Elmer Paul, was the spark plug. Paul grew concerned after his work as a trooper took him to deadly accident scenes. He became interested enough to attend a lecture given by the staff of the Crash Injury Research Project, which had been established by Cornell University. Paul's and Indiana's first fatal accident reports published in 1950 were surprisingly accurate in predicting that as many as 40 percent of the highway deaths they investigated could have been avoided with safer interiors and by keeping the occupants from being ejected from the vehicle.[35] Thus the earliest focus on safer vehicle design was triggered by aeronautical engineers, university researchers, policemen, and emergency room doctors. It was not initiated by the motor vehicle industry, or by the government.

There were some attempts to actually produce safer cars, such as that of a potential new industry competitor, Preston Martin Tucker. The Tucker Torpedo, introduced by Tucker's short-lived company in the 1940s, was a safety-oriented car. Standard features included seat belts, shatterproof glass, and a padded dash board. But Tucker could not compete with the industry giants, despite his expenditure of $22 million on the start-up company. It soon folded. So did Kaiser Corporation in 1955, after obtaining government and private loans of over $100 million. It sold over 700,000 "safer" cars, but it could not compete with the Detroit Big Three.

Their virtual monopoly in the automobile industry not only drove up their profits, but it affected the nature of their thinking toward their product and customers. In a meeting in Dearborn in 1968 regarding his company's lack of safety innovation, Henry Ford II told Don Randall, a Senate Antitrust Subcommittee staff counsel: "I am making 18 percent in profit a year. I can't be making any mistakes."[36]

But Ford, GM, and Chrysler were making mistakes, big mistakes. The oligopoly power of the industry was a major factor in its promoting and advertising annual styling and horsepower "improvements," like Oldsmobile's overpowered "Rocket V-8" engine, rather than new technologies, such as three-point seat belts (first made standard equipment by Volvo in 1959), rollover protection, and disc brakes (introduced first by Mercedes-Benz in 1958).[37]

That attitude may have been a major factor in the automotive industry's failure to react more quickly to the growing consumer demand for smaller, more fuel-efficient cars. The void was filled quickly by foreign manufacturers with cars such as the Volkswagen Beetle and the Toyota Corolla. It ultimately cost Detroit one-half of the American automobile market and was a big factor in requiring a government bailout in 2008 to save most of the American automobile industry from bankruptcy.

NOTES

1. The current death rate used is for 2012. See Traffic Safety Facts, 2012, U.S. DOT HS 812032, table 2, at 18. It increased somewhat in 2013. Some experts believe a more relevant number is deaths per 100,000 people in the country. The comparable numbers are 25.89 (1966) and 10.69 (2012).

2. Interview by the author with Louis Lombardo, January 2, 2013, formerly Research Scientist, National Highway Traffic Safety Administration, author, "Vision of a Safer America," http://www.careforcrashvictims.com. No federal or state agency compiles exact data on serious injuries. The serious injury numbers used are estimates by NHTSA and safety experts.

3. NHTSA, "The Economic Impact of Motor Vehicle Crashes" (2014) DOT HS 809 446, table 3 at 9. The total societal cost of automobile accidents was $871 billion by 2010, including estimates for loss of life, pain, and suffering. See DOT HS 812 013 (May 2014).

4. Fiscal Year 2014 Budget Overview, National Highway Traffic Safety Administration (NHTSA), 5. NHTSA also spends about $561 million for state highway safety grants, much of which affects highway and driving safety.

5. Jeffrey O'Connell and Arthur Myers, *Safety Last* (New York: Random House, 1966), 3.

6. Ibid., 4.

7. Laminated glass, which is now mandated in windshields by Federal Motor Vehicle Safety Standard 205 (49 CFR 571.205), is made with a clear plastic sheet between two layers of windshield glass, thus strengthening the windshield and inhibiting glass shattering and related injuries. Tempered glass, another type of safety glass, is not as strong and not as effective in preventing ejection of the passengers from windows. It is utilized in side windows of many cars.

8. *Historical Statistics of the United States*, millennial ed. (2006), vol. 4, part D, table: df488-456.

9. See appendix A for a current list of fifty-four primary federal safety standards.

10. James J. Flink, *The Automobile Age* (Cambridge, MA: MIT Press, 1988), 27.

11. Ibid.

12. Quoted in ibid., 129.

13. Ibid.

14. The increase from 1945 to 1952 was from 26,785 to 36,088 annual fatalities. *Historical Statistics,* ibid. See DOT HS 811 346, A-1 "Motor Vehicle Fatalities" (2008). Also available at www.careforcrashvictims.com click on MV-TRAFFIC FATALITIES (1899–2009).

15. In estimating the size of the automobile industry, we include substantial portions of the automotive parts, petroleum, tourism, and road-building industries. Direct automobile manufacturing is among the top ten industries.

16. See Jonathan Mantle, *Car Wars: Fifty Years of Greed, Treachery, and Skulduggery in the Global Marketplace* (New York: Arcade Publishing, 1995), xiii.

17. Ibid., xiv.

18. See "Ten Largest U.S. Manufacturing Industries, 2010," iStock Analyst, http://www.istockanalyst.com/finance/story/5289514/ten-largest-u-s-manufacturing-industries-2010. (Motor Vehicle manufacturing ranks ninth; World Almanac (2012), from R. L. Polk, "Top Motor Vehicle Producing Nations 2010" (the U.S ranked third worldwide).

19. See John D. Graham, *Auto Safety: Assessing America's Performance* (Dover, MA: Auburn House Publishing Co., 1989), 17.

20. Diana Kurylko, "Ford Had A Better Idea in 1956, But it Found That Safety Didn't Sell," *Automotive News,* June 26, 1996. http://www.autonews.com/apps/pbcs.dll/article? Accessed May 7, 2014.

21. Ralph Nader, *Unsafe at Any Speed* (New York: Bantam Books/Grossman, 1972), ix–xi.

22. Ibid., lxxvi.

23. Joel W. Eastman, *Styling Versus Safety* (Lanham, MD: University Press of America, 1984), x.

24. "For Federal Auto Registration," *New York Times,* December 6, 1908, 54 (ProQuest Historical Newspapers).

25. See *Wickard v. Filburn,* 317 U.S. 111 (1942).

26. Eastman, *Styling Versus Safety,* ibid.

27. Ibid.

28. Theodore Sky, *The National Road and the Difficult Path to Sustainable National Investment* (Newark: University of Delaware Press, 2011), 154–55.

29. Ibid., 170.

30. The flow of federal dollars to construct highways and roads and ultimately complete the interstate system under the Federal Highway Act of 1965 was consistently supported by motor vehicle manufacturers during the same sixty-year period that witnessed the great increase in highway deaths and injuries.

31. Louis Lombardo, "Vision of a Safer America" (12-18-08), http://www.careforcrashvictims.com, accessed 5/23/2012.

32. Ibid.; "Traffic Safety Facts, 2012," NHTSA, DOT HS 812 032, table 2, 18.

33. See Louis Lombardo, "Vision of a Safer America," supra.

34. Total vehicle registrations in 2012 were 265,000. NHTSA, Traffic Safety Facts (2012) DOT HS 812 032, inside cover and table 2, 18.

35. Eastman, *Styling Versus Safety,* 215.

36. Interview by the author with Donald A. Randall, January 3, 2013.

37. Flink, *Automobile Age,* 292.

TWO

Voices in the Wilderness

"And Sudden Death" is painful to read. The article, which appeared in the August 1935 issue of the *Reader's Digest,* came with a warning label.[1] The editor of what was then America's most-widely read magazine wrote: "The sickening details of this article will nauseate some readers."

J. C. Furnas, the author, wrote about motor vehicle accidents, deaths, and injuries. But publicizing the large numbers alone he said, "never gets to first base in jarring the motorist into a realization of the risks of motoring." Figures, he said, "leave out the pain and horror of savage mutilation . . . which means they miss the real point."

Furnas set out, thirty-one years *before* the enactment of the first national automobile safety act, to describe or stun his readers into understanding how, "Every time you step on the throttle, death gets in beside you, waiting for his chance." Even witnessing a single horrible motor vehicle accident is not enough, Furnas wrote, because this is no isolated horror story. Even a mangled body on a slab in the morgue is nothing. That picture would need to be multiplied a thousand times to include the groaning and creeping pain of dying victims as the shock wears off, the twisted legs, the crushed bones of children's bodies, the screaming of the injured, the blood dripping from shattered skulls and torn flesh.

The automobile can "become a treacherous, deadly missile." Sixty-five miles an hour "feels like nothing at all" to the driver. But "it is a speed which puts a viciously unjustified responsibility on brakes and human reflexes."

Foreshadowing the medical and engineering battles that were then decades in the future, Furnas wrote: "Collision, turnover . . . each type of accident produces either a shattering dead stop, or a crashing change of direction . . . and since the occupant continues in the old direction at the original speed, every surface and angle of the car's interior immediately becomes a battering, tearing projectile . . . [it is] inescapable. There is no bracing yourself against these imperative laws of momentum."

"Flying glass—safety glass is by no means universal yet—contributes more than its share" to the mayhem inside a crashing car. And "even safety glass may not be wholly safe when a flying human body makes a neat hole in it . . . the shoulders stick and the raw edge of the hole decapitates the body as neatly as a guillotine." In a clue as to the source of his information, Furnas wrote that what he was describing was not "just scare fiction, it is just the horrible raw material of the year's statistics as seen in the ordinary course of duty by policemen and doctors picked at random."

"If ghosts could be put to a useful purpose . . . every bad stretch of road in the United States would greet the oncoming motorist with groans and screams . . . and the educational spectacle of ten or a dozen corpses, all sizes, sexes, and ages, lying horribly still, on the bloody grass."[2]

In 1935 the *Reader's Digest* had a circulation of 1.4 million American readers. Probably some were executives or employees of motor vehicle manufacturers, or members of Congress. In a postscript the magazine offered reprints, at less than two cents a copy, to automobile clubs, schools, and "other groups interested in public welfare." Presumably, millions of copies of the magazine, or the reprints, were distributed nationally and worldwide.

There was no measurable effect. The effort failed, in terms of public reaction, legislative action, or safer automobile designs. There was no reduction in the rising numbers of deaths and injuries. They continued their seemingly inexorable increase for another thirty years.

It is inconceivable that the message of "And Sudden Death," together with the article's obvious automobile design implications, were lost on automobile industry engineers and management. The plea for the manufacture of motor cars that did not decapitate and mangle their occupants after impact could not have escaped the notice of organizations like the National Safety Council, the Automobile Club of America, the automobile industry, and governments at the federal and state level. Yet it and others like it appear to have been ignored. Little of any significance happened for a very long time.

From the beginning of the twentieth century when the "horseless carriage" was first produced commercially to the present day, the automobile became the backbone of the new consumer goods society.[3] It fueled the American economy, triggered the growth of suburbs, employed millions of workers, and supported other industries such as oil, steel, rubber, road building, and travel.

Motor vehicles have also killed more than 3.5 million Americans.[4] One historian suggests that overselling of the new machines in the roaring twenties and the growth in installment financing of car purchases created a kind of economic "bubble," which played a major role in the Great Depression of 1929.[5]

Some people were concerned about the rising death and injury rate in those early decades. But not many.

Buried on an inside page of the *Wall Street Journal* of January 12, 1927 is an article reporting on a speech by an automotive engineer who worked for the long-defunct Stutz Motor Car Company. Charles Crawford, the company's chief engineer, told a gathering of the Metropolitan New York Section of the Society of Automotive Engineers, "Safety must be the keynote of automotive engineering . . . to meet traffic conditions that are fast approaching the perilous."

Crawford quoted statistics to show that "poor design of chassis and bodies were, in many cases, contributing causes of serious accidents." He added that outside the United States, European companies had innovated four-wheel brakes and other advances. He criticized American engineers for contenting themselves with "mass production and sales." Crawford offered some specific ideas to improve the design of motor vehicles: Low center of mass to eliminate overturning, steel running boards that would act as side fenders . . . narrow corner posts, non-shattering glass for better protection of the occupants.

These were just some of his recommendations to the automotive industry and his fellow engineers.[6]

There is no record of what, if anything, happened to Charles Crawford because of his critical comments on the design responsibility of automotive engineers and of the industry. There is, however, a clear historical record that, other than a few meetings, such as a series of National Conferences on Street and Highway Safety initiated by Commerce secretary Herbert Hoover in 1924, nothing effective was accomplished to reduce the death and injury toll for another forty years.[7]

One minor exception to the years of laissez-faire came with the arrival of the New Deal in 1933. Submerged in the flood of new agencies and policies that were issued at the advent of Roosevelt's administration was the action of FDR in establishing an "Accident Prevention Conference" in 1936. It was charged broadly with investigating the causes of automobile accidents in the United States and, more important, proposing remedies. The first report of the Conference suggested a new approach to automobile safety might be near:

> A change in the power and design of cars to protect the motorist against his own folly appears to hold out the only possible hope of solution of the problem of deaths and injuries on the highways . . . slower speeds, better lights, safer body construction . . . and generally strengthening of bumpers and body parts to increase safety in cases of collision seem desirable.[8]

The FDR conference had proposed a new type of action. Much of it appeared to be based on minimizing what was later called the "second collision." The difficulty was that the Conference appeared naïve in its further conclusion about how to get from here to there: "Voluntary industry action would be more effective than compulsory action from other sources, which a growingly impatient public would demand."[9]

As it turned out, voluntary action was not merely *less* effective. It was a pipe dream.

By 1946 automobile sales, in reaction to the pent-up demand after World War II, were up to six million vehicles per year. At the same time highway deaths had risen to almost 32,000 people per year, which translated into 9.35 people for every 100 million vehicle miles traveled.[10]

Yet no one seemed to focus much on producing more crashworthy motor vehicles. The automobile safety establishment, including the National Safety Council and the President's Committee on Traffic Safety (which was reestablished by president Harry Truman in 1946) and a mesmerized public focused on producing better drivers, not better-designed cars.

The process of understanding why so many drivers and passengers were being injured and killed took a long time. A few people built on the work of others, with little help and sometimes active obstruction, from the "safety establishment." The key to reducing death and injury in motor vehicle accidents was understood to include such things as driver education to attempt to avoid accidents, stricter enforcement of traffic laws (which called for more police and more money), and construction, mostly with federal dollars, of better-designed highways. This, of course, was always the focus of the automobile safety establishment and the industry that built the cars.

Over the decades of the first half of the twentieth century, there were some investigators who began to see that the death and injury toll could also be reduced by minimizing post-crash injury and the "second collision."

The "second collision" is now well known. It is the collision of the occupants of a vehicle with its interior, or the road, after the initial impact of a car crash. Ultimately the creativity of a few scientists, doctors, and investigators, none of them a part of the automobile industry with its legions of engineers and designers, developed an understanding of what actually happens to a human body in a car crash.

It became clear that if unrestrained in a manner described in Furnas' 1935 *Reader's Digest* article, a driver or passenger would smash into something like a wall of steel, glass, or pavement. Researchers gradually developed ideas they hoped would prevent this second collision.

There ought to be an honor roll somewhere of the people who first observed the "second collision" in automobile crashes and searched for ways of avoiding or minimizing it. It seems obvious now. Eliminating all or even most driver mistakes seemed, at least by the 1930s, impossible. A certain number of drivers were going to make a driving error. Preventing or minimizing devastating injuries and deaths after a crash was something more realistically possible. Over the long decades before 1966, doctors and investigators, often working alone, came to understand that better-engineered cars might achieve that goal.

The pioneering engineers, researchers, and doctors, who often risked their lives and devoted their careers to this cause, deserve to be remembered. Their lives and labors are mostly lost now in the mists of time. They were, and will remain, unsung heroes; voices in the wilderness. How these people, sometimes accidently, stumbled upon progress is instructive.

THE FIGHTER PILOT WHO SURVIVED

The most significant development in crash-injury research may have started with the work of one man—a self-trained engineer with a doctorate in pathology named Hugh DeHaven.

In 1916 as World War I raged, DeHaven left Cornell University as a student to join the Canadian Air Force. He went to Canada because he had failed to pass the physical examination for the U.S. Army Air Corps. During flight training, DeHaven observed some of the precautions that were being taken to avoid crash injuries. Pilots wore lap belts, primarily to keep them from falling out of the cockpit, rather than for impact protection. In order to protect their heads, trainees were instructed to fold their arms and place their heads on their arms on the instrument panel in the event of an impending crash. It was not much, but it was a beginning.

Then DeHaven's plane crashed during a training exercise. The other airmen involved were all killed. It was a relatively low-speed crash with another Canadian Air Force plane. Having followed his instructor's advice by covering his head with his arms, DeHaven's head was not injured, but his arms were cut, both his legs broken, and his pancreas ruptured. That nearly proved fatal. [11]

DeHaven recovered from his injuries. He went back to the scene of the crash and examined the wrecked plane. He wanted to understand why he had survived the crash. DeHaven thought that the design of the safety belt had actually caused some of his internal injuries. But survival in airplane crashes, he came to believe, normally resulted when the pilot remained in the cockpit and, as was the case with his relatively slow-moving biplane, the cockpit remained intact.

DeHaven went on to a financially successful business career. But he never forgot his brush with death. Almost twenty years later, in 1935, he witnessed a deadly automobile accident. It revived his interest in applying his understanding of aeronautical crash survival concepts to motor vehicles. He began a long series of crash survival experiments, which included dropping raw eggs from buildings, simulating a human head, onto padded surfaces. The eggs did not break.

> I again realized that engineers didn't know, and that nobody knew, how many times people were hurt or killed by things that could be easily changed. I had seen identical injuries in airplanes, and I naturally wondered if 10, or 100, or 1,000 people had been thrown against this knob in automobiles, and if using a rubber knob would have eliminated their injuries. [12]

After years of effort and a skeptical response from almost everybody he talked to, DeHaven got an article published containing eight case studies of crash injuries. The article "War Medicine" appeared in the *Journal of the American Medical Association* in July 1942. He wrote: "It is reasonable to assume that structural provisions to reduce impact and distribute pressure can enhance survival and modify injury within wide limits in aircraft and automobile accidents." [13]

DeHaven wrote a second article four years later for the *Journal of the American Medical Association* emphasizing that, as a result of studies made at Cornell Medical School's aeronautical labs, aircraft manufacturers were already redesigning instrumental panels and control wheels to cushion impact. He thought the findings applied to automobile crashes as well. The motor vehicle industry chose mostly to ignore him.

Dehaven's lifelong effort and the work of the Cornell Automotive Crash Injury Research Program of which he was a cofounder in the 1940s and which received some modest financial support from the automobile industry was crucial. It became one of the most important leaders in the development of crash survival technology and in the six-decades-long struggle to enact federal motor vehicle safety standards.

A DOCTOR WRITES TO MR. CHRYSLER

Dr. Claire Straith has been called "the first hero of the auto safety movement." [14] About the time Hugh DeHaven was trying to get someone to pay attention to his crash-survival ideas, Straith, a practicing plastic surgeon, was seeing some terrible things in his Detroit operating room.

One of the doctor's specialties was reconstructing the faces and skulls of automobile accident victims. He noticed that accidental injuries to occupants of the front seat of automobiles were so typical and repetitive that he could easily classify them into repetitive groupings. One group Straith described was "steering post injuries." Another was injuries sustained by passengers in the front right seat, which Straith labeled the "death seat." Straith called these injuries "guest passenger injuries." Based on his observations, he wrote that steering post injuries are caused by sudden stops when the driver is jammed against the wheel. He said the victim's chin is often broken or lacerated, the jaw fractured, and the nose broken or gashed. Chest, knee, and ankle injuries were also common.

Guest passengers were in the most dangerous seat in the car because of their unprotected position in the event of sudden stops. Sudden stops caused crushing injuries against the dashboard. Occupants of the "death seat" were, according to the doctor, injured at about three times the rate of drivers.

Straith wrote articles about the kinds of injuries he was seeing in his clinic. He published pictures of the gashed and shattered faces of the victims. He recommended vehicle interior redesign to avoid the kinds of traumas he was seeing in his clinic. As early as the mid-1930s Straith recommended collapsible steering posts and padding of the dashboard in automobiles.[15]

The Detroit surgeon began a one-man campaign to eliminate injuries caused by steel dashboards, protruding knobs, hook-shaped door handles, and other interior hazards. He installed lap belts in his own car. He designed and patented a dashboard crash pad. In 1937, he wrote directly to Walter Chrysler, president of the Chrysler Company. Chrysler was so impressed by Straith's work that he ordered a redesign of the door handles in the 1937 Dodge and other Chrysler cars. Dubbed the "Safety Interior," Chrysler advertisements called it "The greatest advance since all-steel bodies." It included a smooth, flat dash board with no protruding knobs, curved door handles, and padded front seat backs. It was sold and advertised as a $510 optional purchase. Apparently it did not sell, or the company did not believe it sold well enough. It was discontinued a few years later.

Straith continued his one-man safety campaign. His ideas were again published in a 1948 article in the AMA Journal.[16] In it, Straith reproduced more graphic pictures of the disfigured faces of victims of automobile crashes that he had seen. He wrote explicitly of proposed changes in new car models that could eliminate or minimize such devastating injuries:

> For the protection of the driver collapsible steering posts have been advocated . . . raising the padding on the lower edge of the dash lessen knee injuries . . . fewer floor pedals might minimize ankle injuries.
>
> I have advocated the removal of all knobs, cranks, drop-down ash receivers, sharp edges, etc. from the dash, and the incorporation of crash padding in front of the guest passenger. . . . Fortunately some car manufacturers are becoming more aware of these dangers to the guest passenger, and are eliminating dangers . . . adding protection from the dash. It is hoped that others will follow suit to help reduce the staggering toll of accident victims.[17]

Straith's recommendations were not limited to automobile design. His epidemiological approach included (1) better traffic-law enforcement, (2)

better education of drivers and, most significantly, (3) safer vehicle engineering.

Unfortunately it would be almost thirty years before Straith's ideas
were adopted in passenger vehicle design. When they were, it was by no
means by voluntary action.

COLONEL STAPP AND THE ROCKET SLED

About the time in 1937 that Dr. Straith was approaching Walter Chrysler
concerning the interior hazards of automobiles, an obscure government
committee within the U.S. Department of Commerce reported to a safety
conference that high speed and poor exterior lighting were a major cause
of the 36,000 fatalities a year at that time. "Road surface conditions play
only a minor part," said chairman Henry Heimann of New York. "In
some sections, liquor is a factor, but there is no evidence pointing to
drunken driving being materially on the increase. Cars are being driven
too fast for lighting conditions," the report said. "While speeding up to 80
mph is not uncommon, night driving over 50 mph is unsafe." The report
advocated the radical solution of limiting the engine power of automobiles "to protect the reckless motorist against his own folly."[18]

Seventy-five years later, the concept of denying the buying public a
small amount of its testosterone-inducing horsepower seems unthink-
able. But horsepower and high speeds have always played a major role in
automobile safety and highway risk.

The U.S. Air Force was a key factor in dealing with safety and speed.
In 1947 captain Chuck Yeager broke the sound barrier in an experimental
rocket-propelled airplane. His superiors knew that supersonic jets were
just around the corner. What they did not know was whether a pilot
could bail out at such speeds and have any chance of surviving the wind
shear and deceleration forces. Some scientists then believed that the maximum decelerating force the human body could sustain was 18 Gs, or 18
times the force of gravity.

One of the problems in assuring pilot survival was to find out what
stresses an unprotected human body could live through. The Air Force
assigned the question to an unknown flight surgeon, Lt. Col. John
Stapp.[19] Stapp, the son of Southern Baptist missionaries, was born and
grew up in Brazil, received an MD degree from the University of Minnesota, and joined the Air Force medical corps at the end of World War II. A
bachelor, Stapp had a quiet sense of humor, a love of classical music, and
an unquenchable scientific curiosity.

Under his direction a 2,000-foot railroad track, designed for a rocket-
driven sled, was built cooperatively by the Air Force and Northrop Corporation at Edwards Air Force Base in California. Stapp now needed a

volunteer to ride the sled at high speed and crash into a barrier, to determine whether such an impact was lethal, or survivable.

He selected himself as the first rocket sled volunteer.

In December 1954 Stapp, then forty-four years old, strapped himself into the sled, adjusted his helmet, took a deep breath, pulled the release, reached the record-setting speed of 632 mph, and crashed head-on into a fixed barrier. The impact caused Stapp's body to decelerate to zero mph in one second, with a force of more than 40 Gs on it. His body weight had increased to the equivalent of 6,800 pounds in one second.

He was badly battered but he was not killed. Afterwards Stapp described what happened during the test: "It felt as if my eyes were being pulled out of my head. . . . I could not see."

Stapp ultimately recovered his sight. He did however, sustain retinal hemorrhages, broken wrists, and cracked ribs during his twenty-nine rides in the rocket sled. But he survived the tests and in so doing proved that properly belted and cushioned, the human body can withstand great forces in an airplane—and, by extension—in an automobile crash. It was another decade before Stapp's discoveries were mandated.

Out of Stapp's wild rides came improved helmets and better-cushioned aircraft seats. In 1955 (eleven years before the enactment of the the first federal motor vehicle safety law), he convened the first annual Stapp Car Crash Conference to consider applying the lessons of aeronautical safety to automobile design. The twenty-six guests at the first Stapp Car Crash Conference held at Holloman Air Force Base in New Mexico included representatives of the armed services, universities, and automobile manufactures. The Stapp Car Crash Conference became a regular automobile safety meeting. It served for many years as a force in furnishing test and basic data among those active in auto safety—and perhaps some motivation for improved car design.

Stapp's and DeHaven's pioneering research led ultimately to a change in focus, away from one primarily on driver behavior before accidents occurred. It forced new consideration of the structural properties of the motor vehicle as a factor in reducing or eliminating automobile injuries and deaths.

The ideas developed by DeHaven, Stapp, Straith, and other researchers were, in short:

1. build a package [the car] strong enough so that it will not collapse, thus crushing the occupants;
2. construct the doors to stay closed, thus preventing the occupants from being ejected onto to the roadway;
3. restrain the occupants so that they will decelerate with the car instead of smashing into its interior; and,

4. design the interior so that if the occupant were thrown forward, he or she would come in contact with energy-absorbing areas, thus reducing the stopping forces on the body.

The engineering research that broadened the work of DeHaven and Stapp was done at nonprofit institutions such as Cornell Medical College, Harvard University, the University of California, Wayne State University, and the University of Michigan between 1945 and 1965. There was only modest automobile-industry funding or engineering support involved.

DR. WOODWARD AND THE AMERICAN MEDICAL ASSOCIATION

A little-known subcommittee of the United States House of Representatives held an unprecedented hearing on April 23, 1958. The subject was: "Research Needs in Traffic Safety." The hearing was the first of its kind by the U.S. Congress. It focused, somewhat gently, on what additional research needed to be done in order to gain understanding of the nature of the "traffic safety" problem in the country. The automobile and its design were not in any sense the primary subjects.

The witness list was long and scholar-heavy. The subcommittee chairman, representative Kenneth Roberts, said that the subcommittee was mostly "listening," to get a better understanding of the position of professionals in the field of traffic safety, as well as the need for additional research. He noted the "excellent cooperation" the subcommittee was receiving from all concerned.

Included as witnesses that day were experts such as Dr. James Goddard of the U.S. Public Health Service, Dr. Ross McFarland of the Harvard School of Public Health, John Moore of Cornell University Medical College and its Automotive Crash Injury Research Program, and William Johnson of the National Safety Council. Also on the panel was Dr. Fletcher Woodward, a practicing ear, nose, and throat surgeon. Woodward was chairman of the ENT department at the University of Virginia Medical School and was experienced in emergency surgery. The hearing moved to a conclusion over several hours. Roberts called upon the participants for final comments. He was careful not to suggest any particular responsibility by any person or group for traffic injuries.

Fletcher Woodward, who was also serving as the first chairman of the American Medical Association's committee on automobile injuries and deaths, spoke intensely. He did not talk about funding or data gathering, as had the other experts. He spoke about his experience as an emergency room doctor:

> As the chairman for many years of the department at the University of Virginia Medical School we were responsible for the repair for the faces

and jaws of all those who were so injured in automobiles. This took us many hours of the day and frequently all night long and on weekends. Sometimes the next morning, on Sunday, we were still working. We observed . . . these injuries over a period of years. . . . Sometimes they are brought in at one o'clock in the morning as strangers. The father is dead because of an impact against the steering post. The mother is injured because of an impact against the unprotected windshield and dashboard. I recently saw a child who had been sitting on his mother's lap at the time of the sudden impact. The child had pitched forward and the door handle punched out his right eye. Well, we don't have to have a projecting door handle there. Why not a flush door handle? Those are examples of the clinical aspects that daily confront us. That is why we talk a little bitterly about poor automobile design. . . . The question of automobile design is a thing that rankles considerably under the skin of doctors. . . . And we know that automobiles can be designed that will be safer, much safer than anything we have today and it must be done. [20]

Woodward was one of those quiet people who liked to fish and shoot quail. He was soft-spoken. He talked with a leisurely southern drawl, maintained a gentle manner, and generally had a kindly smile on his face. He was not the type of person to engage in a public dispute.

Except on one subject.

As recalled in an article in the *Saturday Review*,[21] there was one thing that really raised Woodward's blood pressure. It was the human suffering of the victims of motor vehicle crashes. In 1948, based on his experiences handling emergency room cases at the University of Virginia Hospital in Charlottesville, he delivered an address to a section of the American Medical Association on "A Medical Criticism of Modern Automotive Engineering." So intense and persuasive was his reasoning that the AMA set up a committee on the Medical Aspects of Automobile Crashes. They made Woodward its chair. He toured the country for years, without pay, with a motion picture depicting the vicious reality of road crashes. He campaigned for seat belts and collapsible steering wheels.

The AMA backed Woodward with repeated resolutions by its House of Delegates and articles in *JAMA* calling for action. But again, no one in the automotive industry and not many members of the public seemed to take much notice.

Toward the end of his career in 1957 Woodward pleaded: "When the automobile death rate ranks next to our main killers—cardiovascular disease and cancer—it is indeed time to answer Cain's query and say, "Yes. I am my brother's keeper."[22]

THE LABOR LAWYER AND AUTOMOBILE SAFETY

Harold A. Katz spent most of his career as a labor lawyer. He was elected to the Illinois House of Representatives from 1965 to 1983. Katz was the author of several books and articles on labor law. In his law practice he represented mostly labor unions. He was the founder of a law firm headquartered in Chicago. Sometimes Katz's firm took on a worthy automobile accident case.

Katz was born in a small town in Tennessee. His father emigrated from Russia. He worked in a general store in Tennessee and later as an insurance salesman for the Metropolitan Life Insurance Company. Katz's father's business and his family were financially devastated by the Great Depression of 1929. Katz swept floors as a teenager to earn money for his family.

As a young man on a scholarship at Vanderbilt University, Katz was an early advocate of racial integration. He also wrote and spoke for an expanded role for labor unions in the workplace. Perhaps because of his hard early life, Katz often saw wrongs in society and wanted to see them righted. He graduated with honors from the University of Chicago Law School in the spring of 1948.

It is a somewhat surprising twist of history that Katz, then a very new lawyer, briefly shifted from his main field of interest to write a now-historic Comment for the *Harvard Law Review* in 1956, fully a decade before the enactment of National Traffic and Motor Vehicle Safety Act. It was about the prevailing legal doctrine the courts used to decide automobile liability cases. Katz challenged the law that an automobile manufacturer could not be held responsible for the negligent *omission* of safer designs, but only for production errors or mistakes.

Katz went far beyond the usual kind of legal writing. He included a section describing existing, documented "evidence of negligent design of automobiles." He referred to the findings of the Cornell Automotive Crash Injury Research Program and said they "might be presented to a jury" as proof that manufacturers should know how to make a safer car. "It has been found that fifteen years of automobile design have produced no improvement as far as their injury potential is concerned, and the data pointedly suggest that the newer model automobiles are increasing the rate of fatalities in injury-producing accidents."[23]

Katz wrote that "since the epic decision of Mr. Justice Cardozo in the *MacPherson* case, the courts have increasingly recognized that the manufacturer of a chattel has a duty of care to the ultimate consumer or user."[24] He wrote that this principle of law, while responsible for the liability of numerous manufacturers for a wide array of product defects, had not yet been applied where an alleged automobile defect was the failure to incorporate a safer design, rather than making a manufacturing error. The courts, he said, "have been reluctant to impose liability on the manufacturer."[25] He argued that the defect principle should be applied to automobile design omissions that would improve safety regarding known dangers, as well as to production defects.

He wrote that common law principles made it obvious that manufacturers should take the steps that any reasonable person in their position would take to protect their customers—the motorist and his passengers. Relying again on the investigative work of the Cornell Automotive Crash Injury Research Program, beginning in the 1940s, he described what he called "a major medical problem of epidemic proportions." He said it could and should be presented to a jury as evidence of design negligence by the car maker.[26]

For the benefit of his readers—and possibly some interested lawyers—Katz detailed some specific design omissions that might be evidence that a manufacturer had not produced a car that would avoid or minimize the "second accident" to passengers. Passengers were, he wrote, "as vulnerable as a teacup shipped loose in a barrel." He suggested these facts should be "persuasive evidence" of negligence to a jury.

His final verdict on automobile safety might have been written in a legislative preamble ten years later:

> A recent booklet by an automobile manufacturer (Ford) succinctly states the problem: "What happens to the passenger inside the car in the event of an accident? A body in motion will continue in a straight line until something stops it. . . . This is the so-called second accident which actually produces the injuries."[27]

Katz went back to police field studies where he found that university researchers and police officers studying fatal accidents in Indiana in 1951 believed that at least one-half of the victims could have survived if the design of the car had been better. In a conclusion that could not have been missed by the automobile industry, passive government officials, and cautious judges, he recommended that the law of design defect liability be changed: "It is indeed striking to observe how ineffective the law has been to date in doing anything about effectuating improvements in design to alleviate the daily bloodbath of automobile-inspired tragedy."[28]

The article seemed to have some effect. Lawyers began bringing automobile injury cases based on the negligent failure to incorporate a known safety improvement, such as collapsible steering shafts, or lap and shoulder belts. Manufacturers began to be held financially responsible by the courts for not designing their cars to avoid the well-known dangers of driving. The highway crash and the "second collision" were such risks, particularly after the publication of Katz's article.[29] Thus, in his detour from labor law, Katz contributed significantly to the automobile safety movement. He lived long enough to see change and died at age 91, in 2012.

And it is probably worth noting that one of Katz's most ardent readers was a student at Harvard Law School named Ralph Nader. "That was the beginning," Nader said fifty-seven years later. "That started it all." [30]

CORPORAL PAUL AND THE INDIANA STATE POLICE

DeHaven's articles and studies had demonstrated the validity of what many people at first viewed as his "crackpot" theories. At least they enabled him to obtain some financial support for further tests from two federal agencies, the Civil Aeronautics Board and the National Research Council. He then had the idea of going into the field to investigate the causes of actual automobile injuries and deaths and the effectiveness of seat belts and shoulder harnesses. He began enlisting state agencies to conduct on-the-ground studies. In late 1948 the Indiana State Police became interested in DeHaven's work. DeHaven visited state police headquarters in Indianapolis and gave two lectures about the Cornell project and its injury-reporting studies. While there, he met Corporal Elmer Paul who told him that he would like to undertake an automobile crash injury project in Indiana.

Paul liked cars. He had worked in an automobile repair shop while attending high school. Having become familiar with the mechanics of cars, he put his car knowledge to use when he was assigned to investigate automobile accidents by the Indiana police department. Paul told Hugh DeHaven he thought he would be able to evaluate with some accuracy the effects on human bodies of different types of accidents in different types of cars. He told DeHaven that, in responding to accidents, he had observed that sometimes people were killed or seriously injured in relatively low-speed, minor accidents. He was puzzled by this fact and motivated by it.

Paul had taken a course given by the National Safety Council at Northwestern University on accident prevention. He enlisted the help of other Indiana State Police troopers in a very preliminary study of fatal automobile crashes.

The data they gathered indicated that a large number of the injuries and deaths that they saw were due to faulty design of automobile interiors. Paul wanted a more comprehensive investigation. [31] His early findings led him to attend DeHaven's lecture, which led to his conversation with DeHaven about a broader field study.

Thus in 1950, under Paul's leadership, Indiana with some technical and financial assistance from Northwestern University and Cornell initiated a statewide study of fatal rural car accidents. An automobile crash injury department was established, with Corporal Paul, now promoted to Sergeant, as its director. After responding to hundreds of fatal accidents, the conclusion of the Indiana study was that many fatal vehicle accidents were survivable and that many people were killed or injured by the placement and design of equipment in vehicle interiors.

A year later, the Indiana State Police superintendent appeared before the National Safety Council to present the findings of Paul's auto crash injury project. Most significantly, Paul's task force had also found that forcible ejection was one of the main causes of fatal injury. At least one door had opened in 80 percent of fatal accidents they studied. The investigators added that being thrown from the vehicle generally increased the severity of injury, a finding that was directly contrary to some current opinions in the field. In the opinion of Paul's investigating police officers, almost half of the fatal accidents they studied were "survivable."

The reaction of the motor vehicle industry, in particular General Motors, to Paul's work was to set out to determine whether any degree of control could be exercised over him and the Indiana State Police department to mitigate the statements contained in future reports or press releases.[32]

General Motors sent its Director of Safety, Howard Gandelot, to Indiana, to "establish a relationship" with Paul and his group. Gandelot assured Paul of GM's "great interest" in his work. He drove Paul to Detroit for a two-day visit in August of 1951. Paul was shown some of the activities of GM's styling section and some engineering work by the company, presumably safety tests. He was hosted at a luncheon with a GM "safety group." Paul's trip to Detroit seemed to convince him that GM was indeed working hard on automobile safety. He later responded to GM's criticism that his work was too "preliminary" to be of much use. He convinced members of an Indiana legislative committee, who had condemned the automobile industry in harsh terms for not utilizing Indiana's crash injury research, to soften and then kill their critical report. With GM's "assistance," Indiana's safety studies soon ended.

One might speculate that Paul was ultimately slowed, worn down, and then co-opted by Gandelot and GM. Even with the best of intentions, an individual within a small organization in a large state department can be overmatched by the pressure and blandishments of an industry giant.

Paul's pioneering work (and the support of the Indiana State Police department) may have been slowed, but it was not lost or forgotten. It was incorporated as a major part of the comprehensive findings of the Cornell Automotive Crash Injury Research Project in 1951 that confirmed Indiana's basic field findings: Many automobile crashes are survivable if the automobile's interior is properly designed and if the occupant stays inside the vehicle.

Sergeant Paul faded from the pages of history. His determination and perceptive investigations did not. They were a forerunner of continued safety efforts. They remained a significant part of the field research that over fifteen years later produced mandatory federal and state vehicle and highway safety standards.

And as it turned out, safety might also sell some cars.

PAT MOYNIHAN'S PASSION

Patrick Moynihan served for over thirty years at the highest levels of government. He is remembered most today for conceiving a major initiative—the "War on Poverty"—while in the Kennedy administration. President Lyndon Johnson eventually adopted it and pushed it through Congress.

When Richard Nixon became president, Moynihan switched allegiances and became a White House advisor. Then he was appointed by President Nixon as ambassador to India and later, ambassador to the United Nations. Moynihan may have set some kind of record by being a cabinet or sub-cabinet officer in the administrations of four presidents: Democrats Kennedy and Johnson; Republicans Nixon and Gerald Ford.

In 1976, Moynihan was elected to the Senate from New York for the first of four terms—once again as a Democrat. He served with distinction for twenty-four years.

But long before Moynihan gained fame at the highest levels of the government, he doggedly pursued a little-known, fiercely held passion. He was committed to forcing American automobile manufacturers to design and produce safer cars. He came to his fervor in a roundabout way.

After earning a degree in economics from Tufts University, a Fulbright scholarship, and a doctorate in economics from the Fletcher School of Law and Diplomacy, he started his political career as a New Deal liberal. He handed out flyers for Franklin D. Roosevelt in the 1940s. Then, rising through the ranks of clubhouse politics, he served on the staff of New York's patrician Democratic governor Averell W. Harriman from1954 to 1958. While in Albany working for Harriman, Moynihan met a young doctor, William Haddon, who was an MIT engineer and Harvard Medical School graduate. Haddon had developed a deep commitment to traffic safety, viewing it as a medical and public health issue. In Haddon's view, automobile accidents were a "national epidemic." He wrote that all elements of the problem, including the engineering of the automobile, needed correction.[33]

Moynihan was drawn to and in some degree expanded on Haddon's idea to single out what he saw as the primary injury-causing agent: the design of the car.[34] Although auto safety turned out to be outside the main focus of his long political career, Moynihan's anger over the national epidemic on the roads and the force of Haddon's ideas played an important role in automotive safety.

In 1959 in an article for *The Reporter* magazine, titled "Epidemic on the Roads," Moynihan wrote:

> By emphasizing the individual's responsibility in automobile acci-
> dents, the Safety Council shifts public attention from factors such as
> automobile design which we can reasonably hope to control, to factors
> such as the temperament and behavior of eighty million drivers, which
> are not susceptible to any form of consistent, overall control.[35]

After setting out a basic multi-cause approach to the epidemic, much as
William Haddon did, Moynihan took on Detroit's specific role in increasing the safety of the vehicle: "Perhaps the clearest illustration of the automobile industry's attitude is the problem of seat belts. General Motors
has opposed them from the very beginning."[36]

At the Department of Labor, five years later, Moynihan initiated what
was to become one of the most significant—and least remembered efforts—to actually do something about the epidemic on the highways.
Despite the fact that the Department of Labor had little or no responsibility for automobile safety, Moynihan boldly authorized a study and report
on the effects on federal employees of unsafe automobiles. It was completed and passed on to the Senate in 1965—a perilous step for a young,
relatively low-level government appointee.

In the next few years, he wrote and spoke extensively on the subject,
including a paper given in 1966 before the Fellows of the Center for
Advanced Studies of Wesleyan University and published that year in
Public Interest magazine.[37] His writing pulled no punches, which seemed
to ensure that he would have a short political carrier:

> [F]or brute greed and moral imbecility the American automobile indus-
> try has no peer. . . . The industry is, for its size, comparably the most
> profitable enterprise in the world. These profits are drenched in
> blood.[38]

After years of involvement with the auto safety issue he had concluded
that the safety record of the automobile industry was very poor. He did
not mince his words: "I believe it can no longer be doubted, that within
the higher executive levels of the industry there has been a conviction
that excessive concern with safety is bad for business."[39]

Moynihan had statistical support for his scathing attacks. The government's National Health Survey estimated that as of 1966 there were as
many as four million persons injured annually in automobile accidents.
At least 100,000 of them were injured permanently. The annual cost to the
country was then estimated by the National Safety Council at $10.7 bil-
lion.[40] It is more than eighty times that amount now including the cost of
death, pain, and suffering.[41]

Moynihan is not remembered now for his passionate commitment to
the American automobile industry's capacity to build safer automobiles.
Nonetheless he contributed much to that result, even if the cause at times
seemed hopeless.

NOTES

1. J. C. Furnas, "And Sudden Death," *Reader's Digest*, August 1935, 21.

2. Ibid., 22.

3. James J. Flink, *The Car Culture* (Cambridge, MA: MIT Press, 1976), 104.

4. Louis Lombardo, "Vision of a Safer America," www.careforcrashvictoms.com (estimate based on data from the National Highway Traffic Safety Administration . See NHTSA DOT HS 811 346 (2010) appendix 27, "Motor Vehicle Traffic Fatalities and Fatality Rates 1899–2009."

5. Flink, *Car Culture*, 157.

6. *Wall Street Journal*, January 12, 1927. Pro Quest Historical Newspapers.

7. The approach of the Hoover Conferences is best illustrated by the remarks of president Calvin Coolidge at the 1924 Conference: "[The] solution does not rest in national action." The final 1924 Conference Report concluded: "The Federal Government's relation to the safety program is one of encouragement . . . distribution of information and use of best practices." http://www.careforcrashvictims.com/assets/24P11.pdf, 5, 15.

8. Arthur W. Stevens, *Highway Safety and Automobile Styling* (Boston, MA: Christopher Publishing House, 1941), 123.

9. Ibid., 125.

10. Susan B. Carter, Scott Sigmund Gartner, and Michael R. Haines et al., eds., *Historical Statistics of the United States*, millennial ed., vol. 4 (Cambridge, UK: Cambridge University Press, 2006), Table Df448-4456.

11. Eastman, *Styling Versus Safety*, 211.

12. Ibid., 212.

13. Hugh DeHaven, "Mechanical Analysis of Survival in Falls," *War Medicine*, vol. II (July 1942): 586–96, as quoted in Eastman, *Styling Versus Safety*, 214.

14. Eastman, *Styling Versus Safety*, 214.

15. http://americanhistory.si.edu/exhibitions/america-on-the-move.

16. Claire L. Straith, M.D., "Guest Passenger Injuries," *Journal of the American Medical Association* (May 22, 1948): 348.

17. Ibid.

18. "Safety Group Asks Limit on Power of Automobile Engines," *The Christian Science Monitor*, February 19, 1937, 2.

19. John L. Frisbee, "The Track to Survival," *Air Force Magazine*, May 1983, 54.

20. "Special Subcommittee on Research Needs in Traffic Safety," Committee on Interstate and Foreign Commerce, House of Representatives, April 23, 1958, 292.

21. Naomi Weber, "The Doctor's Prescription for Motoring," *Saturday Review*, March 2, 1957, http://www.unz.org/Pub/SaturdayRev-1957mar02-00048.

22. Ibid.

23. Harold A. Katz, "Liability of Automobile Manufacturers for Unsafe Design of Passenger Cars," *Harvard Law Review* 69 (1956): 863.

24. Ibid.

25. Ibid.

26. Ibid., 867.

27. Ibid., 868.

28. Ibid., 873.

29. Interview by the author with Joseph A. Page, Professor of Law, Georgetown University Law School, May 26, 2014; see *Larsen v. General Motors Corporation*, 391 F2d. 495 (8th Cir.1968).

30. Interview by the author with Ralph Nader, October 1, 2012.

31. Eastman, *Styling Versus Safety*, 216.

32. Ibid., 218.

33. For more on William Haddon, see chapter 7.

34. Nicholas N. Eberstadt, "Daniel Patrick Moynihan, Epidemiologist," in *An Intellectual in Public Life*, published by the Woodrow Wilson Center Press (Washington, D.C., 1998), 44, 47.

35. Daniel Patrick Moynihan, "Epidemic on the Highways," *The Reporter*, April 30, 1959, 17.

36. Ibid., 21.

37. Reprinted in Daniel P. Moynihan, *Coping: Essays on the Practice of Government* (New York: Random House, 1974), 79.

38. Ibid., 83.

39. Ibid.

40. Ibid., 79. See also Lawrence J. White, *The Automobile Industry since 1945* (Cambridge, MA: Harvard University Press, 1971), 238. According to White the $10.7 billion in economic loss included $2.7 billion in lost wages, $0.7 billion in medical expenses, $3.4 billion in property damages, and $3.9 billion in insurance administration costs. The number does not include any estimate for loss of life or pain and suffering. Another measure of economic loss offered by the author is the $10.6 billion in automobile insurance premiums paid in 1967. Today, the U.S. DOT uses a figure of $9.2 million per lost life (2013) which includes value for both economic costs and other costs including value for pain and suffering.

41. DOT HS 812 013 (May 2014), "The Economic and Societal Impact of Motor Vehicle Crashes, 2010."

THREE

Just a Congressman from a Small State

A thirty-eight-year-old lawyer from Calhoun County, in the hills of northeastern Alabama, was elected to Congress in the midterm elections of November 1950.

Ken Roberts had been the city attorney of Piedmont, the county seat of remote Calhoun County, population around 10,000. There was nothing in Roberts's background to suggest he had an interest in automobile safety, preventing traffic accidents, or consumer protection in general. Calhoun County was then, and is now, a conservative part of a politically Right-leaning state. It voted overwhelmingly for Barry Goldwater in the 1964 presidential election. It went for John McCain over Barack Obama in 2008 and for Mitt Romney in 2012.

There was no Democratic presidential candidate on the 1964 presidential ballot, just a Dixiecrat and the Republican nominee Goldwater.

Congressman-elect Roberts was, however, destined to surprise his supporters and defy his background in the years to come. He had his own ideas. And in the end, he made a lasting impact on life—and death—in America.

Roberts was born in Piedmont in 1912. He went to Samford University in Birmingham. He graduated from law school at the University of Alabama in 1935, and then opened a one-man law office in Talladega in 1936.

Roberts was a low-keyed, friendly Southerner. He was elected to the Alabama State Senate only six years after graduating from law school. He resigned shortly after his election to enlist in the Navy at the height of World War II. He served three years as a lieutenant in dangerous theaters. Except for the war years, when he served in both the Atlantic and Pacific, Roberts spent all of his adult life prior to 1950 as a mostly country lawyer.

Despite his rise to a position of some prominence in national politics, Roberts started his life as a dirt-poor kid during hard times. As a youth in the Depression, he needed to work to help his family make ends meet. He worked on the small family farm in the Piedmont foothills. He was the second eldest of four children. When he was ten, his father died suddenly. Roberts kept on working the family farm throughout his college years. His effort was essential to the family's survival. And he worked his way through college and law school.

Just before his father's death in 1931, something happened that may have had a lasting impact on young Roberts. His father had rented some land to a neighbor, a black farmer, for the purpose of growing watermelons. One night when the melons were getting big and ripe, Roberts and a young friend were tempted to sin. They invaded the tenant farmer's fields; broke open dozens of melons and had a feast. In the process they trampled on and ruined much of the tenant farmer's crop.

The reaction of Roberts's father must have come as a shock to a Southern kid at that time and place. Roberts repeated the story to his own children many years later. He had been scolded in no uncertain terms. Roberts recalled to his children that his father had talked sharply to him; told him he had ruined a poor man's crop, taken the little money the black man could earn and acted in an "unchristian way."[1]

To Ken, a devout Baptist, the reprimand must have lingered. A young man who has lost a beloved father would probably take the memory of such words very much to heart. Roberts seems to have done that. Perhaps they were one reason for his becoming a Southern liberal on racial issues . . . and on other issues as well.

As an adult he was a smallish man, about five feet, six inches in height. He spoke with a soft Southern drawl. He was friendly and outgoing, even courtly in his approach to the people of Calhoun County, his Alabama Senate district . . . and then the Third Congressional District.

"My father was a natural politician," recalled his daughter Allison Sinrod, sixty-two years later. "He had a lot of new—you might say bold—ideas about improving things for his people, black and white. He had been brought up in a small Southern town. He was a religious man. He was definitely not a slick, media-savvy politician. Not the type we have come to know in the big-money era of the new century. He was certainly not a typical Southern Democrat in those times."[2]

Allison recalls that Roberts told her he was once threatened by the sheriff of a town nearby during one of his early campaigns. The sheriff told Roberts: "You don't have to go talking to all those black people at the other end of town. Stay out of those neighborhoods and you will be a lot better off." It was not clear whether the speaker meant politically better off—or physically safer.

Roberts listened. Then he ignored the implied threat. He went back to white and black neighborhoods, shook hands, and talked to anybody he could get to listen to him, all over his district. He did not stay away from anyone. The tactic seemed to work well. He was elected and reelected to Congress and to the Alabama legislature seven times.

Despite representing a conservative district for twelve years in Congress, Roberts developed some progressive ideas, especially for a Southern politician of his era. In his years in Congress, he sponsored legislation to promote consumer welfare and public safety. He often challenged major economic interests.

Roberts introduced and pushed to enactment legislation mandating that household refrigerators be manufactured with safety locks on the inside of the door, so that children who might become trapped in them could push the door open. Not a major law but a signal of things to come. He introduced legislation requiring the labeling of poisonous household substances, promoting public-educational television, and bills providing for health care for migrant workers and Native Americans. Roberts was a congressman, it seemed, who was instinctively concerned about the well-being of a wide range of people.[3]

Of all the progressive legislation Ken Roberts introduced and pushed in his twelve years in Congress, he made his greatest impact on the toughest political issue of his day: automobile safety. In 1956, he came up with the idea of looking for a way to do something about the rapidly growing problem of traffic deaths and injuries.

Seemingly out of nowhere, Roberts introduced a precedent-shattering bill to establish a special subcommittee in the House to "study and report on the large increase in traffic accidents in recent years."[4] It was the first time that any representative or senator had offered anything like it dealing with highway and automobile safety, going back to the invention of the horseless carriage over sixty years earlier.

Roberts's resolution received absolutely no support from the Eisenhower administration, or from most members of the House of Representatives. It was ignored by major interest groups, such as the National Safety Council, as well as the automobile companies. At the time, there were no consumer organizations deeply involved in automobile safety that might have supported him. But, surprisingly under the radar, Roberts's traffic safety resolution slipped through the House and was passed.

According to one leading automobile historian, Roberts's plan to do something about the growing problem of death, injury, and property damage on the highways had very little chance of having any success: "The odds of the Roberts' subcommittee having any real impact were remote. A subcommittee composed of congressmen, little known outside their own districts, without the support of the administration, or a well-organized pressure group had little chance against the largest manufacturing industry in the country . . . ."[5]

It was an unprecedented thing to do. There had never been any general study of "Traffic Safety," much less of automobile industry manufacturing practices, authorized by the Congress. Just looking into the subject was dangerous ground for any politician, especially one who wanted to be reelected. Roberts, just one lone congressman from a small state, was on his own.

The Roberts's special subcommittee held *eighteen* days of hearings in 1956. It continued to annoy the industry and government agencies with hearings, meetings, and manufacturing plant inspections during the next eight years. But Roberts faced a continuing atmosphere of disinterest . . . or perhaps fear, over the issue from his colleagues in the House:

"Roberts was surrounded by apathy and opposition in Congress and with hostility from the automobile industry and its traffic safety establishment. Even taking a look at the problem was suspect."[6]

He became known, somewhat derisively, as "seat belt Roberts," based on one of his seemingly radical proposals to have the automobile companies offer seat belts in new cars. He did not allow the apathy to bother him. He was, in fact, way ahead of his time.

Roberts never got the mandatory federal seat belt law he wanted. Nonetheless, by the time he had finished his so-called "Traffic Safety Study"—halted by his surprising defeat in the 1964 election—it had become much more than a "study." His work led to the first federal law directly mandating the safer design of automobiles—at least for the 36,000 cars purchased each year by the federal government. He also authored a unique, but minor, federal safety law prohibiting something known as "evaporating" brake fluid, which was at the time being sold to car owners.

What led Ken Roberts, a small-town lawyer from a small state, to undertake such a major fight, involving so much political risk? The answer remains mostly a mystery.

Two personal events in his life may have triggered Roberts's long campaign for safer motor vehicles, which started out being innocuously called "Traffic Safety."

One occurred at the time of his marriage to his wife Margaret in 1953. On the newly married couple's trip back to Washington from a honeymoon in Virginia, their car was rear-ended by another vehicle at high speed. The crash threw Roberts's young bride against the glove compartment and the dashboard. Roberts hit the steering wheel so hard that he dented the wheel. They were both badly shaken up, but not seriously injured.

In the trunk of their car the couple had stored their wedding gifts, including cups, plates, and glassware. As they limped back to Washington in their damaged car, Roberts decided to find out what had happened to the glassware gifts. "Don't bother," said Margaret. "It is not even worth looking. They are all smashed up." Roberts thought so too, but he stopped the car anyway. They took the cartons of wedding gifts out of the smashed trunk and began opening them up. To their surprise, nothing had broken. The dishes and crystal had been carefully packaged in boxes, with tissue paper and other wrapping. All of the gifts survived the collision without damage.[7]

It made the young congressman wonder if people in automobiles could be better packaged as well.

The second incident occurred about a year later in 1954. A group of Puerto Rican nationalists attempted to publicize a demand for independence for Puerto Rico by gaining admittance to the House gallery. Then they drew hidden weapons and fired down at the members on the floor of the House. Five congressmen were wounded. One of them was Ken Roberts. He was in a hospital for months convalescing from serious wounds.

Roberts recalled: "While I was in the hospital, I began to think about what I could do to save some lives, since my own had been so miraculously spared. I thought about my experience with the glass stuff in that car collision and realized that no real study had ever been made of this thing, about the possibility of making automobiles safer."[8]

The brush with near death on the floor of the House seemed to lead Roberts to a new cause, one that would stay with him for the rest of his life.

Roberts did not approach the subject of automobile safety, or the giant automobile industry, in an unfriendly manner. He was after all a Southern gentleman at heart. He attempted a voluntary and cooperative solution—at least at first. And he was dealing with the largest, most powerful industry in the country.

At the opening hearing of the Special Subcommittee on Traffic Safety of the House Committee on Interstate and Foreign Commerce in July 1956, Roberts as chairman read from House Resolution 357, which he had introduced and which had established the new subcommittee.[9]

Congress' first effort to broadly investigate the problem of motor vehicle safety was guarded in its wording. The resolution noted the "large increase in traffic accidents during recent years." It referred to "excessive speed, intoxication and lack of adequate inspection" as probable causes of the large increase in the number of highway accidents. It referred to conducting an "investigation and study of measures which *may* be taken by the federal government to *assist* in eliminating such accidents or reducing their frequency and severity."

The wording of the Roberts resolution is significant. It authorized only an "investigation and study"—a report by the subcommittee to the Commerce Committee and then possibly, if approved, to the full House. No federal legislation or even consideration of legislation was suggested in the resolution.

Congress knows very well how to tell a subcommittee to draft proposed legislation. In this case the powers that controlled the House and the Commerce Committee did not do so. The vague wording of the bill does not signal that any major involvement in the traffic safety issue by the federal government was foreseen by the House leadership, Committee chairmen, the House Rules committee, and perhaps even Ken Roberts. As with most House bills, it was a carefully negotiated document. Yet Roberts may have had some new ideas that were not shared by House leadership.

The tradition of state and local regulation of automobile and traffic safety issues remained strong in 1956. That may be why H. Res. 357 slipped through the House almost unnoticed by the economic powers that then controlled automobiles, highways, and traffic safety in America.

Roberts continued the same quiet, cooperative approach in opening the first hearing of the subcommittee:

> Certainly a problem created by human ingenuity in the development of the modern automobile and our national highway network can be met in a measure by giving it serious thought and earnest consideration. By calling attention to some of the problems and pointing out what serious minded and dedicated men in various fields of activity are doing, the subcommittee hopes to accomplish much in promoting efforts to reduce this highway slaughter. . . . The subcommittee is well-pleased with the spirit of cooperation we have met on all sides.[10]

Roberts asked senator Paul Douglas of Illinois to be his first witness. His choice was significant. It is clear that Roberts admired the progressive senator from Illinois. But more likely he invited Douglas because of Douglas's recent outspoken statements on the need for strong action to address the increasing traffic death and injury toll.

Douglas had just lost a fierce fight with the Senate leadership and the automobile industry on the subject. His resolution to set up a subcommittee in the Senate similar to the Roberts subcommittee in the House had been soundly defeated. The Senator was not pleased. He was not as gentle in approaching the safety problem as Roberts.

Douglas told the Roberts subcommittee in 1956:

> The country looks to you with high hopes. Gentlemen, if a scheming enemy of the United States were to touch off a series of catastrophes that in each year took the lives of more Americans [than] were killed in battle in the Korean War, and injured from 10 to 20 times the number wounded in that bloody struggle, the people would demand and get protection against this terrible slaughter and these wanton injuries. The American people are in fact now experiencing just such a destructive slaughter. . . . I would like to particularly stress the need for going into the question of automobile design. . . . Great economic interests and activities are bound up in this question . . . in formulating the resolution I introduced in the Senate. . . . I was convinced that this was one of the most important areas to be investigated.[11]

Roberts continued building a record of that "slaughter" throughout 1956 and for eight years afterward. The House was generally a harder environment for consumer legislation than was the Senate. It was easier for the big-money lobbyists to convince the Representatives, who had smaller, less costly districts in which to run than those of the Senators, of the "wisdom" of their employer's needs and of the political danger of opposing them.

The subcommittee was all over the country: in Columbus, Indianapolis, Chicago, and in several Southern cities. It heard from doctors, judges, engineers, dentists. It met with the American Medical Association, all the automobile manufacturers, and with the National Safety Council.

Most of the hearings that the Roberts subcommittee conducted between 1956 and 1963 were technical—even dull. They focused on the need for better traffic-law enforcement, more crash injury research data, and, ultimately, on better car design. Roberts called researchers from the Cornell Automotive Crash Injury Research Project to testify, including its director John Moore, a supporter of seat belt requirements. He called Air Force Colonel John Stapp, who had risked his life repeatedly, crashing a rocket-propelled sled into fixed barriers to test the human body's resilience. Then Roberts called Dr. Fletcher Woodward, chairman of the Committee on Automobile Injuries and Deaths of the American Medical Association.

Woodward's testimony suggested that something of a change of attitude might be taking place in the medical community, among some automotive engineers, and perhaps in the country; a movement that might be asking for government action on the problem. But Roberts continued with his cooperative attitude toward the automobile industry and the apparent public indifference toward automobile safety and deaths. "We have asked a number of leaders in several diversified fields of research to come here today to tell us what progress has been made . . . ," he said gently a couple of years later.[12]

He said the subcommittee was functioning "largely as a listening post, so that we may better understand the position of the professionals in the traffic safety field." Clearly Roberts was treading carefully.

Buried deep in the record of the fifty-year-old hearing is the testimony of Dr. Fletcher Woodard on behalf of the American Medical Association, with surprising recommendations for action:

> The engineers and designers of the automobile, a relative handful of men in the industry, virtually control the destinies of the American public on the highways. They are the men who decide which of safety designs we put into, or are left out of next year's new automobiles. . . . There is presently an ample body of research data which clearly indicates the definite values of certain safety features of automobile design, construction and equipment. Yet these safety features are all too often made available as optional equipment at extra costs . . . in recent years

safety has generally been ignored in favor of other developments. The following suggestions have been repeatedly advanced by physicians, researchers and safety engineers with little success: anchorages for seat belts, an improved steering wheel, safety door locks, elimination of sharp pointed hood ornaments . . . . [13]

Woodward also reported on a 1955 resolution adopted by the AMA House of Delegates. For the first time the AMA had called for "The President of the United States to request legislation from Congress, authorizing appointment of a national body to approve and regulate safety standards of automobile construction."

It was a stunning proposal, orchestrated in large part by Woodward himself. After many years, the cautious AMA had urged federal automobile safety legislation. But the testimony compiled by Roberts's subcommittee over eight years, including the legislative proposal by the American Medical Association, seemed to fall on deaf ears.

Roberts spent a week in Detroit with the subcommittee, visiting manufacturers of cars and manufacturing facilities, in an attempt to stir up press and public interest in obtaining new state or federal safety legislation—or even voluntary action by the automobile industry. There was little interest in the issue by the industry or the press, and less by the general public. [14]

It was almost as if people were not interested in facts. They had already reached their own conclusions about what was killing people on the highways. They had come to accept the safety establishment's assertion that it was not the car, or the roads. It was irresponsible drivers that were the real cause.

It is not easy to change people's minds once they have made them up.

Timothy Wilson, a professor of psychology at the University of Virginia, has written about how and why people change their minds and their behavior. [15] Real-life stories seem more powerful than data, said Wilson, as reported in the *New York Times*. [16] Stories allow people to identify with the problems of other people because they identify with them emotionally. The same was undoubtedly true of politicians and executives who had for decades, publicly blamed irresponsible drivers for motor vehicle deaths and injuries and downplayed the role of the vehicle. They had the culprits. They needed something more than some "facts" such as Roberts was developing to change their already firmly made-up minds. So did the American public. They needed war stories.

That facts have far less impact than real life stories in changing people's minds was established by Roberts in his eight years of auto safety fact gathering. The public (and the safety establishment) had a conceptual—and often economic—stake in the belief that bad driving causes most accidents and their deadly results.

Perhaps the public did not know enough personal, real life stories about some individual they might have known and loved to induce them to rethink the established wisdom on the causes of automobile deaths and injuries. Nor did they have the information necessary to visualize what happens to a human body in a crash. The minds of the public and the industry, not to mention the press, seemed closed to the facts the Roberts subcommittee was regularly putting on the public record.

Eventually, about 1957, Roberts came to the reluctant conclusion that "the industry was dragging its feet. From the first day in Detroit, I came away feeling they were never going to do anything unless you made them do it. They just didn't want to be bothered. They would come around with the business of putting the blame on the driver. It's hard to change human nature. So if you take that attitude you are licked to start with."[17]

As a result of its first series of hearings the subcommittee filed a report recommending the use of seat belts in all automobiles, presumably voluntarily by the car makers and hopefully, by drivers and passengers. It got some publicity, but it was a subject of much humor in the House and was brushed off by fellow House members. Roberts said, "We were laughed at. They called me 'Seat belt Roberts.' The members just didn't take any interest."[18]

So Roberts tried to get the states involved in his automobile safety campaign. He cosponsored something called the Beamer resolution, after its sponsor Republican John Beamer of Indiana. It recommended that the states "coordinate national efforts" on automobile safety voluntarily. It passed easily, with the enthusiastic backing of the automobile industry. It was a clear effort to divert and sandbag Roberts, submerge major safety issues, and to get the federal government out of the picture. But Roberts, seemingly blocked on all other fronts went along with it.

In fact, over time the Beamer resolution may have helped stimulate states like New York, Iowa, and Massachusetts to hold hearings and propose new state laws, particularly seat belt laws, promoting safer automobile designs. Some states began to put pressure on Washington to take some action.

In 1957, the persistent Roberts led his subcommittee in a report proposing that uniform highway safety laws should be enacted by all states. The report recommended expanded research on accident causes, expanded driver education, and improved court administration, but no new federal law. It did not focus at all on vehicle design.[19]

Roberts was not deterred by the lack of much response. But perhaps he was becoming a bit frustrated. He was quoted in the *New York Times* in 1957, with a not-so-conciliatory message to the industry.

At a hearing in Michigan, General Motors' vice president for engineering, Charles Chayne, had defended the new higher-powered "muscle cars" then being intensely marketed by all American companies, with an incredible argument.

With a straight face and no apparent factual support, Chayne claimed that the reason for the manufacturers' new emphasis on increasing the horsepower of current models was that it actually made them "safer to drive."[20] GM followed up with a demonstration that day. It was designed to prove to the subcommittee (and whatever members of the press happened to be in attendance) the surprising claim that in many situations, such as passing another car on a two-lane road, or in crossing a busy intersection, more horsepower actually made cars safer for the occupants.

Chayne told the Roberts subcommittee, "The advantages of higher horse power cars manifest themselves in a car's performance—its ability to accelerate, its ability to respond to the driver's command."[21]

In other words, when in doubt GM's witness suggested . . . floor it.

Roberts and fellow subcommittee member Sam Friedel of Maryland seemed shocked. They expressed doubt about GM's theory as expressed by Chayne. And they added that the automobile industry would accomplish more by installing safety devices such as seat belts, as *standard* equipment on their cars. Chayne replied: "It is customary to offer many extra cost items as optional equipment first, to ascertain whether the public likes them and would use them."[22]

Roberts was unconvinced. He said the subcommittee was getting a lot of mail "criticizing the automobile companies for overselling speed and underselling safety."[23] It seemed to the subcommittee that if speed and style, not safety, was being advertised almost exclusively—well that was what buyers would ask for.

A second report issued by the subcommittee in 1957 went further: "All known and tested safety devices such as crash padded paneling, padded windshield visors, dish type steering wheels, safety glass, etc. [should] be included as *standard* equipment on all model cars."[24]

The press quoted Roberts as saying, "Safety requirements come first . . . and the car manufacturers should understand that. We would prefer them to take protective action voluntarily, rather than to have corrective federal legislation."[25]

The industry ignored him. Their approach was captured later by Elizabeth Drew in an article in *The Atlantic*: "And back in Detroit the giant $25 billion-a-year auto industry nestled comfortably in its corporate cocoon, content in the knowledge that this was the pride of private enterprise, the backbone of the American economy (accounting for nearly one sixth of it) and the only major transportation industry free of government regulation."[26]

But Roberts was beginning to be noticed. He spoke at the Governors' Traffic Safety Conference in Sacramento in 1958. He sounded uncharacteristically angry. "I'm frankly tired of hearing that our drivers are delinquents, alcoholics, and incompetents." According to the *New York Times* report on the event, Roberts blamed the automobile manufacturers for a "large percentage of the increasing highway traffic death toll." [27]

By 1962, Roberts had had about enough of volunteerism. He was the keynote speaker at the Governors' Conference on Metropolitan Washington Traffic Problems. He acknowledged that maybe effective auto safety measures might still be taken at the state and local level, but he criticized the automobile industry for refusing to adopt many recommendations, some of them his own, that would immediately make cars safer to drive.

And Roberts issued a prediction that he could not possibly have known would ever come to pass. He said, without much legislative support for his position, that the federal government may assume "a larger role in traffic safety enforcement if local officials failed to curb the annual highway slaughter." [28] Roberts was ultimately unsuccessful in his attempt to obtain voluntary action from Detroit, in altering motor vehicle design and deemphasizing horsepower.

So, in 1958 he changed course. He proposed legislation requiring that the 36,000 automobiles purchased by the General Services Administration for the federal government be required to meet mandatory safety standards to be set by the federal government's GSA. Roberts thought if he could get the government to require safer designs, the rest of the automobile market would soon be forced by public opinion to follow suit for all models.

The GSA bill was passed by the House of Representatives three times between 1959 and 1962. It was opposed by the General Services Administration itself. it was supposed to run the program and set the safety standards—not a good sign. It was also opposed by the automobile makers. Surprisingly, it could not get past the Senate, [29] which in later years would be a driving force for automobile and consumer safety bills.

It was not until 1964 that Roberts found a way to get the GSA bill through the Senate and enacted into law. It developed out of a conversation he had with senator Warren Magnuson, the powerful chairman of the Senate Commerce Committee.

Roberts later described how he worked a classic Washington end-run maneuver to rescue his GSA standards bill. [30] He said, "Basically it was a matter of lobbying. There are only 100 senators, and the auto boys are very effective. They have about 30 people working on the Hill." [31] That was more than enough to handle the U.S. Senate, at least until Roberts and Magnuson had their talk in 1964.

After three failures at trying to get the GSA measure out of the Senate Commerce Committee, Roberts at last succeeded. Perhaps it was because of Magnuson's newly appointed, consumer-sensitive staff, Jerry Grinstein and Mike Pertschuk. They proved to be masters at moving many consumer safety bills over the years. Or perhaps it was because of some horse trading regarding a commercial fishermen's health care bill. Magnuson badly wanted it reported out of Roberts's House Commerce Committee. Either way, Roberts got the support of the senator for a possible deal.

Roberts managed to get Magnuson's fishermen's health care bill out of the House Commerce Committee. It was no easy task since it would cost the government some money. Magnuson, in return, pushed Roberts's GSA automobile safety bill through his Senate committee and then the Senate. The General Services Administration safety standards law may have seemed small potatoes at first, covering only about 36,000 government purchased vehicles a year. But it turned into a precedent. [32]

The GSA, in response to the Roberts's legislation, proposed seventeen modest safety standards which would be required, as standard equipment, in all 1967 cars bought by the federal government. The standards included:

Anchorages for seat belts;
Padded instrument panels and visors;
Impact-absorbing steering wheel and column displacement;
Safety door latches and hinges;
Stronger anchorage of seats;
Safety glazing materials for windows;
Dual operations braking systems. [33]

"Seat belt Roberts," whom the Birmingham Chamber of Commerce had derided as a "do-gooder," had triumphed over the automobile industry.

Detroit did not take the defeat lying down. It reversed course. The car manufacturers immediately installed most of the required, minimal equipment on all vehicles purchased by GSA and all others in the United States. They could now claim credit for having acted voluntarily, before the government standards could actually go into effect. Then the Automobile Manufacturers Association went about attempting to lobby a *reduction* of the specific levels of the standards that the General Services Administration was writing. This was not difficult. The GSA had little expertise in car design and less money to hire engineers. It was forced to rely on industry expertise. The industry urged limitations on the scope of standards on protruding door knobs and controls and also on impact-absorbing steering wheel assemblies. And it succeeded in reducing the GSA specifications for those and other safety standards. The auto manufacturers then increased their prices to the public and the GAO $50 per car in exchange for the "safety package." And this despite the fact that when mass produced the features involved arguably cost no more than a few dollars per vehicle. [34]

Ken Roberts never could get his big federal law, mandating national safety standards for all new cars, passed by Congress. The opposition from the industry was just too strong. The government was uninterested. Buyers seemed unconcerned. But Roberts accomplished something very important. Powerful senators like Abraham Ribicoff (Connecticut), War-ren Magnuson (Washington), Bill Nelson (Wisconsin), Robert Kennedy (New York), and John Danforth (Missouri) began to see the possibility of a change in public thinking on the subject and thus in the possibility of national automobile safety legislation.

"Roberts couldn't get any publicity on what he was doing. He was just a congressman from Alabama," said one historian."[35]

Shockingly, Roberts was upset in his run for reelection for a seventh term in November 1964. It is not clear if the motor vehicle industry ac-tively recruited or aided his virtually unknown opponent. But the circumstantial evidence is damning.

Roberts was a popular congressman. His previous margins of victory were large. He was a six-term incumbent. They are usually quite hard to beat. The man who beat him was Glen Andrews, a little-known Republi-can who had just jumped from the Democratic Party to side with Barry Goldwater in his unsuccessful run for president that year.

Andrews then served just one term in Congress before losing his seat to a Democrat in the 1966 election. During his one term, Andrews gained notice as something of an extremist, by voting against the Voting Rights Act of 1965.

Did the automobile industry help defeat Ken Roberts in 1964 because of his sponsorship of automobile safety bills? Its exact role in Roberts' defeat remains a mystery.

While on a train in 1964, Roberts heard he had lost his reelection bid. He was returning from Alabama to Washington with Margaret and his two children. They heard reports of his defeat on the radio. "I remember my Mom broke down and cried," said his daughter Allison. "My dad just shrugged it off. He went back to mostly being a small-town lawyer. He continued to work for safer automobiles for the rest of his life."[36]

President Johnson put Roberts on the National Transportation Safety Advisory Committee after his defeat in 1964. He was appointed counsel to the Interstate Vehicle Safety Commission created by the Beamer bill he had sponsored. But he never had a chance to vote in Congress for what he really wanted: a National Traffic and Motor Vehicle Safety Act. It was passed, in a major shock to the automobile industry, two years later. Roberts was back practicing law in Alabama and in Washington when the law was passed by the House and Senate and signed by President Lyndon Johnson in 1966.

Before he died in 1989, Roberts went back to live in Anniston to be near his Alabama family. He was old and sick. Allison, who was hoping to improve his health, asked him to come to Maryland, where her family lived. "I was very close to him," she recalled. "I tried hard to get him well. He could no longer talk. But I knew he would want to see the U.S.

Capitol again. So I had the ambulance drive from Union Station, around the Capitol where he had served so long ago. He saw the big white dome, all the American flags flying and it really perked him up. He got stronger. He seemed to rally."[37]

Ken Roberts died three days later. The last words he heard, spoken by his daughter were "We love you, Dad."

NOTES

1. Interview by the author with Allison Sinrod, February 8, 2012.

2. Ibid.

3. Tribute to Congressman Kenneth Roberts, Congressional Record, 101st Congress, June 21, 1989, by Senator Howell Heflin at http://thomas.loc.gov/cgi-bin/query/z?r101:S21JN9-76:

4. H. Res. 357, 84th Congress, 2nd Sess. (1956); printed in hearings, "Traffic Safety," (committee print) Interstate and Foreign Commerce Committee, July 16, 1956.

5. Eastman, *Styling Versus Safety: The American Automobile Industry and the Development of Automotive Safety, 1900–1966* (Lanham, MD: University Press of America, 1984), 242–43.

6. Ralph Nader, *Unsafe at Any Speed* (New York: Grossman/Bantam Books 1965), 253.

7. O'Connell and Myers, *Safety Last*, 215.

8. Ibid.

9. H. Res. 357, 84th Congress, 2nd Sess. See Hearings Before a Subcommittee of the Interstate and Foreign Commerce Committee, Investigation of Highway Traffic Accidents, House Doc. July 16, 1956, 1 ("Roberts Hearings").

10. Roberts Hearings, 1.

11. Ibid., 2.

12. Roberts Hearings, Committee on Interstate and Foreign Commerce, Special Subcommittee on Traffic Safety, April 23, 1958, 1–3.

13. Ibid., 39.

14. Morton Mintz, "Capitol Reading," the *Washington Post*, March 29, 1966, A14. Mintz wrote, "*Safety Last* contains some criticisms—some justified, some not—of the press. But it slights the biggest blooper of them all—the totally inadequate coverage of the auto-safety hearings started a decade ago by former representative Ken Roberts. Had these hearings been properly reported, it is possible that an aroused public would have spurred auto safety legislation long ago."

15. Timothy D. Wilson, *Redirect: The Surprising New Science of Psychological Change* (New York: Little Brown and Co., 2011).

16. Maggie Koerth-Baker, "How to Move a Mind," *New York Times Magazine,* August 19, 2012, 14–15.

17. O'Connell and Myers, *Safety Last*, 216.

18. Ibid.

19. "House Unit Urges U.S. Highway Code," *Christian Science Monitor*, January 7, 1957, 5.

20. Damon Stetson, "High-Power Cars Defended By GM," *New York Times,* August 28, 1956, 29.

21. Ibid.

22. Ibid.

23. Ibid.

24. "Traffic Danger Factors Listed by House Group," *New York Times*, January 8, 1957, 18.

25. "U.S. Law on Safe Car Construction Seen," *New York Times*, August 4, 1956, 14.

26. Elizabeth Drew, "The Politics of Auto Safety," *The Atlantic*, October 1966, 95.

27. "Car Makers Blamed in Highway Deaths," *New York Times*, October 3, 1958, 56.

28. "Federal Program on Traffic Safety to Curb Deaths Seen," *Washington Post*, September 26, 1962, A-1.

29. O'Connell and Myers, *Safety Last*, 217.

30. Ibid.

31. Ibid., 218.

32. Ibid.

33. P.L. 88-515, 1964.

34. O'Connell and Myers, *Safety Last*, 220–21.

35. Ibid., 222.

36. Allison Sinrod interview, February 8, 2012.

37. Ibid.

FOUR

Safety Doesn't Sell

"I believe it can no longer be doubted that within the higher executive levels of the industry there has been a conviction that excessive concern with safety is bad for business."[1] These were the words of future senator Pat Moynihan in 1966, repeated in 1974, in his book *Coping*.

When Moynihan, then a mid-level appointee at the Department of Labor under President Kennedy, first offered this assessment of the automobile industry's safety record, it was a dangerous thing for a bureaucrat to do. It was, however, based on Moynihan's experience. He had served several years as governor Averell Harriman's chairman of the New York State Traffic Safety Policy Committee. It was also, from Moynihan's point of view, based on the explicit statements of automobile industry executives. And it was documented by the unremitting annual increases in highway deaths and injuries since the invention of the automobile at the dawn of the twentieth century.

The National Safety Council estimated that in 1966 there were 1.9 million people injured annually in automobile accidents.[2] At least 100,000 of them were injured permanently. The annual economic cost to the country in 1967 was estimated by the National Safety Council at that time to be $10.7 billion.[3]

It is more than eighty times that amount now based on government (NHTSA) estimates.[4]

During the first six decades of the twentieth century the American automobile industry seemed wedded to the idea that safe design was not its responsibility. There was no public demand, it was said, for safer automobile design. Nor did the industry seem to think it had much responsibility to inform the public about the risks of vehicle design and the omissions such as lap and shoulder belts.

In the years before the enactment of the National Traffic and Motor Vehicle Safety Act in 1966, better-designed motor vehicles might have saved millions of drivers and passengers from death and injury in what had by then become known as the "second collision." This is the collision of the driver and passengers with the interior of their own vehicle during a crash.

The basic physics of the "second collision" were described by Hippocrates in the fourth century BCE when he contrasted the greater severity of wounds inflicted by a sharp penetrating object with the less-serious wounds produced by a blunt weapon. This established that when force is distributed over a larger area (say by safety belts over the shoulders, chest, and pelvis) rather than a small area (the face or head of a driver or passenger) the force per unit of area is much less.

Similarly, two centuries before the invention of the automobile, Sir Isaac Newton defined the relationship between velocity and deceleration of a moving object. Simply put, the *greater* the distance over which vehicle deceleration occurs the *less* injurious the force that is imparted to the occupant body, such as the head and neck. For example, the two-foot deformation, or crushing of the front end of a vehicle, is the stopping distance of an unrestrained passenger before striking the interior of the vehicle. In the same car, the stopping distance of the same passenger wearing a lap-shoulder belt, would be much greater, as the car decelerates over many feet, causing less injurious forces to the neck, skull, and body.[5]

Detroit automotive engineers, of course, knew about these basic principles and problems of the physics of automobiles. Since at least the 1930s they had also known of some promising solutions.[6] But their employers who called the shots were deterred either by cost, perceived engineering problems, or marketing considerations from doing anything much about applying them. Mostly the companies sold annual styling changes and more horsepower.[7]

The reaction of the motor vehicle industry, dominated by General Motors, Ford, and Chrysler, to the increasing toll of death and injury (from about 33,000 deaths per year in 1950 to 53,000 in 1969)—was consistent. The manufacturers placed primary blame on the driver and on driver attitudes.

Joel W. Eastman, in his seminal work *Styling Versus Safety*,[8] summarizes the conscious oblivion of the manufacturers:

> Automobile manufacturers, echoing the reasoning of the highway professionals, took the position that it was not normal for a motor vehicle to be involved in an accident, and that therefore, they were under no obligation to design for that circumstance. Manufacturers asserted that not only were automobiles "safe" when properly utilized, but that they were also becoming "safer" as a result of improvements introduced with each new annual model.[9]

Eastman disagreed with that conclusion:

> In reality, the industry had found it difficult to use engineering improvements to a technically complex product as a means of selling automobiles to relatively uninformed consumers. Instead the industry had come to emphasize fashion or "styling" altered on an annual basis in order to make previous models appear old fashioned. . . . Rather than producing safer automobiles . . . competition in styling resulted in motor vehicles that were sometimes even more hazardous than previous models. [10]

Executives of the major automobile manufacturers were quite explicit in expressing their attitude toward the safety of their product and the absence of any pressing need to improve it. As automobile accidents increased in number and severity from the 1920s through the 1960s manufacturers responded by increasing their support of and influence over the "highway safety movement." It emphasized driver education and driver responsibility for accidents. It was led by the National Safety Council and motoring clubs such as the American Automobile Association, with financial assistance from the manufacturers.

Lee Iacocca, general manager of Ford Motor Company in the 1960s—and later president of both Ford and Chrysler—put it simply: "Styling sells cars," he said, "and safety does not." [11]

Writing years later Iacocca had seemingly changed his views:

> Ever since the 1956 [Ford safety] campaign I have been quoted as having said that "Safety doesn't sell," as though I was making an excuse for not making safer cars. But that's a severe distortion of what I said and certainly of what I believe. After the failure of our campaign to promote safety features, I said something like: Look fellas, I guess safety didn't sell even though we did our damnedest to sell it. . . . I was a safety nut and I still am. [12]

About the same time, William Mitchell, director of styling for General Motors, was sufficiently unconcerned about the safety issue to tell a *Fortune Magazine* reporter in 1956 that safe cars would appeal "only to squares—and there ain't any squares no more." [13]

This is not to say that the American car industry completely ignored the safety of its products in the decades before the 1960s. It was simply not a priority. For example, in 1908 John O'Leary patented a "smart fender" that was designed to deploy a net to push pedestrians out of the path of an oncoming car. Henry Ford was an early advocate of stronger door latches to keep occupants inside the car. Cadillac developed an electric starter, largely to end injuries caused by cranked starter kickbacks. [14]

In a full-page advertisement published in the January 1935 issue of the *Journal of the Society of Automotive Engineers* [15] Ford emphasized its "center-poise," a new suspension design that "combines comfort with stability and safety as never before."

In 1937, Norman G. Shidle, editor of the *Journal of the Society of Automotive Engineers*, surveyed the new models. He wrote,

> Further attention to safety and safe driving features is evident. . . . In this category perhaps may be listed devices for keeping windshields clear of frost and snow; driver seats which adjust vertically as well as horizontally; refinements in steering mechanisms . . . detailed improvements in the size and functioning of brakes. [16]

In contrast to the words of Iacocca and Mitchell was the statement of at least one automotive engineer. In 1956 Roy C. Haeusler, Chrysler's first chief safety engineer, seemed to break ranks, saying that his job and Chrysler policy was to "provide all *practical safety features* [emphasis added] that appear likely to reduce the driver's probability of having an accident—or to reduce the severity of injury should an accident occur." [17]

In retrospect, Haeusler deserves credit for raising safety issues, particularly in the face of the lack of priority expressed by much of the industry's top executives. But Chrysler's safety chief added a kicker:

> By practical safety features we mean those that are likely to be accepted, used and appreciated by the driving and riding public. When considering the possibility of offering [the] shoulder harness, for example, we must face the fact that [the] shoulder harness is less convenient to use than the lap type seat belt and it is only natural that a smaller segment of the public is likely to accept it." [18]

So speaking for Chrysler in 1956, Haeusler said that one of the most effective safety devices known at the time—the three-point lap and shoulder belt—which is now required by the government in all cars—was conditional on its use and acceptance by the driving public. The public, however, was simultaneously being bombarded with advertising that promoted styling and horsepower. It had little information about the life-saving potential of three-point belts.

The universal use of combined lap and shoulder belts did not happen for another twenty years. And when it did happen, it was by no means a voluntary change by manufacturers.

In the early 1960s, a modest cloud appeared on Detroit's horizon in the form of state legislation offered in New York, Massachusetts, and Iowa to mandate lap and shoulder belts and a few other vehicle safety standards. The attitude of the manufacturers to these bills was predictable. John F. Gordon, then president of General Motors, found them infuriating. On October 17, 1961, addressing the National Safety Congress in Chicago, he called the trend toward regulating the safety of vehicle construction "radical and ill-conceived." [19]

"Resist the siren call of alleged panaceas" he told the assembled safety-conscious audience. "The traffic safety field has in recent years been particularly beset by self-styled experts who believe . . . that cars could be made virtually foolproof and crash proof under government regulation. This thesis is wholly unrealistic. It is also a serious threat to a balanced approach to traffic safety." [20]

Jeffrey O'Connell and Arthur Myers, authors of *Safety Last,* which was based in part on interviews with industry leaders in Detroit and a meeting with GM's safety director, had a different view. They found that General Motor's "balanced approach" to automotive safety was first, the driver was to blame; second, the roads were to blame; and finally, take a look at the vehicle. "They simply don't feel there's any money in safety," the authors concluded. [21]

As late as January 1965, when the annual death toll on the highways was almost 50,000 people a year, Harry F. Barr, vice president of engineering at General Motors told the *New York Times:* "We feel our cars are quite safe and quite reliable. The driver is the most important, we feel. If the drivers do everything they should, there wouldn't be accidents, would there?" [22]

Just after Ralph Nader published his groundbreaking book *Unsafe at Any Speed,* in 1965, attacking the overall safety record of the industry and General Motors, in particular for its design of the 1960–1963 Chevy Corvair, Henry Ford II spoke out. The chairman of Ford Motor Company told the *New York Times* that the industry was being subjected to "harassment" with regard to safety:

> "You will all agree," he said, "that we are being attacked on all sides and we feel that these attacks are unwarranted. . . . Naturally, when 50,000 people a year are killed on the roads of the United States, this is a bad situation. On the other hand, to blame it solely on the automobile is very unfair. We build safe cars and have always built safe cars." [23]

Mr. Ford went on to say that everybody was getting into the safety act.

> "We have a fellow called Nader who this morning has taken out after Volkswagen. . . . [W]ell I say we've got jobs for rear axle engineers and if he is that good we'll be happy to give him a job. But frankly, I don't think he knows very much about automobiles. . . . I don't think he knows anything about engineering safety into automobiles." [24]

So, in response to the rising public interest in safer vehicles—and on the eve of the industry's fast-approaching Waterloo—Henry Ford II was saying in 1966 that Ford had always built safe cars and that Nader was a phony.

Mr. Ford went on to assert what would become an underlying industry rationale for nonregulation or voluntary self-regulation over the coming years. He said the industry is "most important in the economic picture of the United States. . . . . Consider the problems Washington may force on the industry and the economy even before any safety law is passed." Ford warned that federal safety legislation can "upset the economy of this country very rapidly." His comments on Nader's lack of knowledge and his assertion that the industry "had always built safe cars" are refuted by the history of vehicle fatalities and injuries over the preceding six decades and by the motor vehicle's role in causing or compounding many of them.

Deep in the stacks of the Library of Congress rests an out-of-print, battered book with the intriguing name: *Old Car Wrecks*. In it anyone can see the evidence of the industry's neglect of occupant safety in its products.[25] The author of *Old Car Wrecks*, Ron Kowalke, reprints photographs of many cars involved in deadly accidents. One picture is of a 1930s sedan of unidentified manufacture.[26] The author notes many dangerous design features are obvious in the picture. The car, we are told, was involved in a head-on collision. With no seat belts to restrain the occupants during the crash, they were all hurled forward on impact, or else ejected onto the pavement. Aside from the impact on the driver of the rigid steering column and steering wheel, the windshield shows cracks from the force of at least one passenger's head hitting it. In addition, the dashboard is loaded with sharp knobs and edges that clearly did serious harm to human bodies.

Also visible in the *Old Car Wrecks* picture, with an arrow superimposed on the photo for emphasis, is a broken door hinge, a problem that plagued GM for years. According to the author, the doors were blown open in the crash, due to the car chassis flexing and the primitive design of the door-latching mechanisms. They spelled death or serious injury for the people who were riding in the car.[27]

Old Car Wrecks also includes a photograph of a rollover accident that occurred in 1952. It involved a 1948 Packard. The car rolled on its roof, which was flattened directly over the driver's compartment—and over the driver. It is highly unlikely that anyone inside could have survived.[28]

The reader can also see a shocking photograph of a car virtually identical to the 1949 Ford convertible that had given me so much youthful driving pleasure. The author comments: "Whatever this 1950 Ford convertible had a run-in with destroyed the car to the point of sheering off the carburetor and air filter canister from the top of the engine and peeling back the rag top. The crash occurred in 1954."[29] One glance at the condition of the driver and passenger compartments makes it clear that the occupants probably died or were seriously injured—in large measure because of the design of the Ford convertible involved.

Kowalke says that he did not write his book to be in any way critical of the automobile industry. He simply shows pictures of the car wrecks he and other photographers saw through the decades from 1920 to 1960.

A statement written by Ford Motor Company is also included in *Old Car Wrecks*. It reflects one industry view of that era:

> Accidents are primarily caused by attitude. One cure for accidents is to make them social errors. The automobile has created a new social order on the streets and highways and we haven't yet had time to evolve social customs such as we have in other fields of human relations. The time is coming when traffic accidents will be looked upon much as lying, rudeness, or dishonesty is now and people will refrain because of social pressure.[30]

Over the years, while death and injury on the highways rapidly increased and the economic costs soared into billions of dollars a year, the American public, according to Ford, had a bad attitude toward driving— one that could be corrected, in due course, by improved manners.

The history of the automotive industry's seemingly unyielding attitude toward the rising fatality rate in car crashes and the recommendations of critics like test pilots DeHaven and Stapp, plastic surgeon Straith, emergency room doctor Woodward and young Ralph Nader, raises a puzzling question. It is not a question of technical knowledge of what might be viewed as obvious facts, such as the field investigation results of actual second collisions, the conclusions of test pilots about the effectiveness of lap and shoulder belts, the American Medical Association's reasoning about safer car bodies and interior designs, or the Indiana police department's findings about the survivability of almost half of the fatal crashes it investigated.

The question is why the leaders of the automobile industry, the government, and a public that avidly consumed its products did not change their minds as the evidence mounted? Why is it so hard to change people's minds, whether it is about the dangers of smoking, the warming of the planet, or the design of automobiles?

One view of the attitude and reasoning of GM was offered by Marina von Neumann Whitman, who served as GM's chief economist and public affairs vice president for thirteen years, starting in1979. Whitman writes that she was forced to come to terms "with GM's deeply imbedded and profoundly dysfunctional culture." She says the automotive industry's leader had a parochial worldview, leadership by the numbers, and a "contemptuous paternalism." The result was GM's "lack of understanding, not only of its Japanese competitors' sources of strength, but even of its own customers' attitudes."[31]

The period of Whitman's service at GM (she had previously been a board member of at least six other major American corporations) put her on the executive level, the 14th floor in the GM building during the era of both new federal safety and clean air standards. Many of these, including the proposed air bag standard, were opposed and delayed by GM and other car companies for years.[32]

Another view of the automobile industry was articulated by Michael Stanton, then president of the Association of Global Automakers, which represents most foreign-car manufacturers selling cars in the United States.[33]

Stanton says that in the decades before the 1970s, industry trade associations and the U.S. manufacturers did not believe government regulation was or should be a factor in their business: "I think that for the most part, other than things like highway infrastructure, government was irrelevant to the automobile industry in the manufacture and sale of their cars . . . they didn't even have Washington offices."[34]

Stanton, who also served as manager of federal affairs and president of the Motor Vehicle Manufacturers Association (representing all the U.S. car companies) for almost twenty years, says the immediate reaction to the government getting involved in automobile design safety in the 1960s was "to push back because suddenly the legislators and regulators were telling them how to do their business. . . . The paradigm was changing as the role of government expanded. It goes to the status of the industry being newly regulated, or potentially regulated. I think there probably was a sense of Detroit knows best . . . and maybe a little bit of arrogance."[35]

Stanton says safety definitely sells cars now and they are built in a more crashworthy manner. In the 1950s and before, the belief was that safety did not sell. "Consumers value safety more now and they will pay for it,"[36] Stanton says, adding that government and the motor vehicle industry had to learn how to work together. "It is a healthy tension," he said. "We are still struggling with it."[37]

A former Department of Transportation safety attorney who dealt extensively with GM and other automobile companies for seven years in the late 1960s and 1970s, recalled his own experiences:

> I found GM's people to be superb engineers and solvers of engineering problems. For example in 1969 they came up with the solution to a complex and critical safety problem: where to place the release point of the newly developed airbag in the car without killing anybody. They did it in ninety days. But, they were totally under the control of the money guys and the design departments.[38]

GM executives were in fact intentionally insulated. They rode a special elevator directly from the parking garage to the executive floors to bypass the ordinary employees. They maintained separate, side-by-side "salaried men's restrooms" and "hourly men's restrooms," so that higher-paid employees would not have to mix with lower level workers.[39]

Understandably the industry tried to ignore Washington's ideas about building cars and the politics of public auto safety. They pushed their own view of the importance of safety in automobiles and what the public would be willing to pay for.

Until it was too late.

There are other well-documented examples of the difficulty of changing people's minds, even intelligent and well-informed minds like the top executives of major car producers.

Today, cholera remains a deadly killer in some poor, undeveloped parts of the world. But in the nineteenth century, it ravaged humans worldwide, including those in the major cities of Western Europe and America.

The cholera epidemic of 1848–1849 killed 50,000 people in England and Wales. It killed them painfully (from a lack of water in their bacteria-ravaged bodies) and quickly. In a day or two, whole families and neighborhoods were decimated.[40] No one knew the cause or the cure for this killer disease until 1849 when John Snow, a respected English doctor, published an article in *Lancet*, the medical journal, asserting that cholera was caused by water supplies polluted with sewage containing human waste which carried the disease into the stomachs of its victims. Snow based his initial findings on detailed empirical research, mapping of the locations in London of hundreds of cholera cases, and their proximity to sewage-polluted water from a single source: the Broad Street pump.[41]

Unfortunately, Snow's maps and reasoning, although well-documented, were greeted with skepticism by the British public health and medical communities. The prevailing view was that cholera was airborne. It was, according to the prevailing "miasma" theory, based on the obvious putrid smells and fetid air of most large cities. It and other theories were held by a majority of the London governing establishment, including private water companies that supplied the city's drinking water. The idea was: get rid of the stink and cholera will fade as well.

It took Dr. Snow's supporters long decades to gain acceptance of the bacterial, water-borne cholera theory that Snow convincingly documented in 1849. And the solution was very costly. It required rebuilding the entire London sewerage system and fully separating sewage from drinking water. Meanwhile, thousands of people continued to die of cholera in London and elsewhere. Ultimately London did what Snow wanted, but it finally happened long years after his death. The overhaul of the London sewage system took place in the 1870s. It was one of the largest public works projects ever undertaken.

Snow did not live to see his theory accepted and put into practice. He and his maps and research were, in fact, belittled in 1855 by the leading British medical journal *Lancet*. One hundred and fifty-five years later the editors of *Lancet* apologized in print for the journal's harsh and incorrect treatment of Dr. Snow's evidence.[42]

Why were knowledgeable British government and health professionals wedded to the false miasma theory? Different reasons can be advanced, some more persuasive than others. There were prior, incorrect scholarly reports and eminent reputations at stake. Water companies, which controlled the existing sources of supply, stood to lose a lot of money if the water they sold, and not the air, was the true cholera source. The anti-Snow forces saw obvious proof through the ever-prevalent stench of the city that everyone could plainly smell.

The rigid mind-set of London's medical establishment and political leaders is discussed in Steven Johnson's eloquent book detailing the difficult path toward change of Dr. Snow and his colleague the reverend Henry Whitehead.[43]

Ghost Map tells us something about why the important change in thinking about the cause of cholera took decades of intense effort. There are many other historical examples of the difficulty of convincing people to change their thinking to fit newly discovered ideas and facts.[44] The American experience with automobile safety is surely one of them.

No American automobile manufacturer had a designated safety department or safety engineer until about 1950.[45] Ford Motor Company did not appoint an official safety engineer until about 1955. Chrysler appointed safety engineer Roy Haeusler about 1952. General Motors established the largest department dealing with design safety within its engineering department, about 1950.[46]

Despite their apparent lack of major interest in producing cars with safer vehicle design, American automobile manufacturers had known since at least 1942 that many automobile crashes were survivable and that redesign of their vehicles could save thousands of lives and avoid hundreds of thousands of personal injuries each year. By 1942, university researchers, independent engineers, and doctors had at least preliminarily concluded that a large percent of deaths and injuries in car crashes were preventable. Editorializing in June 1946, *The Journal of the American Medical Association,* surely no bastion of radicalism, referred to crash research that began in 1942:

> Research on injuries and crashes was begun in 1942 by the National Research Council working with the Safety Bureau of the Civil Aeronautics Board and study groups in the Army, Air Force and Navy. The research was pioneered and is being carried on at Cornell University Medical College in consultation with members of the staff of Cornell and the New York Hospital. Results already available indicate that the ability of the human body to withstand crash force has been greatly underestimated. . . . Serious and fatal injuries can be avoided in many future accidents when the nature and cause of typical injuries are known. Much that is being learned about airplane crashes has applicability in the field of motor car accidents. The value of physicians' contribution to future safety through this work cannot be overemphasized.[47]

If the medical profession, observing "survivable aircraft accidents" in 1942, could see a clear parallel with the prevention of typical car injuries, would motor vehicle manufacturers, with their large engineering staffs, see it as well?

The safety consciousness of the driving public was not much better than the industry's. To some extent, the scope of the growing tragedy and economic loss on the nation's highways was obscured. Fatal and serious automobile accidents were decentralized. They happened separately on the millions of miles of federally and locally funded highways. They happened in thousands of different communities across America. Some were reported in newspapers. Some were not. More importantly, they were not collected and reviewed on a national basis.

Perhaps the only people who could have firsthand knowledge of what happened when a car collided with another object were the emergency room doctors and police officers who responded to the scenes of accidents and treated victims, or removed the remains. Some of them became advocates in the seemingly endless struggle to improve car design. Their protests were overwhelmed by the industry's attitude of "blame the driver," as well as by its advertising: attractive women posing with their stylish cars and later more horsepower in "muscle car" engines.

Joan Claybrook, who became administrator of the federal auto safety agency many years later recalls,

> The great advantage I had was that by the time I came into office (1977) television was rampant. I decided that we had to be a media regulatory agency. So we took films of all our crash tests. We promoted them on television.
>
> We had a research-safety car built [the Research Safety Vehicle] that we crash tested and filmed to show how it worked. We took it on tours all over the country. We took it up to the *Today Show* in New York and we went on the Donahue television show. We did everything we could to demonstrate to people what actually happens to your body in a car crash and why lap and shoulder belts and air bags work to protect you. Now, over the past fifteen years, since around 1995, the automobile companies have been showing their own crash tests on television as a way to sell cars. [48]

But it had become accepted wisdom by mid-century that the cause of car accidents was primarily the driver, not the car. Americans accepted the automobile industry and the safety establishment's repeated assertion: "Cars are safe. Drivers cause accidents." One could view it as a highly effective public brainwashing.

Certainly the car manufacturers did not do a lot to temper dreams of power and adventure in the minds of potential buyers. Dr. Paul Gikas, an emergency room physician in his youth, recalls a twelve-page Ford advertisement in *Time* magazine urging motorists to "cultivate a safety state of mind" even as it named one of its cars the "Marauder"—which is

defined by Webster's as one who (roams about and raids) . . . and lays
waste and pillages the countryside."[49] General Motors, not to be outdone,
published a 1965 advertisement for its Pontiac GTO that read: "There is a
live one under the hood. Have you priced a tiger lately? . . . A V8, standard in the Pontiac GTO . . . 335 horsepower. Want something wilder?
Got it. 360 horsepower."[50]

The GM advertisement was accurate as to the GTO's specifications.
What was left out was the fact that such a car and its invitation to aggressive driving was an invitation to disaster. The advertisements were made
more irresponsible by the failure of manufacturers at the time to incorporate well-known safety designs. As Ford learned the hard way in its 1956
safety campaign, derailed by GM, if one company attempts to sell safety
and its competitors do not, it might incur a price or competitive disad-
vantage in car sales.[51]

It is true that drunk driving was and is a major cause of highway
accidents. It is still a major cause of over ten thousand automobile deaths
annually.[52] It was and remains true that reckless driving was and is responsible for thousands of deaths and injuries, often among younger
drivers. But the design of the motor vehicle plays a major role—and it did
then too.

If the seats in the 1963 Chevy that Bill drove into a telephone pole had
been anchored properly; if the occupants had seat belts available and had
worn them; if the instrument panel was properly padded, seventeen-
year-old Helen might have survived a mere 35 mph crash. If the air bags
that save lives now had been made standard sooner, not as options in a
few experimental models, deaths and injuries would have been reduced
by thousands every year.[53]

There were some exceptions to the general rule that the industry did
not focus much on safety and that the motor vehicle manufacturers sold
styling and horsepower. An advertisement for a 1937 Plymouth told buyers: "Safety Interiors. . . . Every detail inside the car recessed, or padded
or redesigned for the protection of passengers . . . to eliminate minor
mishaps inside the car, bruises in case of sudden stops, torn clothing . . .
barked knuckles."

The Plymouth's safety features notably included recessed controls on
the instrument panel and "double action" hydraulic brakes."[54] But the
groundbreaking safety engineering of the 1937 Plymouth and of Ford's
similar effort in 1956 did not last, and did not warrant any mention in the
prestigious *Journal of the Society of Automotive Engineers.* The 1937 Plymouth was not an economic success. The "Safety Interior" was soon discontinued.

The motor vehicle industry did contribute some funding to safety
research. In 1958 the Automobile Manufacturers Association donated
$150,000 to Cornell University's medical school to study car crash inju-
ries.[55] Ford and Chrysler also furnished modest funding. The Cornell

program was one of the first to investigate vehicle crashes to find out how people were actually being hurt. The grants were miniscule in comparison to the profits of the major automobile manufacturers.

Despite rare exceptions, American motor vehicle manufacturers (Japan and the European companies were not yet on the scene) continued to promote driver education and better roads rather than safer vehicle design.[56] The industry strongly supported and financially assisted driver organizations, like the American Automobile Association, and independent safety organizations, such as the National Safety Council.[57] They were part of the safety establishment, which adopted the same line: driver education is the best way to reduce the toll. That—and the claim that the public would not pay for safer cars.

In 1956, Robert McNamara, later president Kennedy's secretary of defense, was head of the Ford Division of the Ford Motor Company. He was one of the so-called "Whiz Kids," most likely heading for the presidency of the company. But 1956 turned out to be a bad year for McNamara. General Motors tried to get him fired from the Ford Motor Company "for committing the sin of safety."[58]

General Motors was not without friends at the Ford Motor Company. A GM executive, acting with the express approval of the president of the company, Harlow Curtis, called Walker Williams, a Ford vice president, to express GM's "strong disapproval of Ford's safety campaign for its 'Lifeguard Safety' options in 1956 models."[59] In his autobiography, Iacocca noted, "McNamara almost lost his job because of it."

Curtis and GM were so disturbed about the heavy promotion by Ford of safety options, such as padding of instrument panels (a reprise of the 1937 Plymouth) and optional seat belts that they delivered a warning—perhaps a threat. Safety engineers in McNamara's office, particularly Alex Haynes, had convinced McNamara that safety would sell and that this was the way for Ford to outsell GM's new Chevys during the 1956 model year. Ford's sales brochures were filled with comparative crash pictures of Fords and Chevys. The Fords came out much better in crash testing. The brochures were sent to the company's dealers. Ford mounted an aggressive campaign capped by a major safety conference and seminar in Detroit.

Ford executives, many of whom had previously been employed by General Motors, understood the market power of the industry giant that had over 50 percent of the market at the time. The only slightly exaggerated saying at Ford at the time was that Chevy could drop its price $25 to bankrupt Chrysler and $50 to bankrupt Ford. When GM said "stop," Ford screeched to a halt. Ford executives got McNamara to switch gears to an advertising campaign that emphasized styling and performance rather than safety.[60]

Ford's bimonthly newsletter to its dealers, with safety brochures attached, ceased publication. Ford's advertising agency, J. Walter Thompson, scrapped its safety ads. McNamara suddenly came down with the flu. He went to Florida for a long vacation. His career hung by a thread. He later returned and came up with a successful sales year in 1957 (minus the "Lifeguard Safety" package). It secured his rising executive stature at Ford—and his appointment with destiny in Vietnam.[61]

The auto industry's most durable myth began to grow: "Ford sold safety while Chevy sold cars." The belief continued until after the enactment of federal safety legislation ten years later and a change in public attitude. It helped perpetuate another myth: motorists would reject safer cars. Sales and safety strategies don't mix.

The untruth of this claim is documented in a 1956 press release issued by Ford before the GM threats. It was called "The Public Will Buy Safety." The release stated that "since two of the five safety features—crash padding and seatbelts—[which Ford was offering that year] were optional with the customer, it was possible to measure demand by totaling up the number sold."

The demand surprised even the then-optimistic Ford staff. No optional feature in Ford history caught on so fast in the first year: 43 percent of all 1956 Fords were ordered with safety padding. Even the "Fordomatic" automatic transmission, one of the most popular options ever, was ordered by only 23 percent of Ford's customers when it was introduced in 1951. Power steering, introduced in 1953, was first ordered by only 4 percent of buyers. But during that first Ford safety campaign one of every seven buyers (17 percent) ordered the optional cost seat belts.[62]

More than half a century later, in 2012, *Consumer Reports* magazine conducted a poll of its readers on which of seven features were most important to them in the purchase of a car.[63] The responses looked like this:

Table 4.1.

Safety	90%
Quality	89%
Value	85%
Environment	65%
Performance	83%
Design/style	65%
Technology	68%

In 2013 the poll results varied only slightly, with safety placing second in consumer preferences.

Testifying before Congress in 1957 McNamara, by then rehabilitated from his case of the flu and out of the executive doghouse, testified that "the demand by the public for safety extras far exceeded our expectations. All of a sudden, instead of supplying 50 seat belts a month, or 500 buckles a month, we demanded 1,000 buckles a day . . . it was impossible to supply our dealers with stocks adequate to meet the demand at that time."[64]

But based on either General Motors' warning, or the supposedly modest sales results of the Ford safety campaign, the number two auto manufacturer dropped it and returned to pitching style and horsepower. General Motors, Chrysler, and Ford went back to business as usual. The safety features that were developed by the Big Three auto manufacturers in the next decade mostly stayed on the shelf, or were sold with minimal promotion as "extras."

Ford later reported in internal studies that its 1956 safety package, to the extent it was put on the road, minimized injury and death in automobile accidents. The safety door locks reduced door openings in collisions by up to 60 percent; the safer recessed steering wheel cut crushing injuries to the chest by 50 percent.[65]

As Pat Moynihan wrote in 1966, the automobile industry's not inconsiderable profits in the decades before the advent of federal motor vehicle safety standards were "drenched in blood." Perhaps that was a bit of an overstatement. But looking back now at the industry's efforts to delay, limit, or defeat federal safety standards it was not much off target. The industry compiled an impressive record of opposition to many obvious automobile safety improvements. It has since resisted such things as public availability of information about automobile deaths and safety defects under NHTSA's "Early Warning System," federal standards requiring three-point seat belts, passive restraint systems, better visibility and stronger roofs.[66]

Moynihan was not wrong, although perhaps he exaggerated a little. And he did something else that proved important in changing the way the government and the public viewed automobile safety. In 1965 he called Ralph Nader at his small Hartford law office. He offered Nader a part-time job in Washington to write a technical report for the Department of Commerce on automobile safety.

Nader accepted the offer.

NOTES

1. Daniel P. Moynihan, "The War Against the Automobile," *In the Public Interest* (Spring 1966), 13, reprinted in, Daniel P. Moynihan, *Coping: Essays on the Practice of Government* (New York: Random House, 1974), 83.

2. National Safety Council, "Accident Facts," 1966, 3.

3. Lawrence J. White, *The Automobile Industry Since 1945* (Cambridge, MA: Harvard University Press, 1971), 238. According to the author, the National Safety Council's $10.7 billion in annual economic loss in 1967 included: $2.7 billion in lost wages, $700,000 million in medical expenses, $3.4 billion in property damages, and $3.9 billion in insurance administration costs. The annual economic cost as calculated by the

NSC did *not* include any estimated value for pain and suffering of the deceased and injured. Today, NHTSA uses a comprehensive cost methodology and a value of about $9 million per life lost, which among other factors, increases the total estimate to $877 billion a year as of 2010. See NHTSA, *The Economic and Societal Impact of Motor Vehicle Crashes* (2010), DOT HS 812 013 (2014). According to U.S. DOT, $877 billion *includes an amount for pain and suffering in its cost estimate.* Another measure of economic loss offered by White is the $10.6 billion in automobile insurance premiums paid by car owners in 1967.

4. See NHSTA, *The Economic and Societal Impact of Motor Vehicle Crashes — 2010*, DOT HS 812 013 (May 2014), 1.

5. Paul W. Gikas, "Crashworthiness as a Cultural Ideal," in *The Automobile and American Culture* (Ann Arbor: University of Michigan Press, 1983), 329.

6. Ibid.

7. O'Connell and Myers, *Safety Last*, 5–7.

8. Joel W. Eastman, *Styling Versus Safety: The American Automobile Industry and the Development of Automotive Safety 1900-1966* (Lanham, MD: University Press of America, 1984), xiii.

9. Ibid.

10. Ibid.

11. O'Connell and Myers, *Safety Last*, 5.

12. Lee Iacocca, *Iacocca: An Autobiography* (New York: Bantam Books, 1988), 313.

13. O'Connell and Myers, *Safety Last*, 5.

14. Jerry L. Mashaw and David L. Harfst, *The Struggle for Auto Safety* (Cambridge, MA: Harvard University Press, 1990), 30.

15. *Journal of the Society of Automotive Engineers*, January 1935, 42.

16. Ibid., 15. Norman G. Shidle, ed., "Looking at the Future of Car Design," *Journal of the Society of Automotive Engineers* (January 1937): 13–14. Shidle wrote, "Economics dominate and will continue to dominate the automotive picture in America. We will get sudden changes in design when we get sudden changes in economics."

17. Roy Haeusler, "The Automotive Safety Engineer and Company Policies," *Journal of the Society of Automotive Engineers* (September 1956): 44. By 1967 (a year after the enactment of the National Traffic and Motor Vehicle Safety Act), the *S.A.E. Journal* was writing about dual and disc brakes and breakaway steering columns that were about to be mandated by the new federal safety agency (NHTSA).

18. Ibid., 45.

19. O'Connell and Myers, *Safety Last*, 5–7.

20. Ibid.

21. Ibid., 4–5.

22. Ibid., 6.

23. *New York Times*, April 16, 1966, ProQuest Historical Newspapers, 22. See http://query.nytimes.com/mem/archive/pdf?res=F5091EFF3E59117B93C4A8178FD8 5F428685F9.

24. Ibid.

25. Ron Kowalke, *Old Car Wrecks* (Iola, WI: Krause Publications, a division of F+W Media, Inc., 1997), 11.

26. Ibid.

27. Ibid., 11.

28. Ibid., 82.

29. Ibid., 96.

30. "Freedom of the American Road," published by the Ford Motor Company, 1956, cited in Kowalke, *Old Car Wrecks*, 104.

31. Maria von Neumann Whitman, *The Martian's Daughter: A Memoir* (Ann Arbor: The University of Michigan Press, 2012), 223–24.

32. Ibid., 248.

33. Interview by the author with Michael Stanton, President and CEO, Association of Global Automakers, August 28, 2013. The members of the association include Toyo-

ta, Honda, Subaru, KIA, Nissan, Peugeot, Mercedes and other foreign manufacturers of automobiles and equipment.

34. Ibid., 5, 6.

35. Ibid., 3.

36. Ibid., 21.

37. Ibid., 31.

38. Interview by the author with Isaac D. Benkin, NTSB/FHA legal staff (1967–1974) by email, May 22 and June 3, 2013.

39. Paul Ingrassia, *Crash Course: The American Automobile Industry's Road from Glory to Disaster* (New York: Random House, 2010), 9.

40. Steven Johnson, *The Ghost Map: The Story of London's Most Terrifying Epidemic and How It Changed Science, Cities, and the Modern World* (New York: Penguin Group, 2006), 34, 45.

41. Ibid., 139, 153–56.

42. *The Lancet Corrects Obituary . . . From 1858.* "[A]fter an unduly long period of reflection . . . [t]he Editor would also like to add that comments such as . . . 'Has he any facts to show in proof? No!' . . . were perhaps somewhat overly negative in tone." http://www.poynter.org/latest-news/mediawire/210113/the-lancet-corrects--obituary-from-1858/ (April 12, 2013).

43. Johnson, *Ghost Map*, 213, 226.

44. Two contrasting examples of the difficulty of changing public and professional perceptions are those of the rapid adoption of anesthetics and the opposite, tortuous path toward minimizing infections in hospitals. See Atul Gawande, "Slow Ideas," *The New Yorker*, July 29, 2013, 36. http://www.newyorker.com/reporting/2013/07/29/130729fa_fact_gawande.

45. Eastman, *Styling Versus Safety*, 209.

46. Ibid., 210.

47. The *Journal of the American Medical Association*, June 8, 1946, 524.

48. Interview by the author with Joan Claybrook, former administrator, National Highway Traffic Safety Administration; November 16, 2011, 10. As discussed in chapter 12, all models of the Research Safety Vehicle were destroyed by the government for disputed reasons in the 1990s.

49. Gikas, "Crashworthiness," *Automobile and American Culture*, 232.

50. Ibid.

51. Michael Stanton of the Association of Global Automakers said: "Why would one company incur additional costs to try to change people's minds, when another company is not going to do it?" Stanton interview by the author, 15, 22.

52. NHTSA, *Traffic Safety Facts*, DOT No. HS 811 552 (Rev. Feb. 2012), 2. http://www-nrd.nhtsa.dot.gov/Pubs/811552.pdf.

53. NHTSA estimates that frontal air bags saved 2,387 lives in 2009 and about 34,757 since 1975. NHTSA Traffic Safety Facts, 2011 Data, June 2013, Table 4. http://www-nrd.nhtsa.dot.gov/Pubs/811729.pdf.

54. Kowalke, *Old Car Wrecks*, 218.

55. "Cornell Gets Grant," *New York Times*, September 15, 1958, 23. This 1958 article noted, "The Cornell investigators found in earlier studies that the use of seat belts could cut deaths and injuries 50 per cent." http://query.nytimes.com/mem/archive/pdf?res=[[FA061FFF3D591A7493C7A81782D85F4C8585F9]].

56. "Automobile Occupant Crash Protection, Progress Report No. 3, NHTSA, DOT," July 1980, 65, quoted in *Retreat From Safety*, Joan Claybrook and the Staff of Public Citizen (New York: Pantheon Books, 1984), 166, footnote 2.

57. Carol A. MacLennan, "From Accident to Crash: The Auto Industry and the Politics of Injury," *Medical Anthropology Quarterly* 2, no. 3 (September 1988): 233–37.

58. Ralph Nader, *Unsafe at Any Speed*, 2nd ed. (New York: Bantam, 1972), ix; Dan Cordtz, "The Face in the Mirror at General Motors," *Fortune*(August 1966): 206–207.

59. Nader, *Unsafe at Any Speed*, ix. "The Face in the Mirror," *Fortune*, 206–207. See Iacocca, *Iacocca: An Autobiography* (New York: Bantam Books, 1988), 313.

60. Ibid., ix.

61. Ibid., xi.

62. Nader, *Unsafe at Any Speed*, xi.

63. "2013 Car Brand Perception Survey," *Consumer Reports* (February 5, 2013)(February 5, 2013), http://www.consumerreports.org/cro/news/2013/02/2013-car-brand-perception-survey-reveals-the-brand-loyalty-purchase-intent-leaders/index.htm.

64. Testimony of Robert S. McNamara before the House of Representatives, Subcommittee on Traffic Safety, Interstate and Foreign Commerce, 1956, cited in Nader, *Unsafe At Any Speed*, xii.

65. Ibid. Eastman, *Styling Versus Safety*, citing House Subcommittee on Traffic Safety, Interstate and Foreign Commerce, Traffic Safety Hearings, 1956, 493; Ford press release, November 18, 1956; McNamara interview cited in Eastman, *Styling Versus Safety*, footnote 71, at 240.

66. See Testimony of Joan Claybrook, president, Public Citizen, before the Senate Subcommittee on Competition, Foreign Commerce and Infrastructure, June 3, 2004 regarding industry opposition to disclosure of defect information under the TREAD Act, P.L. 106-414, codified at 49 CFR 30101–30170; see General Motors failure to report to NHTSA and to recall Chevrolet Cobalt and other cars with defective ignition switches, discussed in chapter 11; see Ford's proposed ignition interlock system offered to replace mandatory air bags in chapter 10. Virtually all manufacturers opposed a stronger federal standard for vehicle roof strength for thirty years; see chapter 12.

FIVE

General Motors Meets Ralph Nader

During the early months of 1966 calm seemed to settle over the automobile safety wars. Deaths and injuries had risen to record levels. Public interest remained low. People still seemed willing to accept, or ignore, the increasing number of dead and injured (as well as the huge economic cost) involved. It appeared to be the price they had to pay for the convenience of the automobile, now the dominant part of America's car culture.[1]

There were several reasons for the steadily rising accident toll. In addition to the long-accepted causes—driver error and poor highways—there were major new developments.

A large number of younger drivers, the "baby boomers," more accident-prone than older drivers, now had licenses. In catering to the growing youth market, manufacturers began producing much more powerful cars. This included a high-powered class of new "muscle car" with over 300 HP motors, Like the Oldsmobile "Rocket 88," the Ford Mustang, the Chevy Camaro, and the Pontiac GTO.[2] What the muscle cars did not include was enhanced handling and braking capacity necessary to control the extra horsepower and speed the manufacturers were selling.[3] The combination proved deadly.

Carl Nash, an engineer who spent his career working as an expert in car safety and for NHTSA, is critical of the design of the muscle cars and their built-in attractiveness to young drivers. "It was a deadly combination," Nash says:

> The term "muscle car" refers to cars that had very powerful V-8 engines and little else. Cars such as the Chevy Camaro, Ford Mustang and Dodge Challenger and Pontiac GTO, starting in the early 1960s. To be a muscle car they had to have the V-8 engine, with at least 300 horsepower. . . . The muscle cars of the 1960s also had mediocre handling, cheap bodies and inadequate brakes. They were designed to

accelerate quickly and appeal particularly to younger drivers who
tended to push them beyond their safe limits. Muscle cars, which have
made a comeback in recent years, contributed a lot to the rising death
rates of that era. They have been improved, with better brakes, tires
and handling and are safer now.[4]

Perhaps a new generation of "muscle cars" will be safer, but with so
much unnecessary horsepower they will present an invitation to further
disasters on the highways.

Senator Abraham Ribicoff, a newly minted first termer, had finished
eleven days of hearings on "Traffic Safety" during the summer and fall of
1965. Ribicoff chaired the Subcommittee on Executive Reorganization of
the Senate Government Operations Committee. The hearings were intended to be a broad inquiry, the first ever by the Senate, into all aspects
of traffic safety. Presumably that included safer motor vehicle construction. Ribicoff was aware of the almost futile effort of congressman Ken
Roberts to move automobile safety legislation through the House of Representatives during the prior decade.

Undeterred, Ribicoff called more than fifty witnesses. The structure of
the hearings reflected the raw political power of the largest industry in
the country. General Motors, Ford, and Chrysler controlled 94 percent of
the American car market. Thus the hearings were cautiously titled: "Traffic Safety: Examination and Review of Efficiency, Economy and Coordi-
nation of Public and Private Agencies' Activities and the Role of the
Federal Government." With that mind-bending name, it is a wonder that
anybody understood what Ribicoff was up to. Perhaps he was not sure
himself where his "examination and review" might lead.

The sleep-inducing name of Ribicoff's hearings also reflected the power structure of the Senate in 1965. The Subcommittee on Executive Reorganization, buried deep within the Government Operations Committee,
was directed by Senate rules to deal with creating new or restructuring
unnecessary federal agencies. It had absolutely no legislative jurisdiction
over automobile safety, highway construction, or the automotive industry. In other words, it could listen and talk about "traffic safety." It could
not report any bill that would really change anything. It was toothless on
the subject of automobile safety. The Senate's rules on committee jurisdiction are inviolate.

If ever there was a "poor boy makes good," "rags to riches" story, it is
the life of Abe Ribicoff. Except that something more appeared to drive
him. He was born in 1910, in a tenement building on Star Street in New
Britain, Connecticut. His parents, Samuel and Rose, were part of the ear-
ly-twentieth-century wave of Jewish immigrants from Poland. "My
father was a factory worker and we were really poor," he recalled. "But

everything I earned peddling papers and working in stores, he made me put aside for a college education."[5] Ribicoff ran errands and worked in a New Britain zipper and buckle factory to get money to go to New York University. His obvious intelligence gained him rapid acceptance at NYU, right out of New Britain High School in 1928.[6]

Short of money, Ribicoff dropped out of NYU after just one year. He took a job with a manufacturer, the G. E. Prentice Company, to manage its Chicago button and zipper office. While working for Prentice he made time to take late-afternoon classes at the University of Chicago Law School. He used his salary from Prentice Zipper to pay his way through law school.

Ribicoff shone brightly as a law student at the University of Chicago. He became an editor of the prestigious *University of Chicago Law Review*. After graduation in 1933 he passed up big-money offers with law firms to become what he called "a small-town Connecticut lawyer." But whatever Abe Ribicoff did, he seemed to do it well.

In 1933, only five years after returning to Hartford as a "small-town" lawyer, Ribicoff was elected to the Connecticut legislature. He was immediately noticed by the press, called the "most promising new legislator" and a "rising star" in state politics. Eight years later, he resigned from the legislature to accept an appointment as a Hartford Police Court Judge. He was elected chairman of the state assembly of municipal court judges. By then known statewide, Ribicoff had his eye on larger horizons.

He ran an unsuccessful campaign for an open U.S. Senate seat in 1952, losing to the wealthy Republican Prescott S. Bush. Bush was then serving in Congress, from Connecticut. He was, respectively, the father and grandfather of two presidents-to-be: George W. Bush and George H. W. Bush. Undaunted by his defeat, Ribicoff tried again two years later. This time he narrowly won the governorship of Connecticut, defeating a sitting governor John Davis Lodge, by a razor-thin margin of 3,200 votes.

As governor, Ribicoff developed a deep concern over what he viewed as preventable highway accidents caused by speeding and reckless driving. He was known as a "highway safety governor" and a "tough cop" who, long before to his election to the U.S. Senate, pressed for more vigorous enforcement of vehicle safety laws in his home state. Drivers entering Connecticut were warned to be very careful to avoid exceeding, by even a few miles an hour, the posted speed limits when they crossed the state line. At the insistence of the governor the speeding laws were fiercely enforced by the state police.

So when Ribicoff was finally elected to the U.S. Senate ten years later in 1962, he was no stranger to the growing traffic and automobile safety problem.

Ribicoff's Senate hearings on "Traffic Safety" were held during the spring and summer of 1965.

As a freshman senator, elected in 1962, Ribicoff had searched for good issues with which to launch his long-sought Senate career. His subcommittee had what amounted to a hunting license. It could hold hearings on almost anything that affected the executive branch of the federal government. But—and it was a big but—it could not do much about any traffic safety or motor vehicle safety problems it might find. It looked like a perfect setting for advocates of the status quo—primarily the car manufacturers and the safety establishment.

In hindsight, they do not appear to have taken Senator Ribicoff seriously enough.

The power to write and pass legislation that might actually affect automobile safety belonged to the Senate Commerce Committee. It was led by the burly, cigar-chomping Warren G. Magnuson, a very senior Democrat from Seattle. The Senate Public Works Committee had jurisdiction over the closely related issue of highway safety— mostly interstate roads and driver qualifications. It was chaired by another old bull, Jennings Randolph of West Virginia. The Public Works Committee had enormous clout: it controlled federal funding for state highway construction, which gave it a lot of dollars to hand out to the states. But it stayed well clear of Magnuson's turf—the design and safety of the motor vehicle.

Magnuson had many other things on his mind in 1965, including an embarrassingly narrow reelection victory in 1962. Magnuson's committee, which had a lot of real power to do something about motor vehicle deaths and injuries, initially appeared otherwise engaged. With a new consumer counsel Michael Pertschuk in charge of carrying out Magnuson's often very general directions, the Commerce Committee was conducting a series of consumer protection hearings into things like truth in packaging, cigarette labeling, hazardous toys and, at the request of Wisconsin's senator Gaylord Nelson, automobile tire safety. It was also considering dozens of other major and minor items of legislation, including matters of great importance to a senator from a maritime state. This included the bargaining rights of longshoremen, the safety of cruise ships, and the membership of the Federal Maritime Commission. All were on Magnuson's very crowded 1965 committee agenda.

Ribicoff's traffic safety hearings in 1965 heard witnesses from almost every federal agency that had even a remote interest in vehicle and highway safety. They included the Departments of Commerce; Health, Education and Welfare; Defense; Labor; the Post Office and the General Services Administration. Most of them knew very little about the subject— and wanted even less to do with such a political hot potato. The Post Office, for example, knew something about the operation of mail delivery trucks, but not much about safer vehicle design. The GSA purchased a lot of vehicles for federal government agencies, but it did not have much technical engineering knowledge. The March 1965 hearings tended to put their small audiences to sleep, generated only modest press coverage, and got almost no public attention.

The Senator's chief committee counsel, Jerry Sonosky, had happened upon the subject of "traffic safety" almost by accident. Ribicoff, newly elected, read what he thought was an interesting book by a Dr. William Haddon, then with the New York State Department of Health, entitled "Accident Research." It may have given him some ideas about auto safety strategy, or perhaps reminded him of his "tough cop" reputation as governor of Connecticut. Ribicoff mentioned the traffic safety issue to Sonosky, among several other subjects, as possible issues for the subcommittee to look into.

It is not clear how Sonosky first heard of Ralph Nader—or vice versa. However it happened, Nader, who was not known at all on Capitol Hill at the time, seemed to be well prepared when Sonosky called and asked to meet with him. The interview with Nader lasted three hours. To say that Sonosky was impressed with Nader's knowledge of the complex automobile safety issue would be an understatement. Sonosky's report on the interview persuaded the Senator to look into the issue. The Subcommittee on Executive Reorganization had found its first target.

At the time, Nader was working at the Department of Labor as a part-time consultant. Assistant Labor Secretary Pat Moynihan had invited him to come to Washington a few months earlier. Nader's first assignment, in fact his only assignment, was to write a report on a proposed federal role, *any role*, in automobile safety.

Nader had just about completed the report for Moynihan when he received the phone call from Sonosky asking if he would drop by his office on Capitol Hill to discuss automobile safety issues. Would he? This was exactly what Nader had come to Washington hoping to do. Ultimately, he spent a lot of time furnishing Sonosky and the Senate staff with information and ideas about causes and possible cures for the "epidemic" then raging on the nation's highways. At some point it became clear that following Nader's ideas could lead to a head-on confrontation with the automobile industry and its supporters.

Ribicoff and the subcommittee pushed ahead anyway.

In July 1965 the second round of the largely ignored traffic safety hearings began. Having heard from government witnesses, Ribicoff now summoned the heads of General Motors, Ford, Chrysler, and American Motors to testify about how to reduce the highway injury epidemic. Unlike the March hearings, July caused fireworks. In retrospect, the industry was not well prepared.[7]

One big issue that arose was the question of how much the motor vehicle manufacturers spent each year on safety research. At first the leaders of the companies did not appear to know the answer. There was then an unfriendly exchange on the subject between senator Robert F.

Kennedy (then the junior senator from New York) and James Roche and Frederic Donner, president and chairman respectively of General Motors:

Kennedy: What was the profit of General Motors last year?
Roche: I don't think that has anything to do . . .
Kennedy: I would like to have that answer if I may.
Donner: The one aspect we are talking about is safety.
Kennedy: What was the profit of General Motors last year?
Donner: I'll have to ask one of my associates.
Kennedy: Could you please?
Roche: (Pause)—$1,700, 000,000,000 ($1.7 billion).
Kennedy: What . . . ?
Donner: About a billion and a half.
Kennedy: About a billion and a half?
Donner: Yes.
Kennedy: And you spent about *one million dollars* on this [safety research]?
Donner: In this particular facet we are talking about . . .
Kennedy: If you gave just one percent of your profits [to safety research] that is $170 million.[8]

This rare challenge to the car manufacturers was reported by the press. General Motors promptly released a "corrected" statement saying that it had actually spent $193 million on "safety programs." The figure was immediately challenged, since it appeared to include many activities that were unrelated to automobile safety.[9] But, even if true, the figure was a small percentage of GM's $1.7 billion annual net profit.

Chrysler and Ford also released statements saying that smaller amounts had been spent on safety research by those companies. The industry total allegedly came to something close to $400 million.[10] There was some surprise and press interest in the relatively small amount of money (compared to industry profits and revenues) that the manufacturers were spending on the third largest killer of Americans (behind cancer and heart disease).[11] But the safety issue still failed to gain much public traction.

In their testimony before Ribicoff's subcommittee, the motor vehicle manufacturers had continued to emphasize that the driver was primarily responsible for preventing accidents. They said the public would refuse to pay for safety additions to the vehicle, a few of which they sold on some models as options, or "extras." They proposed a voluntary approach toward improving a bad situation. They said, once again, their cars were safe and no additional mandatory design changes were necessary.[12]

At the same hearing Henry Wakeland, an automobile safety consultant working for senator Edward Speno's New York State legislative committee, submitted a study listing four design changes that would reduce pedestrian accidents, which then killed 7,800 people a year. They included modifying sharp hood and rear-end ornaments (such as tail fins), changing the slope of the front end, and removing protrusions that dragged pedestrians to their deaths.[13] The Wakeland study was ignored.

In the House, representative Ken Roberts, the small-town lawyer from Alabama, had been defeated in the 1964 congressional elections. Almost alone, Roberts had for a decade championed the issue of automobile safety in Congress. His Special Subcommittee on Traffic Safety had not been reauthorized by the House after Roberts lost. And no new leader had emerged to take up the cause he had championed.

At the same time there was growing interest in the states in building more crashworthy automobiles. Iowa, New York, and Massachusetts, where seat belt and other bills had been introduced, were among the most active states.

In Iowa, attorney general Lawrence F. Scalise conducted hearings on automobile safety in January 1966. The hearings opened to a sizeable audience in the ornate state capital in Des Moines. The carmakers sent only second- and third-tier representatives to Iowa. The witnesses included some independent advocates and researchers, including young Ralph Nader and Dr. Paul Gikas of the University of Michigan medical school.

Dr. Gikas was a dedicated auto safety investigator and writer. He described for the Iowa officials a real-life field investigation of 125 fatal car collisions in Michigan in which he participated between 1962 and 1965. "There are essentially two ways in which a person is killed in an automobile," he said. "The individual dies of a result of being ejected from his vehicle, or he dies from injuries sustained in the secondary collision between him and the inside of his vehicle." Gikas singled out steering assemblies, dash panels, projecting knobs and levers, door latches opening, and poor crash resistance of passenger compartments as particularly deadly in the crashes he had witnessed.[14]

Gikas had given this same testimony in other state legislative hearings and before the Roberts subcommittee in the House of Representatives. This time he illustrated his study with color slides, including gruesome photographs of impaled corpses that he and his fellow Michigan researchers had seen. There was a deceased man with a gash on his back made by the edge of the car door, incurred when the car rolled over and threw him onto the roadway. There was a picture of a young girl with a hole in her skull in which was embedded the dashboard knob that had inflicted the injury.[15]

Gikas's graphic testimony and the Iowa hearings received little national attention.

In New York State, there was an effort to enact legislation requiring the design and production of a "prototype safe car" which was to be funded by a combination of state and federal money. The leader of that effort was state senator Edward Speno, a Republican from Nassau

County, with a commitment to crashworthy motor vehicles. The project ultimately failed to receive funding from either the state or federal government. Years later the federal government did fund the development and construction of several advanced Research Safety Vehicles. They played an important role in changing public attitudes toward car design.

The state legislative efforts were of some concern to the motor vehicle industry. Fifty different state laws would be a regulatory nightmare for the manufacturers. But most new state laws proposed were not being enacted, or emerging as a serious problem for the motor vehicle industry.

Thus as 1966 began, the automobile safety front, which pitted the overwhelming power of the car manufacturers and their safety-establishment allies against a few professors and doctors, a young safety advocate, and one or two state and federal legislators, appeared stalemated.

Before he burst spectacularly on the national scene, Ralph Nader was an unknown lawyer from Connecticut and before that a 1958 product of Harvard Law School. He had created barely a ripple with his automobile safety report written for Pat Moynihan at the Labor Department.

In 1965 Nader had published a book called *Unsafe at Any Speed: The Designed-In Dangers of the American* Automobile.[16] Nader's small publisher, Richard Grossman, who liked the book so much that he personally edited it, tried feverishly to generate some interest in Nader's work. He achieved only minimal success.

Lawyer Nader, now deeply involved in hands-on automobile safety activities, found time to organize a citizen car safety protest outside a new car show held at the New York Coliseum. The little group of protestors was joined by Dr. Seymour Charles, founder of a group called the Physicians for Automotive Safety and by a few Harvard friends of Nader's.

His mother Rose also came to the rally. She carried a hand-lettered sign bearing the none-too-snappy slogan: "The people in the cars may cause accidents, but it is the vehicles that injure them. Back the drive to build safety in our automobiles."[17]

Grossman traveled around the country with copies of Nader's book, trying to get newspaper editors interested. Major publications, such as *Life* magazine, declined to review *Unsafe at Any Speed*, without giving any reason. Grossman received a more direct answer from the book review editor of *The Houston Chronicle*: "Are you out of your f . . . ing mind? I wouldn't touch that book with a ten-foot pole."[18]

Unsafe at Any Speed did get some press coverage. The *San Francisco Chronicle* called it "A searing document that may become the 'Silent Spring' of the automotive industry." But despite a few endorsements, most of the press ignored *Unsafe at Any Speed*, as did official Washington and, most important, the automotive industry. They ignored it—at least at first.

The book did have one positive effect: it enhanced Nader's potential value to the Ribicoff subcommittee as a witness. He was invited to testify for the first time before Congress, on February 10, 1966.[19]

What made *Unsafe at Any Speed* such an unusual book was that it was a flat-out, well-documented attack by an unknown writer on the largest industry in the United States and on the product Americans loved best. Nader argued that financial considerations had led Detroit to promote style over safety for decades. He catalogued poor engineering decisions in the design of its cars, ranging from the windshield wipers to the decision not to include lap and shoulder belts. He repeatedly referred to the theory of the "second collision," which he pointed out had been advanced many decades before by Canadian Air Force pilot Hugh DeHaven after a training crash during World War I.

Nader devoted the first chapter of his book, entitled "The Sporty Corvair," to discussing what he termed the "inherent flaws" of one of General Motors most popular-selling models—the 1960–1963 Chevrolet Corvair. Over a million 1960 to 1963 Corvairs were sold before General Motors made improvements in the suspension system of the early models to correct severe handling problems.[20]

From the beginning GM was excited about the marketing potential of the new Corvair. It included many innovative design features, including a rear engine, a rear swing axle, and an air-cooled engine. According to Nader, when the Corvair was first marketed in 1959, the type of design used was known to GM's engineers to be prone to instability and rollover, even at low speeds. John Z. DeLorean, chief engineer at Pontiac, was "absolutely convinced . . . that the car was unsafe" so he kept its design out of the Pontiac line until it was redesigned in the 1965 models. DeLorean then pronounced it "one of the safest cars on the road."[21]

But by 1965 General Motors was already the subject of as many as one hundred lawsuits for deaths and injuries to people who had been driving or riding in Corvairs. Nader's book highlighted the stability problems of the vehicle and the absence of corrective action by GM, even after the injury reports began to pour in.

The company's years of inaction regarding the Corvair were, Nader said, due to what he called "bureaucratic rigidities and the abject worship of that bitch goddess cost reduction."[22] GM claimed the Corvair was perfectly safe and settled most of the lawsuits against it. But Nader's attack hurt the car's sales and GM's overall reputation as the industry leader. At least GM thought so.

GM had introduced the Corvair to its 1959 line to compete with the invading Volkswagen Beetle. The dumpy looking, gas-saving Beetle had been designed in the 1930s in Nazi Germany. It had gone into mass production in Germany as "the People's Car," just after World War II. Once the Beetle hit the American market in the 1950s, it immediately demonstrated that there was a big consumer demand here for small, well-made, inexpensive cars.[23]

Ultimately, on a worldwide basis, the Beetle became one of the four most popular cars ever produced even though it *also* had a tendency to rollover. The Corvair, for all its early success, was done in not so much by competition from the Beetle as Nader's criticism of its tendency to "oversteer" (that is, the car turns more sharply than intended by the driver—it veers sharply *into* the direction of the turn). Oversteer can result in a rollover on a curve, or in any quick maneuver, particularly by an inexperienced driver.

The ironic thing about the Chevy Corvair, the car that started the automobile safety revolution, is that Nader's charges about its dangerous lack of stability were never fully proven or disproven. Tests run by NHTSA, requested by the consumer advocate himself, seemed to show that it was as safe and stable as other contemporary small cars like the Falcon and the Beetle.[24]

But the NHTSA tests do not appear to have been credible. They were run with six passengers in an overloaded test car. Despite the unrealistic test method, the tests were approved by an inexperienced Nader lawyer. He did not appreciate the increased vehicle stability of additional passenger weight. It made the test Corvair heavy enough (with a lower center of gravity) to perform better in turns than when it was normally loaded.[25]

The argument over the Corvair's safety was never settled. But that became irrelevant. In terms of national safety reform, the Corvair and *Unsafe at Any Speed* had served their purpose. They had alerted the public to the built-in dangers of many unsafely designed automobiles in the U.S. market.[26]

Other evidence that Nader incorporated in *Unsafe at Any Speed* regarding the Corvair were extensive performance reviews from automotive magazines. These magazines usually took pains to avoid criticizing the companies directly. By withholding advertising and product information the auto companies could squelch them like small bugs.

Nonetheless, *Car and Driver* magazine dared to suggest that the 1963–1965 Corvair was "one of the nastiest-handling cars ever built. The tail gave little warning that it was about to let go, and when it did, it let go with a vengeance few drivers could cope with."[27] *Road Test* magazine called the 1963- and 1964-model Corvairs "probably the worst riding, worst all-around handling car available to the American public . . ."[28] Nader's conclusion was that GM engineers had emphasized, at the direction of their superiors, lower cost over occupant safety. General Motors flatly denied the charges. Then it proceeded to ignore Nader and his new book.

The new author did get some publicity. The *Washington Post* wrote a feature story about him in February 1966. It referred to him as a tall, lean, dark-haired bachelor with an easy grin and a hard head and said, "He gives no sign of letting up on what he thinks of now as a kind of mission."[29]

The *Post* reported that Nader had predicted that the Johnson administration, which was in the process of drafting automobile safety legislation, would come up with something he called a "no-law law." Nader predicted (accurately) that the administration's safety legislation would *not* mandate that the automobile industry incorporate any new crash standards but would recommend something less: more research, or some sort of voluntary method of attempting to reduce the growing death rate.

Three days later, Nader obtained a leaked copy of the proposed legislation authored by the Johnson administration. The bill made Nader look prescient. It did not, in fact, require any mandatory automobile design safety standards. The draft, according to the *Post*, "fulfilled the prediction made last Thursday by Ralph Nader, author of *Unsafe at Any Speed*, a controversial book about auto safety."[30]

Nader's book was generating only modest publicity. His charges against General Motors and its cars were completely denied by the company. The administration's proposed legislation was of a very mild sort, leaving the motor vehicle manufacturers in a seemingly secure position. They took a wait-and-see attitude. At least that is what they appeared to do in public. Behind the scenes, General Motors did something more. It was something that resulted in a monumental change in the history of American automobile regulation.

And a change in the future of the automotive industry.

Ralph Nader had gotten interested in automobile safety in his days at Harvard Law School. He had been a published author on motor vehicle design at least since 1959, a year after he graduated in Cambridge with his law degree. He then authored an article in the *Nation* entitled "The Safe Car You Can't Buy."[31]

Nader followed his first article with a second critique of the automobile industry's safety record in 1963. Writing again in the *Nation* he noted, "In a speech before the National Safety Congress, John F. Gordon, president of General Motors, ridiculed 'amateur engineers' who were trying to take over responsibilities that belong to competent engineers in the industry."[32]

Nader ignored the personal attack but wrote in the second article that through efforts of engineers and medical scientists at Cornell, Harvard, California, Minnesota, and other universities and through research carried out by Liberty Mutual Insurance Company, "a relationship has been uncovered between automobile designs and our annual 40,000 fatalities and 4 million injuries on the highways."[33]

The new safety advocate listed some of what he saw as the causes:

> Pop open doors, cardboard-like roof structures, uprootable seats, flying cushions, jutting metal dashboards, bone-crushing knobs, chisel-like rearview mirrors, and above all, dangerous shafts and steering wheels, are a few of the more than 100 design deficiencies that Mr. Gordon's "competent" engineers seem to have overlooked."[34]

But Nader's articles in the *Nation* and his report to Pat Moynihan at the Department of Labor caused hardly a ripple in the nation's capital and within the automobile industry. *Unsafe at Any Speed* was just a repetition of a theme he and a few others had voiced before: American cars were built primarily for style and horsepower, not for safety. The *Nation* articles, Nader's book, the state legislative hearings—all were pretty much ignored by the powerful motor vehicle industry and by a passive federal government.

A day of reckoning was fast approaching.

Nader was born in 1934, in the small city of Winsted, Connecticut. His parents, Nathra and Rose, were Lebanese immigrants who operated a small restaurant and bakery in town. Ralph was the youngest of four children. He had two sisters and a brother. Even as a kid, Nader dreamed of becoming a "people's lawyer," whatever as a teenager he thought those words meant. His willingness to delve deeply into safety and environmental issues appears to have been instilled in him in adolescence by his socially conscious parents. It was supplemented by noisy free-for-all discussions conducted as a kind of family dinner table seminar, mostly by his immigrant father Nathra, on the duties of citizenship in the United States.

Nader recalls that he had read all the "muckraker" books before he was fourteen years old, including books by Ida Tarbell, Lincoln Steffens, and Upton Sinclair. He was drawn to their sense of mission, he says, undertaken in the slums, slaughterhouses, and factories in gritty industrial cities like Chicago, Cleveland, and New York. "I read them trembling, literally trembling with excitement. . . . I couldn't put them down. My mother would call me to go out and mow the grass. I'd still be in the middle of a 400-page book."[35]

Nader was an adept student. He was accepted at Princeton University in 1951. He was an outsider there—even in his college days Nader was an outsider.

"I grew up thinking one person could change things," Nader said. "Where did I get that idea? First, from my parents and second, from reading American history. So many of the major steps forward in our society's progress started with just a handful of people."[36] Nader's willingness to take action rather than merely talk was apparent even as a college student. While at Princeton, for example, he noticed there were a great number of dead birds lying on the pavement between campus buildings.

> At first I didn't think much of it. . . . At first I just said, there is a bluebird or a robin. They weren't mutilated in any way. They were just lying on their backs dead. A few days later I saw more birds. It turns out it was DDT. At the time in the early 1950s no one thought that DDT was dangerous to anybody but insects. Well, it turned out it was dangerous right there . . . to the birds. I went down to the *Daily Princetonian*, the college paper, and tried to persuade them to do a story. I had one of the dead birds with me to show them. They said, "No, there's nothing wrong. We have some of the best science professors in the world . . . chemistry, biology. If they had any idea it was harmful, it would be stopped."[37]

DDT was banned in 1972 for use as an agriculture pesticide by the Environmental Protection Agency. Most of its uses were banned internationally by the 2004 Stockholm Convention based on its potential to cause cancer in humans and damage to animal species. But that was years later and by then Nader was well known for his involvement in many consumer and environmental issues. He never forgot the dead bluebirds and robins that he had seen while he was in college at Princeton.

When Nader went on to Harvard Law School he remained an outsider at that elite institution as well, despite his obvious intellect and highly inquisitive character. He lived in an old, ornate dormitory named Hastings Hall. It stands today on the Harvard campus in Cambridge; dull brown bricks, dark-shingled, sloping roofs, pointed turrets—perhaps waiting for future students with inquisitive minds and commitment to a cause.

While he was at law school, Nader would disappear for long periods of time. Often he did not attend class at all. He could get away with it. At Harvard grades were based exclusively on year-end examinations. Nader was evidently smart enough to skip classes and still graduate high in his class.

He was a wanderer who liked to travel around the country. Having no car, he hitchhiked. During his travels he began to notice automobile accidents along the highways. He noticed the number and severity of the accidents and the often deadly results for the occupants.

Then he read an article by a young Chicago labor lawyer named Harold A. Katz. It was published as a short "Comment" in the *Harvard Law Review* in 1956.[38] The Katz article must have fueled Nader's interest automobile design safety—and in the legal protection that was *not* being furnished by courts. At the time the legal system largely absolved automobile manufacturers from liability for failure to install known safety equipment, such as lap and shoulder belts. For Nader it was the beginning of a crusade.

He began to study more about the legal and engineering issues involved in automobile design safety. He considered writing something about his newly discovered interest. After graduating from law school, he hung out a shingle in a small law office in Hartford, Connecticut. He handled wills, estates, and some auto accident cases and continued writing about auto safety.

Pat Moynihan also had a longstanding interest in automobile safety. Nader's and Moynihan's interests coincidently meshed. In 1963, when Moynihan was appointed assistant Secretary of Labor in the Kennedy administration, he called Nader at his small Hartford law office. He asked him to come to Washington to do some research about federal employees and automobile safety.

The young lawyer closed up shop in Hartford and headed south.

By the time Nader met Ribicoff's counsel Jerry Sonosky, he had become a self- taught expert on automobile crashworthiness and design and, equally important, on Detroit's inaction over the years. He had written the 235-page report for Moynihan, somewhat beyond his assigned subject. It had the very academic title, "Context, Condition and Recommended Direction of Federal Activity in Highway Safety." It was meant by Nader and Moynihan mainly for use in convincing federal officials to take some action on the subject. But based on the Johnson administration's meek position as of February 1966, it had failed to cause much reaction within the federal government.

Nader remained a crusader looking for a crusade.

A friend kept telling Jerry Sonosky that if he wanted to look into automobile safety, he just had to meet this young guy Ralph Nader. So Sonosky arranged the meeting in room 168 of the Russell Senate Office Building. He recalled later that Nader walked in "looking then as he looks now, sallow-faced, wearing his long overcoat carrying 1,000 pieces of paper under his arm. His message was that the automobile industry had no right to produce unsafe cars. We talked for hours about . . . where we should go with it." [39]

Immediately following the meeting, Sonosky phoned the senator.

> "We just struck gold" he said.
> "What do you mean?" asked Ribicoff.
> "I just met somebody who knows more about auto safety than anybody I've ever come across," Sonosky answered. "I don't have to run around town gathering up various reports. I just found him." [40]

So Nader became an informal advisor to the Ribicoff subcommittee. He fed the staff documents and helped plan the spring and summer traffic-safety hearings in 1965. In retrospect, the Ribicoff hearings laid the indispensible groundwork for what happened next. But it is quite possible that nothing at all would have happened, if not for the arrogance and poor judgment of General Motors.

On a quiet Saturday morning in February 1966, *Washington Post* reporter Morton Mintz was almost alone in the deserted *Post* newsroom. Mintz had recently published his first book, *By Prescription Only*. It was an exposé about the Food and Drug Administration and a medical officer named Frances Kelsey; an obscure scientist at the FDA. She had almost singlehandedly blocked the marketing of thalidomide. It was a drug submitted for approval to the FDA and promoted for use by pregnant women. It had been found in tests to cause birth defects. *By Prescription Only* won Morton Mintz wide national acclaim and awards. It did not deal at all with automobile safety.

Mintz's telephone rang insistently that Saturday morning. The *Post* operator said: "Mr. Mintz, there is a Mr. Nader downstairs here to see you." The reporter had never met Nader. He was busy on a story and was on a tight deadline. Whatever Nader wanted to say, Mintz thought, it could probably wait until Monday.

The young automobile safety advocate had read *By Prescription Only* and noted the writer had investigated the drug industry and its premarketing safety practices. He had sought Mintz out. Perhaps he sensed something about Mintz's journalistic abilities. It was clear that Mintz had, in the words of one of his editors, "A capacity for indignation." [41]

Mintz told the operator to have the receptionist send Nader upstairs to the newsroom. When Nader walked in he told Mintz a surprising story. Nader said he was being followed around the Senate Office Building and other places by somebody. He did not know who was following him or why. The reason he knew this, he told Mintz, was that a Capitol policeman named Marshall Speakes had stopped him in the hallway of a Senate building the day before and told him he was being followed.

Mintz said he was impressed with Nader's sincerity. Nonetheless, he could not write the story. Under the *Post*'s editorial guidelines and his own, Mintz needed confirmation from a second source before he could write an article making such a serious accusation for his paper. Mintz called Marshall Speakes, the Capitol Hill policeman Nader had named, to check out the story. Mintz asked Speakes if he had in fact told Ralph Nader that he was being followed around. Speakes declined to talk. He said Capitol Hill police policy prohibited him from commenting on stories that did not result in an arrest. [42] So Mintz concluded he could not write Nader's story.

Laurence Stern was Morton Mintz's editor on the news desk that day. Mintz walked over to Stern and told him Nader's tale of the Capitol Hill cop and his belief he was being followed. Stern reacted with surprise:

"What?" Stern said.

"Yes, absolutely," said Mintz. He was surprised at the reaction from the usually cool news editor.

Stern said that he had just spoken with another *Post* reporter, Bryce Nelson, who by coincidence happened to be in the newsroom that morning. Nelson said that he too had been stopped in the Senate Office Building, the day before, by a Capitol Hill police officer. The officer said to Nelson, "Mr. Nader, you are being followed."

Nelson and Nader looked somewhat alike. They were both tall and lean, with dark hair. Whatever the reason for the mistaken identification, Nelson had provided confirmation of the police officer's words to Nader. Suddenly Mintz had a believable, if accidental confirmation of Nader's unlikely detective story. Having at least one confirming source for the claim, he was now able to write the story that Saturday afternoon. The article ran in the February 13, 1966 edition of the *Washington Post*.[43]

It was a modest piece entitled "Car Safety Critic Nader Reports Being Tailed."

The *Post* article was not prominently featured. It did not receive immediate attention by other newspapers and media. But ultimately the story went around the world, with assistance from another reporter.

James Ridgeway was a young writer for the *New Republic*. He was also approached by Nader, who was nothing if not persistent that day in 1966. Nader did not know anyone at the magazine, nor did he ask specifically for Ridgeway. He told the *New Republic* receptionist that he had a "hot story" and was put on the telephone with Ridgeway, whose skeptical reaction was "Hurry up, I am on deadline. I only have five minutes to talk to you."[44]

After hearing Nader's story Ridgeway and the *New Republic*'s editors smelled blood. They spent much more than five minutes tracking down the details of the story and devoted a lot of space to the incident in the March 12, 1966 issue. An article by Ridgeway appeared, entitled, "The Dick."[45]

Ridgeway wrote that Nader first believed someone was "watching" him in January when he testified before Attorney General Scalise's hearings in Des Moines, Iowa. But he couldn't prove it. After his appearance before Ribicoff's subcommittee was announced, Nader had received several odd telephone calls. They increased in frequency until the night before the February 10 hearing, while he was trying to finish writing his statement. He received at least half a dozen phone calls that night. A voice would say, "Mr. Nader, this is Pan American." Or, "Mr. Nader, please pick up the parcel at Railway Express" and then hang up. Then, late that night, an unidentified caller said "Why don't you go back to Connecticut, buddy boy?"[46]

The *New Republic* story went on to detail a bizarre series of events, both before and after Nader's Senate testimony. Nader's landlady got a call from a man checking to see whether he paid his rent on time. Nader's stockbroker received a visit from a man who claimed his client wanted to hire Nader and wanted to know about Nader's credit habits. A professor at Harvard Law School, Harold Berman, got a call from a man who said he worked for a research organization, that Berman was given as a reference for Nader, and could he ask some questions about him? Thomas Lambert, the editor of the *American Association of Trial Lawyers Journal*, said he got a call from a man named Mr. Dwyer who wanted to hire Mr. Nader, who asked about Nader's drinking habits and technical capabilities.

Frederick Hughes Condon had been a classmate of Nader's in law school. He was a lawyer for a life insurance company in Concord, New Hampshire in 1965. Nader had dedicated *Unsafe at Any Speed* to Condon because he had been disabled in an automobile accident. A Mr. Warren called Condon and asked to meet to discuss Ralph Nader.

Condon, who considered himself a friend of Nader's, was suspicious. He agreed that the "Mr. Warren" could come over and talk to him about his classmate. When Warren arrived he held a brief case on his lap. Condon was suspicious that a tape recorder might be concealed in the brief case. "Mr. Warren" said he was looking into Nader's background, partly to make sure he had a "normal sex life" and was not involved in "left-wing politics." The so-called Mr. Warren said he worked with an attorney in New York, a Mr. Gillen, who specialized in investigations and was a former FBI agent.

Mr. Warren then conceded he was really the Mr. Gillen he had just mentioned. He said he had heard Ralph Nader traveled a lot. Did Condon know where he had gone? Why wasn't Nader married? Did he get financial help with his book? Was he anti-Semitic, based on his Lebanese family background? Warren—or Gillen—asked whether Nader had ever met with Senator Ribicoff. What were his connections with the Senator? Condon said he didn't know anything about those things. After Gillen left, he wrote up his notes about the interview and sent them off to Nader. He followed up the memorandum with a telephone call to Nader in Washington.

Later that day, a writer for *Book Week* magazine received a call from a smooth-talking fellow asking about Ralph Nader. The writer, Dexter Masters, had authored a complimentary review of *Unsafe at Any Speed*. Masters said he couldn't tell the caller anything about Nader personally, but he certainly liked the book. Masters, thinking that this was one of the silliest phone calls he had ever received, called Nader's publisher, Richard Grossman and related the incident to him.

The investigation of Ralph Nader was not finished yet. The next week, on February 23, Nader was on his way to meet a friend in downtown Washington. He stopped to buy a package of cookies at a Safeway store near his Dupont Circle boardinghouse. There were perhaps thirty people in the store: a few men, some women, and some kids.

Nader was looking at the shelves for the kind of cookies he wanted. A young woman with strawberry blonde hair and wearing slacks, came up to him. "Excuse me, I need some help. I've got to move something heavy into my apartment. There is no one to help me. I wonder if I can get you to give me a hand. It won't take much time." Nader said he was sorry but he had a meeting to go to; he was already late. The young woman persisted, "Please," she said, "it won't take long." Nader refused. Then, although there were a number of other people in the store who might have helped her, including other young men, she abruptly turned and left the store.

New Republic reporter Ridgeway succeeded in reaching detective Vincent Gillen of Vincent Gillen Associates in New York. Gillen readily admitted a client had asked his company to make an investigation of Ralph Nader. My client, he said, was considering him for an important job, "to do research or something. I don't know what." Gillen said he went out and bought *Unsafe at Any Speed*, read the book, and "I felt like staying in bed. I was afraid to drive a car. . . . I thought at the time he better know what he is talking about, or somebody might yell."

"Is somebody yelling?" Ridgeway asked. There was a pause. Gillen said the investigation was not yet complete. Then he added, "All I can say is it is good for Ralph Nader."[47]

The story about the young lawyer being trailed—in fact harassed—by detectives in Washington and other cities went national. It was reprinted in newspapers and magazines all over the country. There was speculation that, because of Nader's sharp criticism of the automobile industry, the detectives had been hired by someone connected with the industry. Chrysler and Ford promptly issued denials that they were involved. General Motors was silent.

After a week or so, General Motors issued a statement admitting that it had been investigating Ralph Nader. The company denied it was trying to harass or intimidate him. GM said the investigation was "routine." It had been "undertaken because of Nader's extreme criticism of the Corvair, the company's compact [car]." It said it was investigating the young crusader to determine whether he was acting on behalf of litigants or their attorneys in one or more of the one hundred lawsuits then pending over accidents involving the Corvair.[48]

Nader replied: "There is absolutely nothing wrong with representing clients in cases against the Corvair. But I am not representing any clients in Corvair cases and have never done so."[49]

Shortly after that senators Gaylord Nelson and Abraham Ribicoff asked the Justice Department to investigate why the author was being followed. Since Nader had just been a witness before their Government Operations subcommittee looking into the government's role in traffic safety, the incident appeared menacing. It is a federal crime to harass or intimidate a congressional witness. The maximum penalties are a $5,000 fine, five years in prison, or both.

Ribicoff also asked the James Roche, president of General Motors, and detective Vincent Gillen to appear at a hearing of his subcommittee in March 1966. The *New Republic* called the whole incident "gangbusters stuff." Ribicoff, when asked to comment said, "It is amazing how stupid the detective agency was . . . their complete insensitivity. When a large corporation puts its reputation in the hands of men like Gillen, it's tragic."[50]

At a packed Senate hearing on March 22, 1966, James Roche, president of General Motors, appeared as a witness. Roche denied any "personal knowledge" of the events. He said the "routine investigation" was authorized by GM's general counsel, or perhaps by one of his staff lawyers. With candor Roche apologized publicly for any part General Motors may have had in the incident. He disclaimed GM's responsibility for the "sex lures": the strawberry blond in the supermarket, who Nader said tried to get him up to her apartment, and another woman, a brunette in a D.C. drugstore, who wanted to discuss "foreign affairs" with him up at her place. Referring to the routine investigation, Roche told the subcommittee, "I am just as shocked and outraged" as you are. Roche said he hoped the senators, and Nader too, would accept his apology.[51]

The *Post* and most newspapers across the country picked up the story once again. GM's apology to the young author and safety advocate was national news. On its editorial page, the *Post* said, "The entire matter is shockingly distasteful. . . . Indiscriminate snooping into private lives . . . not only violates business ethics but threatens the destruction of the right to privacy, one of the bedrocks of a free society."[52]

Post reporter Morton Mintz, who had almost by accident triggered the story of GM's detective activities, had a final word on the almost unreal events. In an article entitled "GM Goliath Bows to David," Mintz cut through it all. He wrote that what was really at stake was General Motors' statement that automobile safety "has a priority second to none."[53]

"The crucial test" he said, "will be whether GM, at a cost to it not exceeding $20 per car, will recall all of its 1960–1963 Corvairs for retrofitting with devices to correct the rear suspension, that under certain conditions causes the car to flip over."[54] GM never did. It redesigned 1965 and later models of the Corvair, but it did not recall the earlier-model Corvairs. Over one million had already been sold. With sales falling fast, GM discontinued the Corvair a few years later.

With the suddenness of a summer tornado, an unknown young lawyer had gone from being an aspiring author and hopeful "people's advocate" to a national consumer champion. Nader continued his fight for automobile safety for many years. He wrote, for example, that automobile makers were wrong in maintaining secrecy about safety defects in cars that they had already sold, for failing to install seatbelts as standard equipment in new cars, and on similar safety issues.[55]

Years later, Nader said that the motor vehicle auto safety law "[H]as led to far fewer gravestones, fewer hospital beds, less anguish, less money spent on repairs . . . In comparison to other health and safety programs it is a shining example of success." Then he paused, still the young crusader he added: "By comparison to what we should do in the second generation of automobile safety. . . . We have a long way to go." He seemed somehow unsatisfied with what he had accomplished.[56]

Over the years Nader expanded his activities to include other consumer protection issues, such as product safety, clean water, clean air, safer oil pipelines, and the expansion of the Freedom of Information Act. He founded new consumer organizations. He was named "One of the Ten Outstanding Men of the Year" by the U.S. Junior Chamber of Commerce in 1967.[57]

Science magazine editorialized, "One Man Who Mattered":

> To anyone who has lost faith in the power of the individual and his ability to assert himself in the world of industrial giants, the story of Ralph Nader is a reassuring one. . . . Nader, like most crusaders, is a single-minded, demanding, relentless critic. . . . The nation now recognizes that much can be done to improve car safety. Perhaps only a man as uncompromising as Nader could have succeeded against such heavy odds.[58]

Time may have dimmed the memory of Ralph Nader's successful crusade for safer automobiles. The result—remaking of the law and the reality of automobile safety—cannot be dimmed. Nader and GM combined, in very different ways, to change the future of automotive safety in America.

The events of those years would lead to Detroit's worst nightmare—a national motor vehicle safety law.

NOTES

1. See Flink, *The Automobile Age*, 277–79. In 1955, "The United States produced two-thirds of the entire world output of motor vehicles, with 94 percent of the huge American domestic market held by Detroit's Big Three." In 1980 the National Research Council found "competition occurred largely on the basis of economics of scale; styling and sales networks . . . innovation became increasingly invisible." Ibid., 278.

2. Michael Rose, "The Birth of the Muscle Car: The Pontiac GTO at 50," *The Detroit Bureau*, May 13, 2013. www.thedetroitbureau.com.

3. Interview by the author with Carl E. Nash, former senior staff, National Highway Traffic Safety Administration; Adjunct Professor of Engineering, National Crash Analysis Center, George Washington University, January 9, 2013.

4. Interview by the author with Carl E. Nash, by email, July 6, 2014.

5. "Ribicoff of Connecticut Dies, Governor and Senator Was 87," *New York Times* Archives, February 23, 1998.

6. Martin Weil, "Abraham Ribicoff, 87, Dies," *Washington Post*, February 23, 1998, D6.

7. Eastman, *Styling Versus Safety*, 245.

8. Hearings, "Federal Role in Traffic Safety," U.S. Senate, Part 2, 89th Congress, First Session, 681–86, ("Senate Hearings"); Eastman, *Styling Versus Safety*, 246; Nader, *Unsafe at Any Speed*, 267.

9. Elizabeth Drew, "The Politics of Auto Safety," *The Atlantic*, October 1966, 95.

10. "1967 Passenger-Car Engineering Trends," *Journal of the Society of Automotive Engineers* 44, no. 11 (1967): 33.

11. "GM Says It Spent $193 million in 1964 on Automobile Safety," *Wall Street Journal*, July 19, 1965, 5. See also Gikas, "Crashworthiness as a Cultural Ideal," in *The Automobile and American Culture*, ed. David L. Lewis and Lawrence Goldstein (Ann Arbor: University of Michigan Press, 1983), 330.

12. Senate Hearings, (July 1965), 672–82.

13. Senate Hearings, 1051.

14. Quoted in Ralph Nader, "Safer Cars: Time for Decision," *Consumer Reports*, April 1966, 195.

15. O'Connell and Myers, *Safety Last*, 7–10.

16. Ralph Nader, *Unsafe at Any Speed: The Designed-In Dangers of the American Automobile* (New York: Grossman Publishers/Bantam Books, New York 1965).

17. Justin Martin, *Nader: Crusader, Spoiler, Icon* (New York: Perseus Books, 2002), 43.

18. Ibid., 46.

19. Ibid., 47.

20. Nader, *Unsafe at Any Speed*, 11–12.

21. Flink, *Automobile Age*, 288.

22. Nader, *Unsafe at Any Speed*, 30; Flink, *Automobile Age*, chapter 15: "The Insolent Chariots . . . The Dinosaur in the Driveway," 281–87, 281, 283.

23. Interview by the author with Carl E. Nash, November 13, 2012.

24. Carl Nash Memorandum on Corvair history and testing, to the author January 2013, Bethesda, Maryland.

25. Ibid.

26. In 2013 Nader's conclusion about the safety of the Corvair was, "It was on the outer edge of instability. It had handling problems because of the combination of the flexible axle system and the positioning of the engine in the rear of the car. It required a different kind of highly experienced driver to safely handle it. GM decided they wanted to save two bucks a car. They failed to put in a dual axle system which would have avoided the problem and which was known to them, because it was already used on German cars. It was an unstable car, like the VW Beetle." Interview by the author with Ralph Nader, December 12, 2013, 2.

27. Nader, *Unsafe at Any Speed*, 13.

28. Ibid., 14.

29. Richard Corrigan, *Washington Post-Times Herald*, February 21, 1966 (ProQuest Historical Newspapers).

30. Morton Mintz, "Auto Safety Measure's Provisions Disclosed," *Washington Post*, February 14, 1966, A-1.

31. Ralph Nader, "The Safe Car You Can't Buy," *The Nation*, April 11, 1959, 214.

32. Ralph Nader, "Detroit Makes Your Choice: Fashion or Safety," *The Nation*, October 12, 1963, 214.

33. Ibid.

34. Ibid.

35. Martin, supra, *Nader*, 11.

36. Ralph Nader interview, "Academy of Achievement," http://www.achievement.org/autodoc/page/nad0int-1, 1.

37. Martin, supra, *Nader*, 6.

38. Harold A. Katz, "Liability of Automobile Manufacturers for Unsafe Design of Passenger Cars," *Harvard Law Review*, vol. 69, p. 863 (1956).

39. Martin, supra, *Nader*, 44.

40. Ibid., 49.

41. Interview by the author with Morton Mintz, February 12, 2012, 3.

42. Ibid.

43. Martin, supra, *Nader,* 49; interview by the author with Ralph Nader, October 1, 2012.

44. Nader, interview, October 1, 2012.

45. James Ridgeway, "The Dick," *New Republic,* March 12, 1966, 11.

46. Ibid.

47. Ibid., 13.

48. Ibid., 8.

49. Ibid., 8.

50. Ibid., 8.

51. Ibid., 8.

52. "The Corvair Caper," *The Washington-Times Herald* editorial, March 24, 1966, A-24.

53. Morton Mintz, "GM's Goliath Bows to David," *Washington Post,* March 27, 1966, A-7. ProQuest Historical Newspapers.

54. Ibid.

55. Morton Mintz, "Nader Raps GM, Ford on Faulty Seatbelts," *Washington Post,* April 26, 1966, A-1.

56. Interview by the author with Ralph Nader, Washington D.C., December 12, 2013, 22.

57. In 2006 *The Atlantic* asked ten eminent historians to name the one hundred most influential people in American history. They named Ralph Nader ninety-sixth. *The Atlantic* commented, "He made the cars we drive safer; thirty years later he made George W. Bush president." http://www.theatlantic.com/magazine/archive/2006/12/the-100-most-influential-figures-in-american-history/305384/.

58. Henry Brandon, "One Man Who Mattered," *Science Magazine,* May 28, 1966, 9.

My first car: a hot, yellow 1948 Ford. No seat belts, padded dashboard, or other safety systems. Sicnag/Wikimedia Commons.

Henry Ford's Model T: the beginning of the American car era. 15 million were sold from 1908 to 1927. Harry Shipler/Wikipedia.

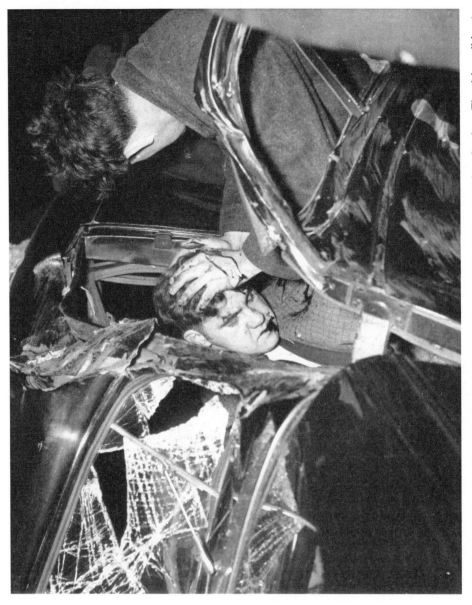

Auto accident, East Hempstead, New York, 1940. No seat belts or safety glass, weak door latches. The driver did not survive. *New York Daily News* via Getty Images.

Car crash 1938. Weak door hinges, roof, and body structure. All four occupants died. New York State Department of Police

The GM/Pontiac GTO: one of the first "muscle" cars, circa 1964. Powerful 340 HP, V-8 engine, weak brakes, and poor handling. Freesek from En-Wikipedia.

A young Ralph Nader. U.S. Library of Congress.

GM's headquarters in Detroit, circa 2000. Ritcheypro/Wikipedia.

A 1964 Chevy Corvair: the rear engine, swing axle car that Nader used to push for a federal safety law. Greg Gjerdingen/Wikimedia Commons.

Dr. William Haddon: the first National Highway Safety Administrator; a leader in challenging the automobile industry to improve automobile safety. Insurance Institute for Highway Safety/Photograph by Tom Brunk.

Senator Warren G. Magnuson: a gruff old pol. Strong on safety, he was the primary author of the first federal Safety Act in 1966. U.S. Senate Historical Office.

Joan Claybrook, fiery National Highway Safety Administrator; later, a tough consumer advocate. Public Citizen/Photograph by Patsy Lynch.

Transportation Secretary Elizabeth H. Dole. She turned President Ronald Reagan around on automobile safety. Courtesy Elizabeth H. Dole.

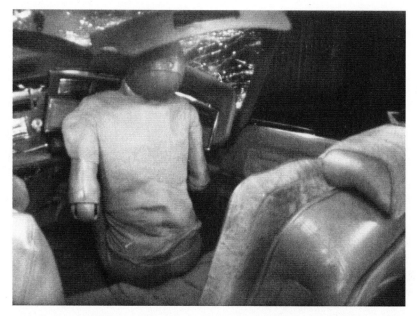

Crushed dummy: test car with no air bag, 35 mph crash into fixed barrier. Insurance Institute for Highway Safety.

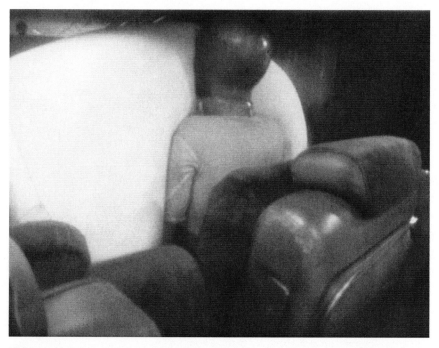

Unharmed dummy, test car with airbag, 35 mph crash into fixed barrier. Insurance Institute for Highway Safety.

Dr. Carl Clark, air bag and safety pioneer, tests an early design. Worcester Poly-technic Institute Journal/Photograph by Michael Ciesielski.

Hugh DeHaven. A 1917 fighter-plane accident led to his crash-impact proposals for cars, such as lap and shoulder belts. Exodyne Inc.

The Research Safety Vehicle, circa 1975. One RSZ was crashed at 50 mph safely into a fixed barrier. The occupants walked away safely. Donald Friedman/Minicars Inc.

A 2008 Nissan Rogue, crash tested at 35 mph into fixed barrier, with dummy unharmed, passing federal and IIHS safety tests. Insurance Institute for Highway Safety.

SIX

A Federal Law

General Motors' big blunder in tailing Ralph Nader had far-reaching consequences. It made America's largest corporation look like a bully—a clumsy bully at that. And all because Nader had the audacity to criticize the safety of American cars and, in particular, the rollover tendencies of GM's hot-selling Chevy Corvair.

It was David versus Goliath all over again. But this time the result would be different than in the earlier skirmishes with little-known doctors, engineers, and professors whom GM and other auto companies had pushed around or largely ignored. The press had a field day criticizing the invasion of Nader's privacy by GM's private detectives and the effort to intimidate a then-unknown safety advocate. The news story went national and then global.

It all came at a terrible time for GM and the American automobile industry. It happened just as a powerful senator with a savvy staff was rethinking the direction of his career. Eventually, GM's monumental error helped destroy its unique and dominant position in the American automobile market.

Warren G. Magnuson was the senator. He served a total of eight years in the House of Representatives and then thirty-six years in the Senate, representing the voters of the state of Washington. In his last two decades, beginning in the mid-1960s with automobile safety, he also represented—in the broadest sense—the interests of all American consumers. Magnuson became, in the opinion of many, "The most important consumer champion in America."[1]

But he was not a consumer champion, or even a great safety advocate, during the early years of his Senate career. He was known at first as an insider, a confidante of presidents, a bearer of federal bucks to his home state—and at times a playboy.[2]

Elected to the Senate in 1944, after four terms in the House of Representatives, Magnuson earned a reputation as a dashing bachelor. He liked his vodka, played poker, and dated several attractive young women, including one aspiring Hollywood starlet named Toni Seven. Once he romanced her all the way to Hawaii, somehow managing to miss the opening session of Congress in the process.

From 1955 to 1979 Magnuson also was chairman of the Senate Commerce Committee. In the early years of his chairmanship the committee was a quiet, business-friendly place.

Mike Pertschuk, Magnuson's consumer counsel and then staff director of the committee in the latter years of his tenure, remembers that the first bill he was directed to work on was actually drafted by the National Association of Manufacturers. It was written to exempt from the antitrust laws "retail price maintenance" of consumer products by their manufacturer. This allowed manufacturers to set retail prices for otherwise competing stores and thus increase prices paid by consumers.[3]

It was not a great start for a so-called consumer counsel. Not until years later did Pertschuk and Magnuson's chief of staff, Jerry Grinstein, recognize that if the senator was to continue his political career, he would have to be "reinvented."

Magnuson's rise as a consumer champion came about almost by accident. In his fourth Senate campaign in 1962, he was the odds-on favorite for easy reelection. With a solid New Deal voting record, a powerful Senate committee position advantageous to his home state, and a reputation as a consummate Washington insider, Magnuson looked unbeatable. He had won reelection in 1956 with over 61 percent of the vote. But things would be different this time around.

In the 1962 campaign, Magnuson faced a virtually unknown opponent, the reverend Richard Christiansen. Christiansen was a handsome young Lutheran minister and, in sharp contrast to Magnuson, a dynamic speaker. He was ahead of his time in organizing often-ignored women voters with an organization he called "Women on the Warpath." Christiansen was an early proponent of "family values." He called Magnuson's support for the United Nations the equivalent to backing a Communist front. The reverend turned out to be a Tea Party precursor and dangerous opponent who, in those Cold War years, did not hesitate to imply in his advertisements that Magnuson was a "Communist collaborator."[4]

The senator survived the challenge from Christiansen. But it was by the narrowest of margins—only 45,000 votes out of almost a million cast. It was a demoralizing win for one of the most powerful politicians of his day.

The fact that Magnuson liked to play cards, drink, and was a stumbling public speaker had not helped him. The fact that he now appeared to be an aging, cigar-chomping power broker, complicated the Grinstein–Pertschuk campaign to make Magnuson "Mr. Consumer."

After his persistent staff convinced Magnuson of the precariousness of his Senate career, the senator seemed at least willing to consider turning his political power toward something more appealing to the voters—such as consumer protection. His sixth sense probably told him Grinstein and Pertschuk were right. He was in jeopardy of being summarily retired by the electorate.

Finally, after one long discussion with Grinstein, "Maggie" gave a brief answer to the new consumer protection image and the political reversal they wanted him to make: "Sounds good to me,"[5] he grumbled. So Grinstein, Pertschuk, and the rest of the staff began the process of reinventing Magnuson as a champion of the consumer.

In his next campaign, Magnuson repeatedly used a message to the voters back home. It was: "Keep the big boys honest." As it turned out, in the years to come, he kept his word.

Magnuson was a strong-willed chair of a powerful Senate committee. He had a creative staff. The combination would be a major factor in his effectiveness, after his face-lift as "Mr. Consumer." In the 89th Congress, which began in January 1965 and adjourned in October 1966, Magnuson's committee used its sweeping jurisdiction . . . and its clout. The chairman led the committee in producing major legislation on a broad variety of consumer issues including the elimination from the market of hazardous toys, inclusion of cancer warnings on the labels of cigarette packages, "Truth in Packaging" regarding the contents and size on the labels of consumer products, tire-safety standards, safety of oceangoing cruise liners, development of high-speed ground transportation, and improved national truck and air service.

It is not likely that Magnuson overlooked the rising profile of the automobile safety issue. Perhaps it was just that he was kept so busy as the chair of a major Senate committee. He and his staff almost missed the rapidly growing and newly recognized problems in the automobile safety field.

But somehow, Magnuson and his staff either did not want the issue in 1965, or they graciously delegated "traffic safety," as it was then called, to the freshman Connecticut senator named Abraham Ribicoff and to his obscure subcommittee. It was the Subcommittee on Executive Reorganization, part of the Senate Government Operations Committee. It had no obvious connection to motor vehicle or highway safety. Its legislative authority on that subject was nonexistent.

Soon, however, Ribicoff and subcommittee member Bobby Kennedy began gaining publicity over their sharp confrontations with the automobile industry over the rising death toll and the industry's seemingly indifferent response to it.

Magnuson took a second look. The industry's consistent position of opposing any federal role at all in vehicle-safety design and performance, other than shelling out billions of federal dollars for new federal interstate highways, caught his attention. So did the miniscule amount that senator Robert Kennedy (New York) established the industry spent for automotive safety, in comparison to its billions in annual profits (less than one percent it turned out). Or the large number of "dealer recalls" for defects (478 in 1965), many of which the manufacturers had not told car owners anything about. And perhaps the General Motors–Nader detective story was a factor too.

Magnuson may also have become a bit jealous of the media attention the Senate Government Operations Committee was getting in an area that he considered directly within his jurisdiction—and within his new role as "Mr. Consumer."

Thus, at the urging of Grinstein and Pertschuk, the senator determined to take the lead in what was suddenly developing as the major consumer protection issue of the year. The Senate Commerce Committee pulled rank and took control of the motor vehicle safety issue in March 1966. This was immediately after the GM–Nader detective story went public.

Magnuson and the Commerce Committee held seven days of hearings starting on March 16 and ending on April 6, 1966. By that time there was broad popular interest and national publicity over automobile safety and the Nader–GM scandal. That was fine with the committee and its chairman. It made doing what they ultimately did a lot easier.

National interest had been ignited by the release of Ralph Nader's book *Unsafe at Any Speed*, by the industry's hardheaded opposition to any real role for the federal government in motor vehicle safety design and performance, by General Motors' bumbling gumshoe attempt to smear the young author, and by the Johnson administration's ensuing decision to ask Congress for the passage of the first federal motor vehicle safety law in history.

It was clear to Magnuson that the ball should be in his court. He was pleased to take it. His staff thought that at long last something needed to be done about the growing motor vehicle safety problem, probably by the federal government. Exactly what that something was remained very much unclear as Magnuson's hearings commenced in March 1966. President Johnson had included a statement on the motor vehicle safety issue in his 1966 State of the Union message to Congress—and to the millions of Americans listening that January evening. Johnson spoke mostly about the two overriding issues of the day—the administration's "War on Poverty" and the quagmire of the bloody, seemingly endless Vietnam War. In his ten-page State of the Union address the President devoted just two sentences to highway safety. He called for the nation to "arrest the destruction of life and property on our highways." And he said he would propose a Highway Safety Act to "end this mounting tragedy."[6]

The President's transportation message released in early March 1966 further spelled out the administration's traffic-safety plan. It forcefully

stated the need for legislation on vehicle design-safety, placing it squarely in the forefront of the public's consciousness:

> Last year, the highway death toll set a new record. The prediction for
> this year is more than 50,000 persons will die on our streets and high-
> ways—more than 50,000 useful and promising lives will be lost, and as
> many families stung by grief. The toll of Americans killed in this way
> since the introduction of the automobile is truly unbelievable. It is 1.5
> million—more than all the combat deaths suffered in all our wars . . .
> No other necessity of modern life has brought more convenience to the
> American people—or more tragedy—than the automobile . . . the carn-
> age on the highways must be arrested . . . we must replace suicide with
> sanity and anarchy with safety.[7]

This call for action by Johnson and the concurrent humiliation of General
Motors over the Nader-tailing incident set the stage for Magnuson and
his Commerce Committee. He opened the March hearings by signaling
that *some* kind of federal legislation was imminent:

> The Senate Commerce Committee opens hearings this morning on leg-
> islation so important that it is likely to mark the second session of the
> 89th Congress as the "automobile safety Congress" . . . the deaths of
> tens of thousands of Americans on the highways each year are not
> inevitable . . . no meaningful program is possible which does not come
> to grips with the design and engineering of the automobile itself.
>
> I know that no one on this committee has any desire to dictate to
> Detroit the style [or] the design of its automobiles. Nor is this commit-
> tee interested in conducting an inquisition into the past practices of the
> automobile industry. But I, for one, feel satisfied that the automobile
> industry welcomes this opportunity to meet its responsibilities to the
> American public.[8]

Was anyone out in Detroit listening? In somewhat mild terms, Magnuson
had offered the automobile industry an olive branch—a last chance to
avoid tough legislation by supporting a federal role, *some* role, in promoting safer American car design. He had also issued a not-so-subtle threat.
It was clear that some legislation would be reported by the committee.
This would not be just a public debate as it had been before, through the
years of the Ken Roberts and Abe Ribicoff investigations. Just what kind
of law would emerge was not at all clear at that point. The manufacturers
totally missed or ignored Magnuson's s hint: if they compromised they
might not have had to deal much with mandatory federal safety standards.

The claimed subject of the hearings was the Johnson administration's
proposed legislation implementing the president's State of the Union and
transportation messages. It was introduced, as drafted by the White
House, by Magnuson as S. 3005 (it was also introduced as H.R. 13228 in
the House). But perhaps because of Detroit's silence on accepting a feder-

al law, in his opening statement Magnuson immediately announced that he would seek to amend and strengthen President Johnson's bill.

The Johnson bill had already been labeled by Nader as something he called a "no-law law." This was because it gave the automobile industry a significant opportunity to delay the effectiveness of federal standards by as much as five years and, in fact, control the entire process.

The White House proposal gave the manufacturers the right to initially write voluntary standards before the federal government would have the chance and the heavy burden of showing that further action was necessary. Detroit should have grabbed the offer. Voluntary industry standards, in any industry, have the reputation of often being weak standards. They are enforceable only through publicity and public awareness, not by government action. The level of such voluntary standards, set by industry committees with limited public participation, can be that demanded by the weakest company, the one with the tightest profit margins. Voluntary standards are "consensus" standards, based on agreement of all industry participants. In dealing with the lives and safety of so many people, safety standards are, and were then, matters not of consensus but of public importance.

Even Maggie's proposed amendments, announced at the first hearing, required only that "interim" standards be issued immediately and left the question of the need for further safety rules open to administrative "discretion." That is, nothing much was mandated. It was all put off to some future date and some unknown future administration. Would the automobile industry take Magnuson's generous offer and support the proposed Magnuson/Johnson law? Or would it adhere to its long history of opposing any significant federal motor vehicle safety role?

Forty witnesses testified over seven days of Commerce Committee hearings. They represented the government (led by secretary of commerce John T. Connor), the automobile industry (represented by John S. Bugas, vice president of Ford, and an officer of the Automobile Manufacturers Association), and consumer advocates like Nader, and Dr. Paul Gikas representing the newly organized Physicians for Automotive Safety. Over several days of hearings, the committee compiled almost six hundred pages of testimony.

The heart of the legislative dispute can easily be summarized from the testimony of just four witnesses. They were: Ribicoff, John S. Bugas of Ford and the Automobile Manufacturers Association, Nader, and Gikas, the little-known doctor then working at the University of Michigan. Each of them focused on the looming issue of what to do about the rising number of motor vehicle deaths and injuries. The sharp differences among them were about the means they urged to deal with the now obvious problem. The motor vehicle industry did not offer a compromise.

Despite all the rhetoric, the main issue was relatively simple. How extensive should the new federal authority be to set enforceable national motor vehicle safety standards? That power was central to the proposed law. It was delegated in the administration's bill to the inexperienced, business-friendly Department of Commerce. Ultimately it was to be transferred to the as yet nonexistent Department of Transportation. Nobody much disagreed with that—there was no place else to put it. But the nature of the standard-setting power was very much in dispute. In effect, the safety devil was in the differing bills' details.

In handing off the issue to his senior colleague Magnuson, Senator Ribicoff was specific in his recommendations. Ribicoff repeated the gruesome statistics of rising deaths and injuries. He asked:

> Could it be that we have reached the point where we simply accept the highway toll as an ordinary fact of life? Is this one of the prices we must pay for the privilege for living in a modern, technological society? I hope not. We must concern ourselves with more than the causes of accidents."

Ribicoff endorsed the decades-old position of doctors, accident investigators, and university researchers, which had long been ignored by the manufacturers and the safety establishment: "We must look beyond the accident to the cause of the injury that results. I am speaking, of course, about the so-called 'second collision,' the often lethal battering which the occupants of a vehicle incur as the result of even a minor crash."[9]

And Ribicoff challenged one of the key arguments of the manufacturers: "The automobile industry seems inclined to believe that the American public will not buy a safe car. In fact, some spokesmen for the industry have stated that safety doesn't sell, and that they have no choice if they want to stay in business but to give the public what the public wants."

But Ribicoff argued that the public and the press were now "aroused" and had finally grasped the "significance of the second collision"—and presumably the need for federal vehicle standards as a means of preventing the deaths and injuries "that inevitably result from accidents."[10] Because the administration's bill made federal safety standards only optional for the secretary, Ribicoff said: "We believe the president's highway safety bill can be and should be strengthened and improved."[11]

Ribicoff's targeting of the need to strengthen the government's vehicle design authority to address the "second collision" in federal safety standards set the stage for the appearance of the motor vehicle manufacturers. Would they concur with such a bill or would they continue their traditional position that a voluntary or delayed approach to safety design (dominated by the companies), coupled with individual state enforcement action and driver education was preferable to federal responsibility?

When Bugas of Ford got his chance to testify for the motor vehicle industry, he did not alter course.

> We believe that our past record in improving the safety of our vehicles is by any reasonable criterion an excellent one. But we know that what we and others have done in the past is no longer sufficient to meet today's and tomorrow's needs. . . . We propose as an alternative the following three-point program:
>
> 1. A commitment by the four automobile manufacturers to a voluntary action program to improve the safety design of vehicles as rapidly as is feasible . . . for establishment and adoption within the industry of voluntary industry-wide performance standards for vehicle safety.
> 2. [That] the governmental role in vehicle safety standards be strengthened . . . to provide a joint federal-state program, one with federal participation in and support for a much more effective Vehicle Equipment Safety Commission [then a virtually invisible state-directed organization].
> 3. A commitment by the automobile manufacturers to "report frequently" to the Congress and the public.

The three-point program amounted to more of the same: industry self-regulation with little federal involvement. Bugas asserted it would achieve the unanimous goal of increased safety by a different road and, most importantly, that Congress should accept that road: "It will achieve the improvement in performance standards for vehicle safety intended by [the bill]. It will do so more effectively and will do so without the very real and serious risks that we have pointed out."

Bugas also restated the industry's argument of the potentially severe economic impact of a federal law: the automobile industry would be seriously weakened as a source of increased employment and higher incomes in a broad area of the economy if the growth of productivity in industry were retarded by "premature or mistaken regulation."[12] Even if the regulations were later rescinded, "poorly conceived standards," Bugas said, could add unnecessary cost, and stop the progress of experimentation that "often leads to safer cars, as well as other improvements."[13]

After this dinosaur-like restatement of the traditional manufacturer anti-regulation position, Nader testified.

> A superficial reading of the administration's bill [not the weaker Detroit position] might lead some to conclude that the federal government was facing up to the fundamental democratic issue of giving a meaningful and continuous voice to the public in deciding how much safety the motorist is to receive. . . . A closer reading of the bill would indicate that such an objective is in no way required.

In fact, said Nader, "Most of the language of S. 3005 rests on the 'shifting sands of discretionary authority' [as given by Congress to the executive branch] and it diminishes much of the significance of the bill's sometimes encouraging prose."[14]

Nader followed with a laundry list of defects in the proposed administration bill:

- It should ensure that motor vehicle safety standards applied to pedestrian safety.
- The federal standards should include their technical or engineering basis, so they could be evaluated by independent experts and the public [these technical specifications might be deemed trade secrets by the carmakers].
- The bill should make government issuance of the standards within one year, mandatory [not discretionary as provided in the administration's bill].
- Court review should be broadened to include a right to sue for "affected parties" and a right of review by "consumers and insurers."
- The production of prototype "safe cars" should be mandated.
- Vehicle manufacturers should be required to submit annual performance [crash] data, showing how well their cars were performing in actual use.
- All car-maker communications with their dealers regarding safety should be submitted to the government and be made public.
- Enforcement should be strengthened to include criminal penalties, because drivers, Nader said, already face criminal penalties for reckless driving and similar offenses.

Was Nader's plan for the legislation a mere wish list? Or might it actually survive the legislative process? The car manufacturers were betting "no." Only time would tell who was right.

Surprisingly, it was the final Senate witness late on the afternoon of April 6, the last day of the hearings, who furnished the most compelling testimony. He was Dr. Paul Gikas, accident researcher, representative of the Physicians for Automotive Safety and a member of the staff of the University of Michigan Medical School.

Gikas had seen the actual results of hundreds of car crashes. He had been at the scene of hundreds of wrecks. Heknew the human part of the debate. He had told the same story before, to no avail, at hearings in Iowa, New York, and Massachusetts. For the Senate he added a refutation of the testimony of the manufacturers that their cars were safe, or at least as safe as they could reasonably be made.

Before a largely empty hearing room (the press having departed to meet their news deadlines) Gikas reviewed General Motors' claim that it had improved the door locks on its new models significantly. He referred to Bugas's testimony the day before when he had said: "With respect to doors, major advances by automobile manufacturers during the past ten years have significantly increased the extent to which car doors stay closed during accidents."[15] This, of course, could prevent people from being thrown onto the pavement, or worse, in a crash.

Gikas thought otherwise. He showed slides of a fatal accident. It involved a 1955 Pontiac with the new, improved GM door locks. He had arrived on the scene shortly after the collision.

> I am going into this one case in detail to point out the in-depth investigation that was carried out. The car was there with the doors open. This is when the man came out. The man was dead at the scene.
>
> An external examination of the body showed very few marks. There was no indication of the cause of death from external examination. It turns out that . . . two marks in the lower back area turned out to be very significant. This man died from a ruptured aorta . . . completely severed.
>
> We are postulating he was thrown out from the car facedown. The two marks in his back correspond with the two rims in the top of the right front door. We feel he was face down. The top of the door came down hitting the back of his spine and rupturing the aorta . . . If this man had stayed inside the car with the use of a safety belt, or if the door had stayed shut, he could have survived this accident.[16]

It was a vivid example of one unnecessary death; a fitting coda to Magnuson's promise that the administration bill would be toughened by his committee.

By the end of the committee's hearings on April 6, 1966, the die had been cast. It seemed clear to most observers, except perhaps to the motor vehicle industry, that there was going to be a tough federal motor vehicle safety law. It was going to include authority for the federal government to set mandatory safety standards for new cars. How strong the authority would be now depended on the industry's willingness to compromise, its lobbying clout, and the effectiveness of outgunned consumer groups.

The industry was betting that its plan for a five-year phase-in and an opportunity to first develop its own voluntary standards would succeed. Perhaps its position would prevail behind the closed doors of the Senate committee markup, or more likely in the House of Representatives, as it had so many times before. If that was what industry leaders were counting on, it was an amazing miscalculation.

The House proceedings on the administration's safety bill started in March 1966. The hearings were before the Interstate and Foreign Commerce Committee, at the time no great friend of the consumer. The committee was led by a new chairman, the soft-spoken, fatherly Harley O. Staggers of West Virginia. According to one journalist, the proceedings were "mired in dissension for weeks."[17]

Joan Claybrook had recently started work as a member of the staff of newly elected congressman James MacKay. He was a Democrat from Georgia. Perhaps because of his support for the Civil Rights and Voting Rights Acts, he was rewarded by the House leadership with a spot on the important Commerce Committee. Claybrook had been hired as a junior staff member by a junior member of the committee. She was the only House staff member who attended all seven days of Magnuson's Senate hearings. She was impressed with the witnesses who testified.

The House committee staff, as well as many Commerce Committee members, appeared skeptical about the broad scope of the Senate bill. As usual, they were under intense pressure from industry lobbyists to take a different path than the Senate and to water the bill down. The House was not known as the "graveyard" of consumer legislation for nothing. The committee staff had scheduled only one day for hearings on the auto safety issue, apparently in an effort to downplay the importance of the legislation—and also the press coverage.

Congressman MacKay, at Claybrook's suggestion, wrote letters to every witness who had appeared at the Senate hearings and asked that they request an opportunity to give their testimony before the House Committee. It turned out to be brilliant idea. The House staff was deluged with requests to testify. They could hardly refuse Senate witnesses a chance to speak. The result was a much longer, more intense series of hearings than had been planned, more press coverage—and a very angry House Commerce Committee staff.

Claybrook said later that the committee counsel who was working on the hearings "came over to our office and screamed like hell at me for interfering with their plan for a one-day hearing, and blah, blah, blah that this would disrupt the committee's schedule and all that stuff. But it built a strong record in the House and may have sensitized some wavering members to the importance of the issue."[18]

There was, in fact, significant support in the House, even among supposedly pro-consumer Democrats, for the industry's voluntary, state-oriented approach. "Your judgment is quite sound" was the comment of representative Lionel Van Deerlin, a California Democrat, generally a proponent of strong federal safety laws to one manufacturer's witness. "An excellent presentation," added representative John Dingell, Democrat of Michigan.[19]

Some of the criticism of the Senate bill came from Republican committee members. Representative Glenn Cunningham, a seven-term member from Nebraska warned that, "If we lead everybody to think the federal government is going to take care of auto safety, then all the local and private groups who have promoted it for years are going to lose support and we will have 100,000 highway fatalities a year instead of 50,000." Representative Samuel Devine of Ohio, who served twenty-two years, suggested that the industry had "caved in to government pressure." Devine added that he still believed "free enterprise is preferable to controls"—whether or not the carmakers did.[20]

Shortly after the manufacturers offered their latest proposal in the House, governor George Romney of Michigan, later president of American Motors, said the bill should be revised to give the states a major role in devising the standards and final authority to enforce them.[21] Romney testified before the House committee that the industry would need five or six years lead time for engineering, design studies and retooling, once the secretary had established vehicle safety performance "guidelines"—which would not have been enforceable as mandatory standards.

According to the *Baltimore Sun*, "This would mean that automobiles equipped with federal safety performance features might be as long as ten years coming off the production lines of Detroit manufacturers."[22]

Congressman MacKay, who had greatly expanded the House hearings, offered a series of amendments to the bill that were based on Magnuson's Senate bill and were designed to bring it closer to the Senate version. Staggers, now apparently leaning toward the merits of the Senate proposal, incorporated most of them in the bill he placed before the House committee as a starting point. Whether they would end up in *any* bill was uncertain for weeks.

The automobile manufacturers' legislative counterproposal offered in the House was supported by the nation's top business leaders. After a meeting at a fancy hotel in Hot Springs, Virginia of a new organization called the Business Council, W. D. Murphy, president of Campbell's Soup Company, reported on the group's position on the bill:

"It's of the same order as the Hula Hoop—a fad. Six months from now we will probably be on another kick." He charged that the publicity being given the current "auto safety kick is unfair, deadly, distorted and harmful" and he said it was the "sole cause" of a recent drop in automobile sales. Murphy was the chairman of the one-hundred-member Business Council that had just been established to advise the government on policy issues affecting the nation's business. Nearly all of the Business Council members were the heads of large corporations. According to Murphy, all of them "feel the same way I do about the auto safety controversy."[23]

With the support of at least one prominent governor (George Romney) and much of the business community (the Business Council), the automobile industry's alternative proposal for voluntary safety standards and state initiatives appeared to have some momentum.

What Detroit was really fighting for in the House of Representatives was to get a final House bill that would be different enough to create a deadlock with the stronger Senate bill. That would force a closed-door conference committee of the two bodies that might write a bill that the industry believed it could live with. For a while that seemed quite possible. The final result appeared uncertain. Nader issued almost daily press releases alleging new vehicle hazards, often based on leaks from inside the industry. Industry lobbyists led by Lloyd Cutler, the eminent Washington attorney, fought back aggressively.

The debate was ultimately resolved in early June by the intervention of President Johnson and his Deputy Attorney General, Ramsey Clark. The president appealed to the state governors for help in speeding Congressional action on the administration's (and Magnuson's) "traffic safety" bill. LBJ took the unusual step of meeting at the White House with a delegation of seven "concerned" governors. He stepped out of the meeting and issued a statement: "The need for national standards is urgent. Every day wasted is a day in which more lives will be wasted. Every day lost puts us that much further behind. So I ask you to work with us with moving this badly needed legislation forward." The governors agreed with the president, according to governor Clifford Hansen of Wyoming. Only Governor Romney seemed to have reservations. [24]

But the final word on the industry's counterproposal, and the final nail in its coffin, was an eighteen-page letter to Magnuson's committee from deputy attorney general Ramsey Clark. Later promoted to attorney general, Clark said the industry's proposed amendments were likely to delay establishment of safety standards for at least five years and severely impair the federal government's authority to devise effective regulations and to enforce them. [25] He characterized the industry proposal as just a "scheme" that involved the possibility of great delay. The president's attack, the support of the governors (but not Romney), and Ramsey Clark's legal analysis pretty much killed the carmakers' alternative proposal. The LBJ White House and Ramsey Clark at Justice had weighed in forcefully—in support of strong automobile safety legislation.

The largest industry in the nation had guessed wrong again. After all the decades of delay, the Senate, led by Magnuson, did not back down this time. With the support of an aroused public and an involved press it was now prepared to get tough. The motor vehicle manufacturers had shockingly misjudged public opinion—and Congress' political will. The provisions of the final Senate legislation (which became almost entirelythe final federal law) were written by the cigar-chomping Magnuson and his staff and by the determined Nader. He was just thirty-two years old at the time.

The Senate moved with lightning speed for such major legislation. Within two months after the conclusion of its hearings the Commerce Committee acted. On June 23, 1966 it unanimously reported out of committee, to the full Senate, the National Traffic and Motor Vehicle Safety Act. [26]

The final Senate bill was a total revision of the Johnson administration's weak initial proposal. It had originally envisioned federal safety standards only if after five years the secretary determined that the automobile industry had not taken sufficient voluntary action in establishing safety standards.

The Senate bill strengthened the administration proposal by directing the secretary to issue twenty-six *interim* vehicle safety standards almost immediately (by January 1967). They were to be based on government purchasing requirements issued by the General Services Administration under Ken Roberts's 1964 bill. Final upgraded standards were mandated one year later, by January 1968. The bill added bus and truck standards to the proposed law. The Senate also required manufacturers of vehicles *and* equipment as well as importers to:

- Maintain records and make reports as required by the Secretary of Transportation;
- Permit inspection of their facilities by federal officials at "reasonable times," to determine compliance with safety standards;
- Notify the purchaser of any motor vehicle containing a "safety-related" defect by certified mail, promptly after discovering the defect. [27]

Notably, even the strong Senate bill omitted any requirement that manufacturers actually repair and pay for safety-related defects. That mandate was added in an amendment to the statute in 1974, sponsored by Magnuson and representative John Moss in the House. [28]

The final Senate bill was shuttled back and forth by Senate staff between two small conference rooms, to be checked separately by Lloyd Cutler on behalf of the manufacturers and Ralph Nader. Then it was unanimously approved by the Commerce Committee and, after almost all of Nader's amendments had been added, sent to the Senate floor. It was passed *unanimously* by the Senate the next day. [29]

After another effort by Cutler and the industry to weaken the bill in the House, the opposition collapsed and the Staggers committee, then the full House *unanimously* approved a bill on August 17, 1966. It was virtually identical to the Senate bill.

At the same time that the Motor Vehicle Safety Act [30] was passed, Congress also enacted the Highway Safety Act of 1966. [31] That companion law gave the federal government the power to require state highway safety rules, such as requiring seat belt usage by drivers and passengers in any state that accepted federal highway funds. That pretty much amounted to all of them.

The bills were sent to the president and signed on September 9, 1966, just four months after the end of the Senate hearings.

Consumer champion Nader was snubbed. He was not invited to the White House signing ceremony. He applauded the final bill, but voiced disappointment that it did not contain criminal sanctions against violators. The opponents of the legislation, mainly the car manufacturers, had lost their bid to prevent federal regulation of safety-related design and performance features of motor vehicles and equipment sold in the United States.

The Senate report accompanying the legislation proved important. It is the definitive legislative history, by the authors, of Congress' intent. For the first time the automakers were identified as having a primary responsibility for the highway death toll. The committee, it said, had met with disturbing evidence of the industry's chronic subordination of safe design to promotional styling and overriding stress on power, acceleration, speed, and "ride" to the relative neglect of safety performance or collision protection.[32] The Senate report also declared motor vehicle safety to be "the overriding purpose" of the bill,[33] a statement that became crucial in the Supreme Court's review of the federal air bag standard years later.

The companion Highway Safety Act also had an impact on the rising death and injury toll, but in a different way. It at first required, and later offered to the states large amounts of federal highway construction money if they would enact vehicle enforcement and use standards. Many, but not all states did. Foremost among the state highway safety laws now are:

- Primary enforcement mandatory seat belt laws for front and rear-seat riders (meaning state and local police can stop a car without seeing a traffic violation).
- Ignition interlock devices (in some states) for convicted drunk driving offenders.
- All-driver text messaging restrictions.
- All-rider motorcycle helmet use laws.
- Child booster seat laws for children under seven years old, at minimum.
- Mandatory graduated driver-licensing laws and mandatory driver education training in schools.[34]

Ten years after passage of the motor vehicle and highway safety laws the House Commerce Committee's Oversight and Investigations Subcommittee, chaired by congressman John Moss, conducted an extensive review of the record of the National Highway Traffic Safety Administration (NHTSA). It was charged with administering the new law within the Department of Transportation.

Moss's subcommittee issued a detailed "report card" noting that as of 1976 a total of fifty federal safety standards had been issued. They were directed at things like: motor vehicle structural design, equipment, tires, child safety seat construction and secure attachment to vehicles, shatterproof windshields, lap and shoulder belts, and collapsible steering columns. The new safety agency had also promulgated a dozen regulations requiring vehicle manufacturers to take on other safety-related activities; for example, promptly reporting safety-related defects to the government and using specified test methods to test for compliance with federal safety standards. The National Highway Traffic Safety Administration had also conducted a compliance testing program and imposed some civil penalties for violations. Through May 1976 the fines totaled a modest $1.1 million, based on 175 separate investigations of violations.[35] Of greater impact than the fines, were 1,500 "voluntary" recalls announced by manufacturers, covering some forty-five million cars over ten years.[36] Years later, in 2014, there were sixty million cars recalled, not all of them brought in for repair by their owners. Though these recalls are labeled "voluntary" most were done after federal investigations or under pressure from NHTSA regulators.

In 1966 and for decades before, the American motor vehicle industry had elected to be a follower, not a leader, in vehicle safety. For example, steel-belted radial tires, which are safer and get better gas mileage than other tires, were available for many years—but only from foreign manufacturers. The value of the "three-point" shoulder and lap belt system was first established by Swedish car manufacturer Volvo. Volvo's experience prompted the issuance of federal standard 208 in January 1968, which over the objections of the domestic industry, required lap and shoulder belts for front seats in passenger cars (they are now required for all front and back seats).

Ironically, the same kind of reluctant industry approach was evident with the introduction of small, foreign, fuel-efficient cars to the American market. Initially it was the Volkswagen Beetle. Ultimately, the Beetle and small Japanese cars claimed a major segment of the new-car market. The failure of the American companies to evaluate consumer opinion and meet the foreign challenge parallels their slow response to the safety challenge of earlier decades.

The American automobile industry's failure to employ its superior technological capability to design safety, emissions control, and better gas mileage into its cars was closely related to its overriding focus on styling and horsepower in its automobiles. One result has been an erosion of its share of the domestic new vehicle market.

One might ask how the American car industry could have come forward with such a weak proposal for "voluntary" safety standards and reliance on the impotent state Vehicle Equipment Safety Commission on the eve of the impending passage of the 1966 Safety Act. It is a question that has been debated endlessly in the decades since. One answer was offered shortly after the events of March–September 1966.

In a feature article published by *Fortune* magazine in August of that year, author Dan Cordtz concluded, "Many strong supporters of auto safety legislation agree that GM's conduct, then and later was the most important single factor in establishing a congressional climate conducive to the passage of a tough safety bill."[37]

The *Fortune* article suggested that there had been a chance for a better result for the manufacturers had the industry taken a different tack. "In spite of the poor impression made before the Ribicoff subcommittee it was conceivable that the industry could have escaped with a relatively mild bill, but for the Nader incident." *Fortune,* certainly writing from a business perspective, said there had been "two decades of warnings of possible trouble to come on safety, but the industry was 'so out of touch . . . they were visibly shocked at the critical onslaught that followed.'"[38]

Most knowledgeable people agreed that the motor vehicle industry and General Motors in particular, was disconnected from Washington and nonresponsive to public opinion at the time the safety legislation was considered.[39] One executive of a General Motors competitor summed the events up: "I get mad every time I think about that stunt [(referring to the trailing of Nader)]. They made the entire industry look bad and we are all going to suffer for it."[40]

Nonetheless, a single event, even the brazen attempt to discredit young Nader, cannot fully explain the historic legislation that followed.

The American Medical Association is not known as a bastion of liberalism or government intervention in the marketplace. For years it maintained a cautious position representing the interests of physicians and the medical industry. The *Journal of the American Medical Association* is its primary voice. A decade *before* the events of 1965 and 1966 highlighted the issue of highway deaths and injuries, the journal published an article in 1957called "Death on the Highways":[41]

> It will be a long while before there is any marked improvement in the prevention of accidents. Therefore, we must be concerned with prevention of injury, or the reduction of the probability of severe injury.

The famous race driver, Barney Oldfield, had made a statement at a national safety meeting after he had become a safety advisor for the automobile makers, in which he proclaimed the arrival [of] "revolutionary new safety features" that year, "greater protection for passengers by the elimination of protruding knobs and handles on the instrument panel . . . and even the key is recessed . . . throttle and choke disappear on slides in the rounded base of the panel . . . and the cushion of the front seats rounds back over the top as a safety pad for those in the backseat.

The journal, referring Oldfield's statement, warned,

> *This was in 1936* . . .This is our number-one public health problem. We are confronted with a massacre without precedent, without good reason and without a ready solution. The welfare of millions of persons can be benefited by a concerted safety design program of the automobile industry.[42] [emphasis added]

Apparently, neither Congress, the motor vehicle industry, nor the driving public were familiar with the *Journal of the American Medical Association.*

Nor with the pledge of the race car driver Oldfield, presumably given with the approval of his employers, in 1936.

The most surprising thing about all of this is that it took so long. Passenger automobiles were, by the 1950s, the only form of interstate transportation that was not regulated by the federal government for safety.[43] A federal steamboat inspection service began before the Civil War. Railroad cars were inspected by 1907. Aircraft safety was regulated by 1926. The automobile industry's products were the only form of transportation that could still be sold to consumers in interstate commerce without government oversight, even after the death and injury of millions of its customers.[44]

Detroit had lost its bid to prevent federal regulation of the safety of motor vehicles and highways. The companies promised to "live with the bill."[45] But the industry continued its efforts to weaken key safety standards under the new act. It had only temporarily lost its political clout. It raised objections to the first standards issued by NHTSA in 1968 and later, to most things the safety agency proposed. Manufacturers sent their chief executives to the White House and to President Nixon. They pressed Secretaries of Transportation. They lobbied administrators of NHTSA. They argued, often successfully, to the House and Senate Appropriations committees for restrictions on the safety agency's funding. The car safety wars did not end.

The enactment of strong federal motor vehicle and highway safety laws marked the single biggest milestone in the century-long fight for safer cars and roads. But the long struggle against death and injury on the highways was really just beginning.

NOTES

1. Shelby Scates, *Warren G. Magnuson and the Shaping of Twentieth-Century America* (Seattle: University of Washington Press, 1998), 80, 339–41.

2. "Ex-Senator Warren Magnuson Dies at 84," *Washington Post*, May 21, 1989, B6 (quoted in S. Doc. 101–13, 1990).

3. Michael Pertschuk, *Revolt Against Regulation: The Rise and Pause of the Consumer Movement* (Berkeley: University of California Press, 1982), 25.

4. Scates, *Magnuson*, 207–8.

5. Ibid. See also Michael R. Lemov, *People's Warrior: John Moss and the Fight for Freedom of Information and Consumer Rights* (Madison, NJ: Fairleigh Dickinson University Press/Lanham, Maryland, Rowman & Littlefield Publishing Group, Inc., 2011), 75.

6. *State of the Union Messages of the Presidents: 1790–1966* (New York: Chelsea House Publishers, 1967), 3171.

7. The White House, The President's Message on Transportation, 1966, cited in Hearings, United States Senate, Committee on Commerce (March 16, 1966) S. Doc. 89–49, 7.

8. Hearings before the Committee on Commerce, United States Senate, 89th Congress, 2d Sess., Serial No. 89–49 (March 16, 17, 29, 30 and April 4, 5, 6, 1966), 1.

9. Ibid., 32.

10. Ibid., 33.

11. Ibid., 34.

12. Ibid., 379.

13. Ibid., 380–81.

14. Ibid., 275, 306.

15. Ibid., 569.

16. Ibid., 570.

17. "House Passage of Automobile Safety Bill Near," *Chicago Daily Defender,* July 27, 1966, 6.

18. Interview by the author with Joan Claybrook, November 16, 2011, 17.

19. "Car Industry Consent to Federal Standards for Vehicle Safety Causes Mixed Response," *Wall Street Journal,* April 27, 1966, 5.

20. Ibid.

21. John D. Morris, "Car Makers Said to Delay Safety," *New York Times,* June 4, 1966, 1.

22. James Macness, "Auto Safety Plan Offered," *Baltimore Sun,* May 13, 1966, 6.

23. "Business Leaders Back Car Makers on Safety Issue," *New York Times,* May 14, 1966.

24. Morris, "Car Makers Said to Delay Safety," *New York Times,* June 4, 1966, 1.

25. Ibid.

26. *Congressional Quarterly Almanac,* 89th Congress, 2d Session, 1966, 269.

27. Ibid., 266–80.

28. The Motor Vehicle and School Bus Safety Act, P.L. 93–492 (1974).

29. *Congressional Quarterly Almanac,* 89th Congress, 2d Session (1966), 269; see also Eastman, *Styling Versus Safety,* 247. The Senate vote was 76–0.

30. P.L. 89–563, 80 Stat. 718, 49 U.S. Code 30101 et. seq.

31. P.L. 89–564. The Highway Safety Act established a national highway (as distinguished from motor vehicle) safety program coordinated between the federal and state governments. The act authorized the states to use federal money to strengthen state safety programs under federal guidelines set by NHTSA. Areas which have since been emphasized include safer road design, required vehicle inspections, driver registration requirements, improved pedestrian and child safety, and traffic law enforcement by the states. The Act has used billions of dollars in federal highway funds to induce the states to strengthen their highway safety standards.

32. Cited in House Commerce Committee, Report of the Oversight and Investigations Subcommittee, (1976) 157–90; see S. Report 1301, 89th Congress 2d Session, 2.

33. S. Report 1301 supra, 6; see also, H. Rep. (1976), 89th Congress, 2d Session,1.

34. As of the date of this writing thirty-four states had "primary enforcement" seat belt laws; twenty had ignition interlock requirements after drunk driving convictions; thirty-eight had text messaging restrictions; twenty had all-rider motorcycle helmet laws; thirty-two had child booster seat laws; many had some kind of partial teenaged graduated (age and education) driving restrictions. See "2014 Roadmap of State Highway Safety Laws," Advocates for Highway Safety (Washington, D.C.), 2014.

35. Oversight and Investigations Report, 159.

36. Ibid.

37. Dan Cordtz, "The Face in the Mirror at General Motors," *Fortune* (August 1966): 117, 210.

38. Ibid., 208.

39. Interview by the author with Joan Claybrook, November 30, 2011, 6–8; see also, Pertschuk, *Revolt Against Regulation,* 15–18.

40. Cordtz, "The Face in the Mirror at General Motors," *Fortune* (August 1966): 117, 210.

41. *Journal of the American Medical Association* (January 26, 1957): 262.

42. Ibid., 262.

43. Other than natural gas pipelines, which were first regulated for safety in 1968, P.L. 90–461.

44. O'Connell and Myers, *Safety Last*, 222–23. See also, S. Report 1301, 3.
45. *Congressional Quarterly Almanac*, 1966, 269.

SEVEN

Dr. Haddon, Detroit, and the New Safety Agency

Just thirty-five days after the new automobile safety law was enacted, on October 13, 1966 Dr. William Haddon, president Lyndon Johnson's nominee to become the first administrator of the federal safety agency, appeared before the Senate Commerce Committee.[1] Haddon's thick, owl-rimmed glasses and close-cropped crew cut were topped off that morning by his trademark bow tie. He had begun wearing it in medical school, out of concern not to bother the patients he would treat.[2]

As it turned out, Dr. Haddon never had patients after finishing medical school and an internship at the Philadelphia General Hospital. He chose a different path in life.

The Committee Chairman, gruff Warren Magnuson, was critical of Haddon's overuse of the word "study" in his prepared answers to the committee's advance list of questions. The senator surely knew Haddon's reputation as a scientist and committed automobile safety proponent. Nevertheless, he pressed his president's nominee hard.

"We have a warehouse full of studies," Magnuson said. "We want you to take some action down there."

With his characteristic caution, Haddon replied that his new agency would "move as rapidly and as practically and as energetically as possible to reduce the tragedy [of automobile deaths] that we are all concerned with."[3]

Magnuson was not satisfied. He cited one of the challenges the nominee would immediately face: "I notice in the morning paper that Chrysler Company has dropped safety disc brakes." The company had eliminated the safer disc brakes from some models of its station wagons in order to cut prices by $97 a car. It had quietly announced this to its dealers, but had made no public announcement—even though Chrysler had earlier

109

touted disc brakes as a standard feature on all its station wagons. "Do you think that is a matter that the owners should be advised of?" asked the Washington senator. "Do you consider that your job will be to take a look at some of these things?"

Haddon's response was: "I certainly do."

Still Magnuson, the primary author of the groundbreaking National Traffic and Motor Vehicle Safety Act, was not fully satisfied. He warned the nominee, "It seems to me that you are going to have to be quite alert to many of these things to carry out the purposes of this bill. You don't need to study that, do you?"

"No, sir." replied Haddon.

The senator's message to Johnson's academic-looking nominee was quite clear.[4]

Haddon came to the job at NHTSA well prepared. Born in Orange, New Jersey in 1927, he attended Boston public schools after his family moved there. During the Second World War he served in the Army Air Force. Haddon received a degree in science from MIT and then a medical degree from the Harvard School of Public Health. His decision not to choose a career as a practicing physician—not to mention forgoing a lucrative private practice—can only be explained by his scientific inclination and his personal values. He later described himself as a medical epidemiologist, fighting an "epidemic" of automobile crash deaths and injuries. It was an epidemic that had by 1966 killed over two million Americans.[5]

Haddon later told the *Los Angeles Times* that the automobile was the "central, largest single health problem in the first half of life, after you get through birth and the first year."[6] He had come to the conclusion that "I could do more for my fellow man as a public health administrator of some sort, than perhaps as just another doctor."[7]

Haddon was foremost a scientist. He "was all business . . . never made a joke, didn't tolerate fools easily."[8] Leon Robertson, in later years a colleague at the Insurance Institute for Highway Safety, said he could have "a very nasty personality and loved to bait people when their logic or research methods did not measure up to his standards. . . . Nearly everyone in the injury field, including me, had encounters with him that were extremely unpleasant."[9] Still, Robertson said "He was the most objective, honest scientist that I have ever known."[10] Most importantly, remembered Senator Pat Moynihan, "He never forgot what we were talking about were children, with their heads smashed and broken bodies and dead people."[11]

Haddon began working for the New York State Department of Health in 1956 while he was still in graduate school at Harvard. He started way down the ladder as, "Acting Assistant Commissioner for Public Health Research, Development, and Evaluation." He moved up to director of

Chronic Disease Services. Eventually, he gained recognition for his detailed research and trenchant analyses of the epidemiology of highway deaths, especially alcohol-related car accidents. In 1958, Haddon crossed paths with Patrick Moynihan, who was then working as acting secretary for Averell Harriman, the governor of New York.

Moynihan was leading a meeting on traffic safety at the state capitol in Albany. Haddon, seated in the back of the room, asked so many pointed questions (such as, "What data are you using?") that Moynihan (then a Democrat) was convinced he was a Republican spy.

After the meeting, Moynihan suggested he and the persistent questioner go across the street to Yezzi's, a local watering hole, for a drink. There, the two men got down to the specifics of traffic safety. Haddon explained his theory that the best traffic safety measures were *passive*, not active, and were injury *preventative*. In later years the word "passive" often became "automatic." "Active," as in seat belts, became known as "manual," which more clearly says to the car occupant that some action is required to safely buckle up.

The best way to reduce deaths and injuries, Haddon told Moynihan, was to make automobiles safer *during and after* crashes without the need for driver action. Moynihan later said he "fell under Haddon's spell."[12] [2]

While at the New York State Department of Health, the doctor was the principle author of a book, *Accident Research Methods and Approaches*. When it was published in 1964, it was the first analysis of automobile accidents based upon a scientific methodology. It included the genesis of the now-famous "Haddon Matrix." The book won the Metropolitan Life Award of Merit from the National Safety Council.[13] Haddon was prouder of the Bronfman Prize, given him by the American Public Health Association. He thought the National Safety Council was weak on some key auto safety issues.[14]

The Haddon Matrix, which was developed from a pure public health perspective, categorized automobile crash causes by three general types: the pre-crash, crash, and post-crash phases. Then it factored in human, vehicle, and environmental error. It would look like this in an analysis of the primary cause of a vehicle injury or death:

	Human	Vehicle	Environment
Pre-Crash	A		
Crash		B	
Post-Crash			C

(The letters are illustrative and would vary).

One of Haddon's most creative contributions to automobile safety (which he spelled out for Moynihan that day in Albany) lay in refocusing the nation's strategy on the prevention of motor vehicle deaths and injuries.

Over time, he led an effort to move the emphasis on primary causation away from Box A (the driver) and towards Box B (the vehicle). Improving vehicle design safety, or "crashworthiness," was where Haddon and most safety advocates thought the focus should always have been. That was where the most substantial payoff was. It was over this change in public perception and manufacturer design focus that Haddon fought his major battles with Detroit and to some extent with public opinion. To achieve such a shift in understanding, he often attempted to force new safety technologies upon a sometimes unwilling industry—and upon an often uninformed public.

Haddon had broad interests. He was an amateur archeologist, a historian, and a fine arts connoisseur. He collected nineteenth-century carpentry tools. As to his car-purchasing practices, he always bought the one "with all the available safety features"[15]—of which there were few at the time. This caution presumably stemmed from his personal conclusion that he was only "an average driver . . . subject to the same hazards as others have to endure." Sooner or later, he knew, he was likely to have an accident.

Despite shifting titles and jurisdictions, what is now known as the National Highway Traffic Safety Administration (NHTSA) was fully Haddon's domain from its creation in 1966, through his resignation, just after president Richard Nixon took office in February 1969. He created what we know today as the National Highway Traffic Safety Administration (NHTSA) from scratch.

His Senate confirmation as administrator was by voice vote, suggesting little or no opposition—at least not at first. That would soon change. Haddon's confirmation by the full Senate took place just one day after his "grilling" by Magnuson.[16]

On October 21, 1966 Haddon was sworn in as the first traffic safety administrator by Alan S. Boyd, who had just become the nation's first Secretary of Transportation. When asked by an aggressive reporter at the ceremony about likely new safety standards that his agency would adopt, the new administrator flatly refused to commit himself on whether he favored the nineteen "interim" safety standards, which had been helpfully prepared by the Automobile Manufacturers Association.[17] In reality he felt they fell far short of the safety standards he intended NHTSA to issue by the fast-approaching congressional deadline just three months away; January 31, 1967.

Haddon might have looked like a bespectacled, lost-in-thought professor of public health, but he acted with political judgment—and some nerve.

About a month after his confirmation, he and his newly created safety agency had their first major skirmish with the automobile industry. A headline from the November 23, 1966 *New York Times* reads: "Defect

Publicity Angers Industry: Auto Companies Wanted Faults Kept Secret." The story reported that Haddon's new agency had made public industry defect reports collected by the federal government under the requirements of the Safety Act.[18] Another *New York Times* article listed in some detail the General Motors, Ford, Chrysler, and American Motors models and the number of cars that were affected by the manufacturer-reported defects. The list was accompanied by a picture of a very stern looking Dr. Haddon.[19]

This sobering event, the publication of defect reports by the new agency told Congress—and car buyers—that more than 500,000 automobiles with "safety-related" defects had already been found and some repaired by automobile companies. An unknown number were still being driven by an unsuspecting public. The disclosure of such previously confidential information was obviously of great interest to car owners and prospective owners. It "apparently caught the automobile industry by surprise and angered it considerably."[20] The car companies had pressured the government to keep the information secret, as it had been before the Safety Act was enacted. They were ignored by Haddon and his new staff.

Failing complete secrecy, the manufactures supported a slow trickle of defect reporting, since "separate disclosures would have involved considerably smaller numbers and presumably would have attracted less attention."[21] "Once again," a source from Detroit complained, "it is made to appear that Washington is the great protector of the public."[22]

Similar controversies regarding when a company must disclose safety defects and delays by manufacturers in reporting them to NHTSA remain unresolved. In 2014, General Motors' long delay in reporting and recalling over two million Chevrolet Cobalt and other GM models with defective ignition switches, involving at least forty-two deaths, illustrates the continuing problem of public information disclosure that Haddon first raised in 1966.[23]

Haddon himself become a near-victim of a safety defect. On November 11, 1966, a week before NHTSA released the list of defects, he was driving his new Ford Fairlane sedan to work at about fifty miles an hour, along the George Washington Memorial Parkway near the Capitol. He pulled his foot up from the gas pedal. Shockingly, the pedal remained engaged and the car continued to accelerate. The pedal, it turned out, had been caught in a fold in the interior carpet. Haddon was able to kick the gas pedal to release it, and the car's speed slowed.[24]

He told the *New York Times* that the car had "developed a relatively fixed and rigid fold in the floor mat as a result of the mat not being completely tied down." He notified Ford and the company fixed the problem "completely satisfactorily and very promptly."[25]

A spokesman for Ford remarked unhappily that the incident was "an incredible coincidence."[26] "We wish it hadn't happened to anybody, particularly not to Dr. Haddon."[27]

Haddon's reaction to the incident encapsulates the pressure exerted on him during his entire public career. He endeavored to force improved safety, while walking a fine line between the automakers (and their political power) and a new generation of consumer advocates pushing for safer cars. In this case, he praised Ford's response to his individual incident; even called it a "freak, one-of-a-kind occurrence. . . . I have no reason to think that this occurred in any other instance." Because he was aware of no other incidents of this type, he did not use his powers to penalize Ford for failing to report a safety-related defect to NHTSA. But he told the *New York Times* that he believed "a safety hazard still existed."[28]

As it turned out many years later, the sticking accelerator pedal was not an "isolated incident." Sudden unintended acceleration remains a major, often hard-to-pinpoint vehicle problem. In recent years, unexpected acceleration has sometimes been blamed on human error, such as drivers mistaking the gas pedal for the brake. At other times, the transmission or cruise control design, or manufacturing error appear to have led to automobiles speeding up, rather than slowing down when the gas pedal is released by the driver.[29] The most commonly alleged cause appeared to be what Haddon experienced driving along the George Washington Memorial Parkway—the gas pedal became stuck under the floor mat, causing the accelerator to remain engaged. But in today's cars with their computerized operating systems, it is still unclear whether software malfunction is primarily responsible.[30]

The largest safety-related reporting controversy of this kind was announced forty-two years later. In November 2009, Toyota began recalling 8.1 million vehicles worldwide that were manufactured either with gas pedal, floor mat, or software defects. Sixty percent of the Toyota models sold in the United States in 2009 had one or more of these defects—or some other still-unexplained accelerator problem.[31] Toyota paid a 1.2 billion dollar criminal fine to the United States government in 2014 for not promptly reporting the problem and for misstating facts to NHTSA.

Haddon's lasting contributions to automobile safety were his agency's issuance of the first federal motor vehicle safety standards and the first proposed passive restraint/air bag standard. The 1966 Act required the establishment of interim federal motor vehicle standards by January 31, 1967, based on existing General Service Administration and other existing standards. They would apply to new 1968-model vehicles. They would then become final standards, unless revised by the government, one year later.[32]

Haddon announced twenty-three proposed standards on November 29, 1966, at the Auto Industry Dinner held at the Detroit Automobile Show. The heads of American Motors, General Motors, Chrysler, and Ford were all in attendance. Although the initial twenty-three standards were called "interim," manufacturers would still be required to meet them at some cost, in the 1968 models. Failure meant potentially stiff fines, as well as a lot of negative publicity. And the industry knew that these standards were likely to form a basis for the final safety standards due to be issued a year later.

Haddon began his speech by reminding the auto executives and others present of the "continuing national tragedy" of nearly three times as many Americans dying "on our streets and highways," as have died in all America's wars. "As civilized people," Haddon said, we can no longer tolerate these fatalities, "year after year, like a medieval plague beyond our power of influence." America must, he said, "manufacture safer automobiles."[33]

The infant agency raced against the clock to issue new safety standards within about one year of its creation by early 1968. It was not an easy task. Its buildings were scattered all over Washington and it was severely understaffed. Only 150 of its authorized 440 employees had been hired, a "blend of good people and gadflies," according to Haddon's successor, Douglas Toms.[34] Haddon himself worked nights and weekends while building the structure of NHTSA and simultaneously writing the final safety standards. The standards were not finished until the day they were due to be issued: January 31, 1968. The administrator stayed awake until 5 o'clock in the morning to finish them on time. "As a doctor, I'm aware of the medical dangers"—presumably to his staff and to his own health—but "the work has to be done," he told the *New York Times*.[35]

Compounding his challenge was a deluge of mail from unhappy automobile buyers. Some of the complaints were not about serious safety concerns, but others focused on potentially fatal flaws. There was a car that "started itself" and crashed into a fence across from the owner's house, and a car that veered out of control every time it hit a slight depression in the road. There was an incident where high-beam lights turned on whenever the driver sat down, and a sports car owner who reported that his brakes failed for the first mile whenever he drove his car in 20° or lower temperatures. One car owner wrote that his Lincoln Continental was "so bad" he painted lemons on it and parked it in front of the dealership.[36]

NHTSA's twenty-three "final" safety standards were drawn mostly from existing General Service Administration standards, from the Society of Automotive Engineers' (SAE) voluntary "guides," and one—banning hubcaps that could become dangerous projectiles—based on a Swedish government standard. They were organized into three categories, paralleling Haddon's original accident matrix: 100-level standards designed to prevent crashes from occurring; 200-level standards designed to reduce the likelihood of injury when crashes occurred; and 300-level standards designed to reduce the risk of injury after a crash occurred. They were issued on time.

Once a federal standard was adopted it had real teeth. It became the law of the land and could not be ignored or offered only as an option by car makers selling motor vehicles in the United States. The scope of federal motor vehicle safety standards (FMVSS) started with the initial twenty-three, but it has expanded and now includes more than fifty major standards, covering passenger cars, pickup trucks, vans, SUVs, motorcycles, large trucks, buses, and school buses. [37]

The initial 1968 standards ranged from relatively modest changes, such as uniform and visible labeling of dashboard controls, to groundbreaking rules, such as those requiring front seat shoulder harnesses and seat belts built to the GSA standard. There were standards that represented major improvements, such as common transmission shifting sequences (Park-Reverse-Neutral-Drive-Low), warning lights for braking system failures, improved exterior lighting, front seat head restraints, collapsible, energy-absorbing steering columns, and safer door latches. [38]

The first NHTSA standards were met with sharp criticism from automobile manufacturers. They derided them as "useless," "inadvisable," "illegal," and "impossible to meet." [39] After the agency had first issued the standards in proposed form, Haddon solicited the manufacturers' further views and recommendations. By early January 1967, each of the four United States manufacturers had formally claimed that it would be unable to meet many of the proposed regulations in time for the production of their 1968 models. These rebuffs came in the form of bulky dossiers of engineering documents, veiled threats of legal challenges, and somber pronouncements that the standards could force the shuttering of auto factories and job layoffs.

Ford and General Motors reported that they could comply with only ten of the twenty-three interim standards in time for the 1968-model production, but could meet several others with "minor modifications." Chrysler told NHTSA that it could implement only eight of the standards without difficulty and could conform to five others if they were slightly changed. As to ten others, it could "not possibly meet" them. American Motors listed seven standards that "it could not possibly comply" with. [40]

The five standards that Ford, Chrysler, and American Motors all agreed they "would be unable to meet" in their 1968 models were not particularly complex or stringent. They were: standard 107, requiring reduced glare from surfaces within the vehicle; 108, requiring lights and signaling devices that produced warnings on the sides of vehicles at night; 201, requiring changes to instrument panels, switches, handles, and arm rests to protect passengers in the event to of a collision; 207, requiring stronger attachment of seats in order to reduce the danger of dislocation in an accident; and 210, requiring stronger lap and shoulder belt anchorages.[41] General Motors offered a different list. GM stated initially that it could not comply with standards 201 (instrument panels), 207 (attachment of seats), 210 (lap and shoulder belt anchorages), 109 (new tire-quality standards), or 202 (which required head restraints).[42]

Henry Ford II, chairman of Ford Motor Company, was one of the harshest critics of the proposed regulations. "Many of the standards are arbitrary and I think technically are not feasible," he said. "If we cannot meet the final version of the standards, we will have to shut down our production lines . . . depending on what the standards might be."[43]

GM vice president Harry Barr took a milder position, arguing that the proposed standards did not take into account lead time necessary for the production of its vehicles (usually 24 to 36 months) and that, perhaps, the anticipated safety value would not be "commensurate with the additional price the customer will have to pay."[44]

By January 1967, four months after the creation of NHTSA, after the sharp industry pushback, Haddon and the agency had softened many of the proposed standards before they became effective. The Act also required them to be reconsidered again before they became final standards in January 1968.

Of the first twenty-three proposed standards, NHTSA "temporarily withdrew" three in January 1967; fourteen others were amended and relaxed to assuage industry concerns (and then adopted); and six were amended and provisionally adopted, subject to further consultation with the industry.[45] The altered standards included 109 (pneumatic tire quality standards), 110 (tire rim standards), and 202 (headrests). These now-weakened standards were changed to incorporate further concerns of the automobile industry.[46] In addition to weakening some of the safety standards, NHTSA also granted the manufacturers an additional four months to comply with all of them, moving the deadline from September 1, 1967 to January 1, 1968.

The *Chicago Tribune* reported that the automakers felt they had gained "considerable ground" in getting the standards modified, but that there was certainly "no gloating."[47] The industry was right not to gloat. The withdrawn standards on tires, rims, and headrests were all reissued in January 1969.[48]

Despite their complaints, the manufacturers incorporated most of the requirements of nineteen of the remaining twenty initial NHTSA standards into their 1968 models as required by the new law. Foreshadowing future fights over passive restraint proposals, they argued that standard 201, a key effort to minimize the "second collision" with the interior of the vehicle during a crash, was simply impossible to meet. This was the standard that required vehicles to have padded vehicle parts, such as seat backs, knobs, and dashboards in order to cushion occupants when their bodies collided with the interior surfaces of a car during a crash. Detroit's hostility toward interior protection anticipated by a few years the commencement of its decades-long fight over another occupant protection standard for "passive restraints," the requirement for installing air bags in vehicles.

At first, the new administrator stood firm on standard 201, interior protection of occupants, refusing to change it barring compelling information from the automobile manufacturers as to why they could not comply. Then on March 30, 1967 the day after his announcement that he would not unilaterally weaken the standard again, the big four major manufacturers took their standard 201 challenge to court.

They filed petitions to set aside standard 201 as authorized under the Act in the U.S. Court of Appeals in Cincinnati. They claimed it was so strict that it violated a provision in the 1966 safety law stating that the "interim" standards must be "based upon existing safety standards." Ford threatened that if the standard was not revised it would "be unable to produce any automobiles for sale in the United States after December 31, 1967."[49] This was a not-so-veiled threat to lay off a lot of American workers.

In May 1967 the government caved. The Sixth Circuit challenge was withdrawn. In a meeting with automobile manufacturers (which Haddon refused to attend), federal highway administrator Lowell K. Bridwell announced that the government would further weaken the interior protection, or "second collision" standard, based on industry input.[50] Three months later, modified standard 201 was finalized. Automobiles would have some increased padding for interiors, including instrument panels, seat backs, arm rests, and sun visors. However, requirements for leg and knee impact protection were dropped.[51] Some new cars now offer such protection as optional equipment, using small air bags at the knee and leg positions.

The key interior protection standard (201) was thus watered down a second time. This and other revisions of the first set of standards gave the automobile industry a partial victory in its initial fight over the government's role in the manufacturing process. Haddon and NHTSA, however, had won a more important victory. The first twenty-three federal automobile safety standards were now law (all the "interim" standards became "final" standards in January 1968).

For the first time, the automobile industry was required to follow federal safety rules in the design of much of its cars. The standards established a base level of safety in automobiles sold to Americans. And they demonstrated that a federal agency could, if it was forceful enough, require automobile manufacturers to change their car designs to produce safer vehicles. They ensured that automobile safety would not become, in the words of Business Council President William B. Murphy; "a fad, on the order of the Hula Hoop."[52]

At the same time that Haddon and NHTSA were struggling with the car industry's attempts to weaken the new safety standards, they were also facing attacks from consumer advocates. Ralph Nader charged that NHTSA was pursuing automobile safety with "too much timidity and too little imagination."[53] The fight was illustrative of the "caught-in-the-middle" position Haddon and NHTSA would find themselves over much of the next four-plus decades.

The most outspoken consumer critic of the agency was Nader. His now-famous book and his continuous advocacy for building safer vehicles had been critical to NHTSA's very existence.

But Nader was now critical of his own creation and of Haddon. He accused the good doctor, who was anonymously labeled by someone in the *New York Times* "a humorless, walking piece of red tape,"[54] of failing to staff the agency with competent officials and for preferring a go-it-alone approach[55]—that is presumably, for meeting with the manufacturers first, rather than consulting with Nader.

Given the safety advocate's lofty, often unattainable goals his criticism might have been expected. And one unnamed observer had described Haddon as so sensitive to criticism that he could be "blistered by moonbeams."[56] Nonetheless, Nader's attack was divisive. He blamed Haddon for supposedly developing a "protective attitude" toward the automotive industry and for avoiding battles that he believed should have been fought.[57] Journalists Drew Pearson and Jack Anderson appeared to support his assertions in a *Washington Post* article, which said that Detroit employed "a combination of threats and personal flattery . . . the motor moguls flatter Dr. Haddon; then threaten to close down production." Pearson and Anderson reported that Detroit's four main goals were to "1) exempt smaller cars from safety standards; 2) give long, unnecessary lead time for adopting standards; 3) accept auto industry language verbatim in setting the standards; and 4) ideally, have the government rubber-stamp existing levels of safety."[58]

When Haddon called a press conference to present his first twenty compromise safety standards, Nader stepped to the podium afterward—totally uninvited—and delivered an attack. He criticized the standards for being weakened to meet industry objections and unsupported by technical data. He charged that "the 1968 models [would] not be much different than they would have been" without the standards. Even the fiery consumer advocate, however, lauded the administration's requirement for lap and shoulder safety belts in the front seats of vehicles.[59]

NHTSA pushed back against Nader's criticisms, noting that the consumer advocate had not submitted any technical comments for the record. Haddon or his staff also met privately with reporters, emphasizing that Nader was not an engineer and therefore did not fully grasp the engineering problems involved.[60]

There was some basis for Nader's criticism. In the rear-view mirror of history, the standards could have been stronger. The manufacturers could have used their immense engineering capacity to meet them sooner. Overall, however, the first motor vehicle safety standards were a public victory for safety regulation and for Dr. Haddon.

The new standards had another important critic. He had less flair for the cameras than Nader. But he was a safety engineer—and a good one. He was NHTSA's chief vehicle safety engineer, William Stieglitz. "The mere mention" of Stieglitz's name made auto industry lobbyists "turn red."[61] This was because of his proclivity not to waiver from his strong positions in favor of tough rules and his scathing testimony to Congress that was extremely critical of the industry. In early 1967, one automobile official even predicted, "If we can get rid of Stieglitz, we'll be able to handle Haddon without any trouble."[62] He turned out to be right about Stieglitz, but dead wrong about Haddon.

Stieglitz had been a "safety pioneer" with Republic Aviation, then a consultant to the FAA (Federal Aviation Administration) and CAB (Civil Aeronautics Board). He was a founder of a consulting firm on aviation and automobile safety matters in Huntington, New York.[63] In a 1950 paper, he was the first to use the word "crashworthiness" to describe the ability of vehicles to protect their occupants in crashes.[64] After serving as director of the first-ever safety design engineering group at Republic Aviation, Stieglitz began focusing on automobile safety in the mid-1950s because he "constantly [saw] basic safety principles that were known in aviation, consistently being violated in automobile design."

In 1966, Stieglitz's firm worked with the State of New York to create an experimental prototype "safety car." It was later built by NHTSA with federal money. After testifying on the need for aggressive federal oversight of automobile safety, Stieglitz began working as the primary consultant for Haddon and NHTSA in the drafting the agency's initial standards in 1966.[65]

Detroit got its wish when Stieglitz resigned in protest over NHTSA's January 1967 weakening of the first standards, which he helped write. After receiving a copy Stieglitz studied them in his hotel room from 5 p.m. until midnight. He then wrote out his resignation and delivered it personally to Haddon on February 2, 1968.[66] Stieglitz criticized Haddon and the agency for acting as a "rubber stamp" for a set of insufficient safety standards that he said had already been developed by the industry.

Haddon was angry over Stieglitz's comments. In rebutting his engineering expert's charges, he said that Stieglitz "pushed very hard for standards which would have been completely impractical and impossible to achieve within the foreseeable future."[67] Stieglitz, he charged, wanted to compel industry to build cars that "approached or exceeded the performance of a Sherman tank."[68]

Stieglitz conceded that the rushed schedule and inadequate staffing levels at NHTSA between the agency's creation and the required date for the presentation of its first regulations (about a year) had created a major challenge. But, he said, Haddon had backed off too far. He said that the most pressing problem was the safety agency's failure to factor in adequate lead time in its new requirements. "My whole argument was recognizing the lead-time problem. If you have a standard and can't meet it, then change the effective date but not the standard. To me this is essential."

Stieglitz pointed to a section of the new safety act that allowed the agency to extend lead times for standards if "good cause" and "justifiable public interest" were shown. Without tougher standards and adequate lead time to engineer them, Stieglitz argued, the end result would continue to be "Band-Aid" safety.[69]

Despite Stieglitz's angry resignation and criticism of the federal safety program, before fading from the scene Stieglitz expressed optimism for the future. "I think a year has been wasted, but I'm convinced we're going to get good standards," he said. He also conceded that the standards banning pointed winged hubcaps and requiring mandatory lap and shoulder belts were genuine steps forward. He was, over time, proven right.

They may have been imperfect, but a fair appraisal of the first Haddon/NHTSA standards establishes that they significantly reduced automobile deaths and injuries. They were an important stride in compelling manufactures to make safer vehicles while being "reasonable, practicable, and appropriate," as required by the new federal law.[70]

The benefit of hindsight also shows that Haddon was decidedly successful in establishing the agency and directing the first years of its existence. By 2015, estimates show that more than 600,000 lives had been saved by NHTSA safety standards since their initial adoption in 1968.[71]

A *New York Times* editorial written during the heat of the first standards fight was prescient:

> Any disinterested inquiry [over safety regulations] is almost certain to vindicate Dr. Haddon. He has been one of the fathers of the revolution in attitudes toward automobile safety, and his contribution, if less spectacular, has been as important as that of Mr. Nader. Beginning nearly a decade ago as a public health officer for New York State, Dr. Haddon has done pioneering research on accidents. His integrity and his devotion to the cause of safer driving are beyond question.

The *Times* said that Haddon's allies and then critics—mostly Nader and Stieglitz—were "true crusaders" who were critical in passing the traffic safety laws. Despite this, "The purity of their motives [was] not proof that their administrative judgment [was] preferable to that of Dr. Haddon." The initial standards at first appeared only a little more stringent than the existing GSA standards, but it was "only after the industry engineers studied them that the toughness of the standards became apparent and the complaints began." The industry also had been "placed on notice" that what was not feasible for 1968-model cars could be demanded in later years.[72]

Haddon and his successors at the federal safety agency would do much of the demanding.

Several studies confirm that Haddon's innovative start for NHTSA was a success in saving tens of thousands of lives. The first, conducted in 1976 by the General Accounting Office, was entitled "Effectiveness, Benefits and Costs of Federal Safety Standards for Protection of Passenger Car Occupants." It analyzed more than two million cars in crashes in North Carolina and New York, comparing driver death and injury rates in different model-year cars. Analysts at GAO found that the 1966–1970 standards saved 28,230 lives between 1966 and 1974 nationwide. Compared to pre-1966 models, they found that from 15 percent to 25 percent fewer deaths and serious injuries occurred in 1966 to 1970 model-year cars. The GAO study also concluded that the 1966–1970 crash survivability standards produced economic benefits "that probably could be greater than the safety cost allocable to these standards."[73]

A second study was conducted in 1976 by the Insurance Institute for Highway Safety (by then headed by Haddon). Entitled "The Effects of New Car Safety Regulation on Fatality Rates," it cited several factors. For federally regulated post-1967 cars, occupant deaths averaged 27 per 100,000 cars yearly, 23 percent less than 1964–1967 models and 39 percent less than pre-1964 models. The insurance industry report concluded that, "state and federal motor vehicle safety regulations issued in the 1960s and thereafter have greatly reduced automobile occupant fatalities. These regulations are not the end, but the beginning of a process to minimize the toll in human life that accompanies motor vehicle use."[74]

Finally, fatality data compiled by NHTSA in 2010 shows that the fatality rate per 100 million vehicle miles traveled has fallen in almost every year from 1966 to 2010. And over 325,000 lives were saved by the new standards from 1968 through 2002.[75]

The development and issuance of new safety standards were not Haddon's only action at NHTSA. Under the companion Highway Safety Act, the agency also issued thirteen standards for state highway safety programs as a condition for receiving federal highway construction money under the Highway Act. These included mandatory state inspection of vehicles, reexamination of licensed drivers at least every four years, and a mandate for state laws prohibiting driving with over specified blood-alcohol levels.[76] Because they could lose up to 10 percent of their federal highway funding by not complying, states, with few exceptions, enacted these rules.[77] NHTSA and the Federal Highway Administration (FHWA) now jointly administer state highway safety grants for high school driver-training programs, reducing impaired driving and improving police enforcement of traffic safety laws.[78]

NHTSA and Haddon also initiated federal crash testing of new models, as well as the use of government safety testing centers. The first crash tests showed that despite the new federal safety standards, a cross section of 1968 and 1969 models had failed 11.5 percent of the safety tests conducted. The results thus emphasized the need for increased federal inspection and investigation of vehicles and the use of mandatory recalls and fines (also authorized by the 1966 law) to ensure that standards were being complied with and that vehicle safety continued to improve.[79] NHTSA's safety testing subsequently evolved into the federal New Car Assessment Program.

The federal test rating known to car buyers as the 5-Star Safety Rating is required to be shown on the side window invoices of new cars. It was formally established in 1979 by Joan Claybrook, who became NHTSA's administrator and who once worked as Haddon's assistant at the agency. Other groups, such as the Insurance Institute for Highway Safety and *Consumer Reports* magazine also conduct frontal, angled, and side-impact tests. They publish the results online and in print.

After the election of Richard Nixon in 1968, the *New York Times* warned that incoming Secretary of Transportation John Volpe has "indicated that he intends to replace Dr. William Haddon Jr. as director of the Highway Safety Bureau. That is his privilege, but we believe that Mr. Volpe will not readily discover a successor as energetic and creative as Dr. Haddon."[80]

On Valentine's Day 1969, Haddon anticipated his firing by the new administration. He resigned from his post at the close of business that day. But the first administrator of NHTSA never left the auto safety field he loved. He went on to become president of the Insurance Institute for Highway Safety (IIHS) and to change it in his safety-conscious image. He was its president from 1969 until his death sixteen years later.[81]

At the Insurance Institute for Highway Safety, Haddon continued crash-testing cars, filming the simulated accidents, and using them to convince Congress to enact tougher damageability and safety standards. He succeeded in improving damageability standards when Congress passed the 1974 Motor Vehicle Information and Cost Savings Act, to require stronger, crash-resistant bumpers and stiffer penalties for safety violations.

Sometimes called "the quieter Ralph Nader," Haddon later played a major role in inducing the casualty insurance industry to align itself with public organizations and oppose automobile manufacturers on key safety issues.[82] Most important was their joint effort to compel installation of air bags in passenger automobiles. Haddon had directed the issuance of such a proposed passive restraint standard in 1969.[83] He called industry's thirty-year resistance to air bags "a scandal comparable to Watergate."[84]

Haddon died suddenly in 1985 of kidney failure. He was fifty-eight years old. In recalling him, his sometime critic Nader praised the first National Traffic Safety Administrator. Haddon, he said, "was very dedicated. He influenced us all. His auto safety campaign represented a spectacular success in the federal government's mission. When the regulations were allowed they worked. And they worked because they deal with technology rather than human behavior. . . . He spent his full professional life in an effort to save other people's lives, through safer engineered motor vehicles."[85]

After Haddon resigned from NHTSA, the Nixon-appointed Secretary of Transportation John Volpe was put in overall charge of the agency. Volpe surprised a lot of people with his tough safety stance. A business-oriented Republican, the former governor of Massachusetts[86] made it clear that he was eager to carry out the "people-orientated" life-saving goals of the 1966 traffic and highway safety acts. Later, Volpe realized the "political sex appeal" and safety potential of the air bag.[87]

Because they feared that Republicans Volpe and Nixon would promote an unqualified politician to roll back the gains of the National Highway Traffic Safety Agency, both Haddon and Nader had alerted their allies in Congress of their intention to fight an "unacceptable" nominee. But in August 1969, Volpe appointed Douglas Toms as director of the agency. There was no fight. Toms turned out to be more than an acceptable successor.

Toms won Volpe's support by recommending that the NHSB (soon to be known as NHTSA) be placed directly under the control of the Secretary of Transportation, so that it could act with greater authority.

Toms was a safety professional. He had received doctoral training in traffic safety at the University of Michigan. He had also served as manager of the state's motor vehicle agency. "I was probably more acceptable to the safety zealots than I was to the White House," Toms later told historian John D. Graham.[88]

Volpe and Toms ran NHTSA in tandem, proving that safety is not necessarily a partisan issue. "Detroit could not drive a wedge between them."[89] The two identified three priority areas: air bags, drinking and driving, and building an Experimental Safety Vehicle.[90] To meet them, they utilized strict deadlines to create test programs that often created new safety mandates and milestones.

By December 1970 under the new Republican leadership, thirteen more final safety standards had been issued. These included standards for hood latch systems; vehicle identification numbers; head restraints—earlier withdrawn after industry opposition; and windshield mountings.

Today, there are more than fifty major federal vehicle safety standards on the books.[91]

According to automotive historian John Graham, Volpe and Toms solidified NHTSA's "reputation for independence and toughness in its role as a 'technology-forcing' safety agency."[92] Despite this success, Volpe and Toms could not succeed in overcoming industry resistance and establishing air bags (passive restraints) as a federal safety standard. That goal was reached many years later.

Ten years after the traffic and highway safety bills were passed congressman John Moss's Subcommittee on Oversight and Investigations issued a detailed report on "Federal Regulation and Regulatory Reform." In his final four years in Congress Moss had moved from sponsoring pro-consumer safety legislation to oversight of existing programs. He said his goal was to defend safety programs from the deregulation efforts of the 1970s under Presidents Nixon and Ford and to ensure that the new safety laws for automobiles and other consumer products worked effectively.

The Moss subcommittee's ten-year analysis of the National Highway Traffic Safety Administration serves as a kind of "report card" on the first decade of federal regulation of auto safety. The report restates a prime reason for the safety act's importance: "For the first time, the automakers were identified as sharing responsibility with drivers, traffic officials, road designers and road builders for the highway death toll."[93]

The Moss subcommittee report praised NHTSA's early work, noting that between 1967 and 1970 the crashworthiness standards had saved thousands of lives. However, the subcommittee warned "that after a burst of activity in the first three years of its existence, NHTSA's issuance of new standards leveled off in the period from 1970–1973, and then fell off precipitously in the 1974–1975 period."[94]

Although acknowledging that "no one method of putting a value on life or injury commands wide agreement"[95]—thus attempting to moot many of the Nixon Council on Wage and Price Stability's negative cost-benefit findings about safety standards—the subcommittee report estimated that tens of thousands of lives and major economic losses had been saved by safety standards costing at the time about $250 per vehicle.[96]

Even considering the reduction in new safety standards issued after Haddon and Volpe, the Congressional report found it "difficult to see in this history a failure of nerve, or integrity on the part of NHTSA."[97] Rather, the Moss report said this was "an instance of the success of regulated industry in organizing enough opposition[98] and generating enough political interference to change or delay safety standards that could hurt their bottom line."

The best way to continue reducing traffic fatalities and costs, the House Commerce subcommittee concluded, was to grant NHTSA "independence from special interests exerted through executive branch offices," provide it with adequate resources, and allow it to focus solely on saving lives. Then, perhaps, it might have a chance of stemming what Haddon had described many years before as "the largest public health epidemic in America."[99]

NOTES

1. Senate Committee on Commerce, *Nomination of Dr. William Haddon, Jr., Traffic Safety Administrator,* 89th Congress, 2nd Sess., October 13, 1966, 11–15; "Traffic Safety Head: William Haddon Jr.," *New York Times,* September 10, 1966.

2. Senate Committee on Commerce, *Nomination of Dr. William Haddon, Jr., Traffic Safety Administrator,* 89th Congress, 2nd Sess., October 13, 1966, 14.

3. Ibid., 17.

4. "Traffic Safety Head: William Haddon Jr.," *New York Times,* September 10, 1966; Walter H. Waggoner, "William Haddon Jr., Dies; Authority on Highway Safety," *New York Times,* March 5, 1985; B. Drummond Ayres Jr., "Haddon at the Wheel," *New York Times,* April 2, 1967; Brian O'Neill, "Accidents: Highway Safety and William Haddon, Jr.," *Contingencies,* January/February 2002, 30.

5. Senate Hearings, October 13, 1966, 17.

6. "Doctor Wages War on Traffic Deaths," *United Press International,* November 24, 1977.

7. B. Drummond Ayres Jr., "Haddon at the Wheel," *New York Times,* April 2, 1967.

8. Malcolm Gladwell, "Wrong Turn: How the Fight to Make America's Highways Safer Went Off Course," *New Yorker,* June 11, 2001, 60.

9. L. S. Robertson, "Groundless Attack on an Uncommon Man: William Haddon Jr. MD," *Injury Prevention* (2001): 7:261.

10. Ibid.

11. Gladwell, "Wrong Turn," *New Yorker,* June 11, 2001, 53.

12. Ibid., 52.

13. "Traffic Safety Head: William Haddon Jr.," *New York Times,* September 10, 1966.

14. Interview by the author with Ben Kelley, September 15, 2013, by e-mail.

15. In 1974, Haddon bought two Volvos, presumably equipped with seat belts and other safety features; "Doctor Wages War on Traffic Deaths," *United Press International,* November 24, 1977; "Traffic Safety Head: William Haddon Jr.," *New York Times,* September 10, 1966.

16. "Senate Confirms Haddon as Road Safety Director," *Associated Press,* October 15, 1966.

17. "Haddon is Sworn in Capital as Traffic Safety Director," *Associated Press,* October 21, 1966.

18. Walter Rugaber, "Defect Publicity Angers Industry," *New York Times,* November 23, 1966.

19. "List of Motor Vehicle Safety Hazards," *New York Times,* November 23, 1966.

20. Ibid.

21. Rugaber, "Defect Publicity Angers Industry," *New York Times,* November 23, 1966.

22. Ibid.

23. The General Motors' ignition and the Toyota unintended acceleration cases are discussed further in chapter 11.

24. John D. Morris, "Safety Chief Has Pedal Trouble; He and Ford Agree It's a 'Freak,'" *New York Times,* November 26, 1966.

25. Ibid.

26. Ibid.

27. "Auto Safety Official Has Kick Coming," *Associated Press,* November 27, 1966.

28. Morris, "Safety Chief Has Pedal Trouble; He and Ford Agree It's a 'Freak,'" *New York Times,* November 26, 1966.

29. Kate Linebaugh and Dionne Searcey, "Cause of Sudden Acceleration Proves Hard to Pinpoint," *Wall Street Journal,* February 25, 2010.

30. See "The Evolving Public Narrative of Unintended Acceleration," Quality Control Systems Corp., accessed 4/17/13, http://www.quality-control.us/evolving_narrative.html.

31. Bernard Simon and Jonathan Sable, "Toyota Recovers after Accelerator Remedy," *Financial Times,* February 3, 2010. See also chapter 11.

32. "Congress Acts on Traffic and Auto Safety, "*Congressional Quarterly Almanac,* 1966, 266.

33. "Text of Speech by Head of National Traffic Safety Agency at Auto Industry Dinner," *New York Times,* November 30, 1966.

34. A later review found that by Fiscal Year 1968 the agency had filled 406 of its 446 authorized positions. House Subcommittee on Oversight and Investigations of the Committee on Interstate and Foreign Commerce, *Federal Regulation and Regulatory Reform,* 94th Congress, 2nd Session, October, 1976, 158. B. Drummond Ayres Jr., "Nader Charges Safety Agency Shows Timidity," *New York Times,* March 22, 1967; John D. Graham, *Auto Safety: Assessing America's Performance* (Dover: Auburn House Publishing Company), 45.

35. B. Drummond Ayres Jr., "Haddon at the Wheel," *New York Times,* April 2, 1967.

36. Robert F. Buckhorn, "Motorists Beset Haddon with All Kinds of Gripes," *United Press International,* June 12, 1967.

37. See appendix A, summarizing existing major federal safety standards as of 2011.

38. A summary of Haddon's twenty-three proposed initial standards, based on the text of a speech by Haddon at the Auto Industry Dinner, November 20, 1966 includes: standard 101, required headlamps, ignition, windshield wipers, and other controls be labeled and within reach of a driver restrained by a safety belt; 102, required automatic transmission shift lever sequences conform to a common, uniform sequence and an interlock to prevent the car from starting in the drive or reverse positions (based on a GSA standard); 103, required the front windshield to have a defrosting and defogging mechanism (based on a Society of Automotive Engineers (SAE) standard); 104, mandated specific requirements for windshield wiping and washing systems (based on an SAE standard); 105, required warning lights indicating failure of hydraulic breaking systems and a parking brake capable of stopping vehicles at 30 percent grade (based on GSA and SAE standards); 106, required standards for hydraulic brake hoses to reduce failures due to fluid leakage (based on an SAE standard); 107, required limiting the reflectivity of bright metal components in the driver's field of vision, including windshield wiper arms and blades (based on a GSA standard); 108, required headlamps, switches, turn signals, parking lights, tail and stop lights, side marker lights, reflectors, and other devices to increase the visibility of vehicles in darkness (based on SAE and ICC standards); 109, required new pneumatic tires that met requirements for endurance and braking capacity (based on Vehicle Equipment Safety Commission, Tire and Rim Association and Rubber Manufacturers Association standards); 110, required tire rims to meet standards to provide proper load distribution and prevent tier overloading (based on tire and rubber industry standards); 111, required rearview mirrors that provide the driver with clear, undistorted, and reasonably unobstructed view; 201, required protection for occupant impact within the interior of the car, including impact with knobs, switches, levers, handles, sun visors, and arm rests (based on GSA and SAE standards); 202, required front seat head restraints to reduce the frequency and severity of neck injury in rear-end collisions (based on GSA standards); 203, required that the steering control system provide impact protection to the driver's chest, neck, and face (based on GSA standards); 204, required that steering column's rearward movement in crashes be limited to reduce the risk of an impalement (based on GSA and SAE standards); 205, required automobile windshields to be treated with safety glazing materials to reduce lacerations and to prevent occupants from being thrown through vehicle windows in collisions (based on USA Standards Institute and SAE recommended practices); 206, required load requirements for door latches and

supports to prevent occupants from being thrown from the vehicle (based on GSA standard and SAE test procedures); 207, required seats, be attached securely enough to prevent their dislocation in a crash (based on a GSA standard); 208, required seatbelts, including lap and chest restraints, on all forward-facing seats except "jump seats"(based on a GSA standard); 209, required seat belt assemblies to meet forthcoming standards specified by the National Bureau of Standards); 210, required standards to ensure proper location of seat belt assembly anchorages (based on GSA standard); 211, prohibited the use of winged wheel nuts, discs, and hubcaps, a hazard to pedestrians and cyclists, (based on a Swedish standard); 301, required the integrity and security of fuel tanks, fuel tank filler pipes, and fuel tank connections to minimize fire hazards in collision (based on GSA standard). See, "Text of Speech by Head of National Traffic Safety Agency at Auto Industry Dinner," *New York Times,* November 30, 1966. See, appendix A for a summary of fifty-four major Federal Motor Vehicle Safety Standards (FMVSS) as of 2011.

39. Drew Pearson, "Auto Safety Pressure Rises," *Las Angeles Times,* January 24, 1967.

40. Walter Rugaber, "3 Car Makers Say They Can't Meet Safety Deadline," *New York Times,* January 4, 1967.

41. Ibid.

42. "16 Safety Rules Endorsed by G.M.," *Associated Press,* January 1, 1967.

43. "Auto Safety Code Row Looms," *Associated Press,* January 2, 1967.

44. Ibid.

45. "Auto Safety," *Congress and the Nation,* Vol. II, *Congressional Quarterly,* 1970, 804.

46. Ibid.

47. "See Safety Over Cars Easing," *Associated Press,* February 12, 1967.

48. U.S. Department of Transportation National Highway Traffic Safety Administration *Federal Motor Vehicle Safety Standards and Regulations* http://www.nhtsa.gov/cars/rules/import/fmvss/index.html#SN101, accessed February 5, 2013; "47 New Safety Proposals for Motor Vehicles Listed," *Associated Press,* October 13, 1967; "Auto Industry," *Congressional Quarterly Almanac,* 1968, 682.

49. The case was filed as a "protective measure" because it was unclear if the conflict over standard 201 would be resolved before the statutory period for judicial review ended. The issue was resolved before a court decision was needed. "Auto Makers Sue on Safety Rules," *United Press International,* April 1, 1967; Crawford Morris, "Motor Vehicle Safety Regulation: Genesis," *Law and Contemporary Problems,* Summer 1968, 542.

50. John D. Morris, "U.S. Will Relax Standards for Auto Safety Padding," *New York Times,* May 26, 1967.

51. "Safety Standard on '68 Cars Eased," *Associated Press,* August 13, 1967.

52. "Congress Acts on Traffic and Auto Safety, "*Congressional Quarterly Almanac,* 1966, 266.

53. B. Drummond Ayres Jr., "Nader Charges Safety Agency Shows Timidity," *New York Times,* March 22, 1967.

54. B. Drummond Ayres Jr., "Haddon at the Wheel," *New York Times,* April 2, 1967.

55. B. Drummond Ayres Jr., "Nader Charges Safety Agency Shows Timidity," *New York Times,* March 22, 1967.

56. Malcolm Gladwell, "Wrong Turn," *New Yorker,* June 11, 2001, 52.

57. B. Drummond Ayres Jr., "Nader Charges Safety Agency Shows Timidity," *New York Times,* March 22, 1967.

58. Drew Pearson and Jack Anderson, "Heat Put on Auto Safety Boss," *Washington Post,* January 24, 1967.

59. Ronald J. Ostrow, "Some Details of Eased Auto Safety Rules Told," *Los Angeles Times,* February 1, 1967.

60. Morton Mintz, "Nader Sees Signs of Auto Safety Lag, Suspects Intimidation of U.S. Agency," *Washington Post,* January 24, 1967.

61. Pearson and Anderson, "Heat Put on Auto Safety Boss," *Washington Post,* January 24, 1967.

62. Ibid.

63. U.S. Senate Committee on Commerce, *The Implementation of the National Traffic and Motor Vehicle Safety Act of 1966,* 90th Cong., 1st Sess. March 20–21, 1967, 154–57.

64. W. I. Stieglitz, "A Note on Crashworthiness," Sherman Fairchild Publication Fund Preprint No. 266, *Institute of the Aeronautical Sciences,* January, 1950.

65. U.S. Senate Committee on Commerce, *The Implementation of the National Traffic and Motor Vehicle Safety Act of 1966,* 90th Cong., 1st Sess. March 20–21, 1967, 154–57.

66. Morton Mintz, "Stieglitz Quits Auto Safety Job After Reading Standards for '68," *Washington Post,* February 3, 1967.

67. Bob Thomas, "Safety Standards Author Denies Being Impractical," *Los Angeles Times,* February 19, 1967.

68. "Auto Safety," *Congress and the Nation,* Vol. II, *Congressional Quarterly,* 1970, 804.

69. Bob Thomas, "Safety Standards Author Denies Being Impractical," *Los Angeles Times,* February 19, 1967.

70. B. Drummond Ayres Jr., "Nader Charges Safety Agency Shows Timidity," *New York Times,* March 22, 1967; "Congress Acts on Traffic and Auto Safety," *Congressional Quarterly Almanac,* 1966, 270.

71. NHTSA, Technical Report, "Lives Saved by Vehicle Safety Technologies and Associated Federal Motor Vehicle Safety Standards, 1960–2002," i, xii; DOT HS 802 069, January 2015.

72. "Dr. Haddon Under Fire," *New York Times,* February 5, 1967.

73. GAO Report CED-76-121, p. ii, , cited in House Subcommittee on Oversight and Investigations of the Committee on Interstate and Foreign Commerce, *Federal Regulation and Regulatory Reform,* 94th Cong., 2nd Sess. October, 1976, 169.

74. Leon S. Robertson, PhD, Insurance Institute for Highway Safety, April, 1976, based on data from the State of Maryland, summarized in the Institute's *Status Report,* May 3, 1976, cited in House Subcommittee on Oversight and Investigations, Committee on Interstate and Foreign Commerce, *Federal Regulation and Regulatory Reform,* 94th Cong., 2nd Sess. October, 1976, 169.

75. Traffic deaths fell from 5.5 deaths per million miles traveled (50,894 total deaths) in 1966 to 1.1 deaths per million miles traveled in 2012 (37,423 total deaths). There were small rises in the fatality rate between 1976–1980s and between 1985 and 1986. The rate declined in every other year. NHTSA, Traffic Safety Facts, 2012 (DOT HS 812 032), table 90 at 142. See also, "An Analysis of the Significant Decline in Motor Vehicle Traffic Fatalities in 2008," June 2010, DOT HS 811 346, 27 and see, NHTSA, Technical Report "Lives Saved by the Federal Motor Vehicle Safety Standards and Other Vehicle Safety Technologies, 1960–2002, DOT HS 809 833, October, 2004, table 1, xii.

76. These levels varied by state, but were originally between .10 and .15 blood alcohol content, a high content. They are now .08. The National Transportation Safety Board now recommends a .05 maximum blood alcohol level, which is the European Union legal limit.

77. "Congress Acts on Traffic and Auto Safety, "*Congressional Quarterly Almanac,* 1966, 281; "Auto Safety," *Congress and the Nation,* Vol. II, *Congressional Quarterly,* 1970, 805.

78. Section 402 State and Community Highway Safety Grant Program, at http://www.ghsa.org/html/stateinfo/programs/402.html

79. "'68–'69 Cars Flunk Six Tests," *Associated Press,* November 11, 1969.

80. "What Future for Auto Safety?" *New York Times,* February 8, 1969.

81. IIHS is an independent, nonprofit research and testing organization funded by the U.S. insurance industry. Its purpose and that of its affiliated Highway Loss Data Institute is "reducing the losses—deaths, injuries and property damage—from crashes on the nation's roads." www.iihs.org

82. "Doctor Wages War on Traffic Deaths, *United Press International,* November 24, 1977.

83. 49 CFR Part 571, subpart B—Federal Motor Vehicle safety Standards, available at http://www.law.cornell.edu/cfr/text/49/part-571/subpart-B.

84. "Doctor Wages War on Traffic Deaths, *United Press International*, November 24, 1977.

85. "William Haddon Jr., Dies; Authority on Highway Safety," *New York Times*, March 5, 1985.

86. Graham, *Auto Safety*, 41.

87. Ibid.

88. Ibid., 44.

89. Ibid., 55.

90. An Experimental Safety Vehicle (ESV) was designed and built by the Ford Motor Company in 1973. The experiment ended in 1974, in part due to high fuel costs. J. Graham, *Auto Safety*, 45. Additional ESVs, by then called Research Safety Vehicles, were later built under NHTSA contract in the 1970s by Minicars, Inc. and Calspan Corporation. They were paid for with federal funds and crashed safely in texts at 50 mph.

91. 49 CFR Part 571, subpart B—Federal Motor Vehicle Safety Standards, available at http://www.law.cornell.edu/cfr/text/49/part-571/subpart-B. See appendix A.

92. Graham, *Auto Safety*, 56.

93. House Subcommittee on Oversight and Investigations of the Committee on Interstate and Foreign Commerce, *Federal Regulation and Regulatory Reform*, 94th Cong., 2nd Sess. October, 1976, 158.

94. House Subcommittee on Oversight and Investigations of the Committee on Interstate and Foreign Commerce, *Federal Regulation and Regulatory Reform*, 94th Cong., 2nd Sess. October, 1976, 167.

95. Ibid., 174.

96. Ibid., 172.

97. Ibid., 189.

98. Ibid., 190.

99. "Doctor Wages War on Traffic Deaths," *United Press International*, November 24, 1977.

EIGHT

Dragon Lady

By 1977 the National Highway Traffic Safety Administration (NHTSA) had been given expanded authority over automobile and highway safety.

It could issue mandatory safety standards for cars, vans, and trucks. It could make comparative automobile safety and testing data public. It could order the recall of motor vehicles containing safety-related defects (at the manufacturers' expense) and issue state guidelines for highway safety regulations. The state rules included vehicle registration, driver training, legal alcohol consumption limits, and many others. NHTSA had also been directed by Congress, in the Clean Air Act of 1970 to set mandatory national fuel economy (CAFE) standards. The broad authority now delegated to the new agency can be viewed as an early vote of confidence in safety regulation by the Congress.

It also made the NHTSA administrator's job a highly sensitive position.

The safety agency was described at the time by a Senate committee chairman as one "whose activities directly affect the health and welfare of both American motorists and the automobile industry."[1]

Eleven years after its creation, NHTSA was responsible for enforcing not only the Motor Vehicle Safety Act and the Clean Air Act fuel economy standards, but for the new Motor Vehicle Information and Cost Savings Act (1974), limiting the damageability of passenger cars. It also had new authority to set safety standards for larger vehicles such as trucks and school buses.

The increased authority of NHTSA to limit the damageability of cars, such as the "no damage" bumper rule, and to disseminate comparative automobile performance data to the public were added, over strenuous manufacturer objections in 1974, by the Motor Vehicle Information and Cost Savings Act.[2] It was signed in April of that year by president Richard Nixon. The era of enhanced regulation of the safety and design of American cars and highways continued.

Someone who has fought publicly with the automobile industry for tougher safety regulation and fuel economy standards is not a likely selection to head the National Highway Traffic Safety Administration. And yet, when Jimmy Carter became president in 1976 he did just that. Carter nominated Joan Claybrook, a full-time consumer safety advocate, to head NHTSA. A safer choice for the newly elected president might have been a scientist, such as Bill Haddon, LBJ's pick to be the first head of the safety agency. Or Carter might have appointed a regulatory attorney with industry experience, such as Raymond A. Peck Jr. who was named by President Reagan in 1980. But Carter, the Georgia populist, with perhaps some advice from Brock Adams, his mild-mannered Secretary of Transportation, chose Claybrook, the fiery consumer advocate and Ralph Nader lobbyist. Their decision to nominate a consumer advocate to oversee the safe design and manufacture of American automobiles precipitated a ferocious confirmation fight in the Senate.

Claybrook was sometimes referred to as "the dragon lady" within the automobile industry.[3] The history of NHTSA and its major impact on automobile safety does not support that title.

An article in the *Chicago Tribune* summed it up: "While it is not unusual for regulatory chiefs to come from the same industry they regulate, it was extraordinary for Carter to appoint a woman who had directed Ralph Nader's most vigorous watchdog group, Congress Watch, to head a regulatory agency."[4]

S. L. Terry, vice president for public responsibility and consumer affairs at Chrysler, said that he (and presumably his bosses at Chrysler) found Claybrook's appointment "appalling. . . . She has always been against the industry. It certainly does not seem to be an evenhanded appointment. I would not expect that the Department of Transportation would appoint an auto executive, but likewise, I wouldn't expect the appointment of an industry critic or a Nader supporter. There must be a lot of people better qualified."

Ford's president Lee Iacocca was more restrained. Iacocca made no direct comment about Claybrook, but his spokesman said that while he was somewhat surprised by the appointment of a consumer advocate, "he would not prejudge her performance."[5]

The *Wall Street Journal* also wrote about the nomination. It called Claybrook a "strong proponent of government auto safety regulation . . . likely to cause considerable apprehension among auto executives. She avidly supports a federal requirement that airbags be installed in new cars to protect the occupants."[6]

Claybrook was, at the time of her nomination, the chief lobbyist for Nader's Congress Watch group. She had worked the for the consumer side in some controversial legislative fights on Capitol Hill. Despite her strong inclination to march to her own drummer, she was at least at the time, a direct employee of Nader and was perceived as the industry's adversary.

Claybrook's road to the 1977 nomination had begun twelve years before when she won an American Political Science Association (APSA) Fellowship allowing her to seek work as an intern for a member of Congress. She approached a little-known House member named James Armstrong MacKay, a Democrat from Georgia. He hired her under the APSA-financed fellowship program. It turned out the young aide was a bargain. She proved a forceful addition to MacKay's staff and later worked with other legislators as well.

MacKay was, or soon became, a supporter of the proposed automobile safety law. In 1966 Claybrook worked with him and other members to get the House to pass a tough auto safety bill. She had first met the little-known Nader during the struggle over the new safety law. After the law was enacted in 1966, she served for several years as special assistant to William Haddon, administrator of the new safety agency she had worked to create. Claybrook played a little-known, but significant role in assisting Haddon in writing the first federal auto safety standards.

By 1977, when the newly elected Carter nominated her to be administrator of NHTSA, she was experienced in the inner workings of Capitol Hill politics and the likely difficulties of regulating and promoting automobile safety. None of her activities could possibly have endeared her to the leaders of the American automobile industry.

Claybrook said she was surprised when she was recommended as administrator to the newly appointed secretary of transportation Brock Adams. Adams, apparently an early feminist, said he wanted "several women at the top levels of his department." He had been a liberal member of the House for six terms and became chair of the House Budget Committee. He asked for recommendations for the head of NHTSA from his former staff and other people around Capitol Hill.

Adams's inquiries were answered with a pile of résumés, including Claybrook's. Hers was sent to him by a former Budget Committee staff director, Linda Kam. She had just been named general counsel of the Department of Transportation by Adams and had, once upon a time, lost no love on Joan Claybrook.

Claybrook and Kam had fought over the Budget Committee's plan to "streamline" and reorganize the House of Representatives. In Claybrook's view (and that of most consumer groups) the House definitely needed streamlining. The plan was a fairly logical, new arrangement of the archaic, overlapping committee structure of the House. But logic is not always practical or even useful, at least not on Capitol Hill.

The proposal, known as the "Bolling Plan" after its respected author congressman Richard Bolling of Missouri, included the logical step of putting all energy jurisdiction in one House committee, rather than spreading it over the several committees that it was located in at the time. It was, according to Claybrook, "a huge gift to the oil and gas industry, which could then focus all its power and money and more easily dominate a single House committee."[7]

The plan would also have taken political power away from some consumer-oriented members of Congress. That included the tenacious Californian John Moss, a coauthor of the 1972 Motor Vehicle and School Bus Safety Amendments, the 1974 Motor Vehicle Information and Cost Savings Act, and other legislation. Claybrook thought the Bolling Plan was detrimental to prospects for future consumer legislation. She and Congress Watch worked hard against it. Reformers Bolling and Kam were furious. Much of their ire was aimed at Claybrook.

In the end, the plan was soundly defeated with the help of organized labor and House members who supported the status quo. Surprisingly, after the loss, which must have been very painful for Kam, she and Claybrook patched things up. At least Kam seems to have come to the reluctant conclusion that Claybrook, whatever disagreements they might have, was an effective strategist. Adams knew Claybrook from her lobbying days. After he heard from Kam and others about her, he thought she just might do.

According to Claybrook, here is what happened next: "I got a call from an assistant to Brock Adams named Woody Price, whom I had known since I was a teenager in Baltimore. He called me up and said 'Brock wants to see you.' I said, 'Really, why?' This was right after his January 1977 swearing in. Price said, "I'll be god-damned if I agree with this, but he wants to see you about being the administrator of NHTSA."[8]

Claybrook went to see Adams about the nomination. Price, who was not shy and could at times be unpleasant, greeted her: "I told Brock you would be nothing but trouble, but he wants to talk to you anyway." Then, she was sent in to the secretary's large office. Adams was a handsome, young politician from Seattle, with Kennedyesque looks and style. His first question to Claybrook was blunt: "Are you going to be Ralph Nader's shadow, or are you going to be your own person?"

Claybrook said, "I have always been totally my own person and I am not about to change that now."[9] That seemed to satisfy the secretary — and apparently the Carter White House too.

But, when Claybrook's nomination got up to Capitol Hill there was a lot of not-so-subtle opposition from the automobile industry. The manufacturers did not testify openly against her. But two automotive experts, one an engineer who had previously worked for Ford and another who described himself as "an independent citizen," raised vigorous objections to her nomination at the Senate hearings. So did the motorcycle industry, which opposed federally promoted biker-helmet laws. They assumed, correctly, that she would fight for them.[10]

One of Claybrook's critics at the Senate hearing was the "interested citizen," C. R. Blydenburgh, who said that he was testifying to "oppose the appointment of a person who has been openly identified with a concentrated movement to mandate airbag crash protection in all passenger cars and certain other vehicles." This, he said, "would deny consumers the right to decide whether they were willing to accept such an expensive and dubious device, which conceivably could kill them."[11]

A second dissenter, Emile Grenier of Ann Arbor, Michigan, indicated his engineering experience had been at the Massachusetts Institute of Technology and as an engineer for Ford, from which he had retired three years before. He said that even before being nominated, "Claybrook had struck a blow at the auto industry" that she had "demanded as a condition of the nomination that Adams reverse the decision of the Ford administration to postpone the airbag requirement."[12]

The charge by Grenier was denied by Claybrook. But nonetheless, the industry lobbied hard behind closed doors to get the votes to defeat her.

One of the main arguments against her confirmation was an article she had written for the *Washington Post* a year or so before. She had defended Ralph Nader and his comment that Nixon's secretary of transportation, William Coleman "should have the moral fortitude to stand up to the giant auto companies and the White House" and sustain Bill Haddon's proposed passive restraint rule.[13] Coleman, Nader's target, did not do so. He ordered more delay and study of the supposedly thorny safety issue. The basis for Coleman's decision was the familiar argument that, although air bags would save lives, he had concluded the public would not pay for them.

Claybrook's *Post* article seemed to show she had already made up her mind on the value of air bags, the biggest issue then facing the safety agency.

The *Post* article by Claybrook was certainly not a balanced appraisal of the seven-year-old passive-restraint proposal. But it said a lot about her and her habit of saying exactly what she thought on an issue—even one she would later have to rule on at NHTSA. She had written to defend Nader and more important, to defend the idea of putting passive restraints in all American cars: "The issue in the controversy is not the efficacy of the airbag as the *Post* suggested," she said. "The life-saving capability of passive restraints is undisputed and the technical feasibility is assured. The only issue facing Secretary Coleman is political: whether or when."

In the same *Post* article Claybrook wrote, "The merits of passive restraints are widely acknowledged. Former President of General Motors, Edward Cole, and former GM Vice President, John Z. DeLorean, have been enthusiastic supporters. The major auto insurance companies . . .

have spent millions educating the public, members of Congress, and federal officials about their unique utility. The airbag device has been subjected to some 260,000,000 miles of phenomenally successful testing in over 12,000 cars on American roads."[14] Claybrook also cited a statement by House member John Moss about Secretary Coleman's review process: "It's a cave-in to industry pressure."

It certainly cannot be said that Claybrook had an open mind about the passive-restraint issue before her nomination. On the other hand, after seven years of heated debate, testing, and analysis almost nobody else in Washington did either.

There were thirty-three votes cast in the Senate against Claybrook's nomination as NHTSA administrator. But the consumer leader was confirmed by a narrow majority. She says that what saved her was "a guy named Keith Crain who was the publisher of *Automotive News*, the automobile dealer's bible and very influential in the industry." One of his reporters was friendly with her and introduced her to the publisher. They got to know each other over dinner. Crain came to think of her as direct and honest at least. The *Automotive News* undermined the manufacturers' opposition to her in an editorial, suggesting that the industry "keep an open mind" on her nomination.

Then West Virginian Robert Byrd, the Senate majority leader, decided he wanted a tough administrator in the job. Because of that, says Claybrook, her nomination was pushed through the Senate, just as the Carter White House wanted. "If it hadn't been for Bobby Byrd and the *Automotive News*, I might not have been confirmed," she said many years later. But she was confirmed. The advocate and former Nader lobbyist wound up heading the multimillion dollar federal automobile and traffic safety regulatory program.

At the time she was confirmed she was earning a whopping $12,000 a year as the chief lobbyist for Public Citizen's "Congress Watch" affiliate. When she realized she might actually get the NHTSA job (at a much higher salary), she asked Nader for a raise, so that her raise at NHTSA would be more justifiable. Nader objected at first. He never paid his people very much. Ultimately he agreed to increase her wages to a munificent $15,000 a year. Members of Congress were, at the time, about to raise their salaries to $50,000 a year. The administrator's job paid about the same amount.

When she arrived at NHTSA, Claybrook convened a meeting of her top staff—all of whom happened to be men. She had the feeling that they were not taking her seriously. She was relatively young and inexperienced. They were veteran engineers, economists, and safety experts. There were also some holdovers from the Ford administration, which had just postponed Haddon's proposed air bag standard (through Secretary Coleman's decision). After an unsatisfactory first staff meeting, she was having dinner with her father who was a Baltimore attorney and former city councilman. He listened to her concerns and then gave her some fatherly advice. "Show them you are no pushover. Fire someone right away." So she did.

Luckily there was one member of the agency staff with weak credentials and a poor performance record. Claybrook fired the staff member on the spot. No one challenged her authority after that. "Smart Daddy," she said later.

Joan Claybrook grew up in the 1940s in racially segregated Baltimore. Her father was elected a member of the city council as an insurgent, anti-machine Democrat. He was a strong advocate of more public housing and of legal services for the poor. He favored racial integration, long before it was mandated by the Supreme Court. He also campaigned on a platform of eliminating "extra" payments to council members for a variety of mostly political services. He was ahead of his time.

Claybrook's first political experience was walking around Baltimore at age ten wearing a sandwich board that said she was an "unpaid volunteer." It was a way of contrasting many of the campaigners for other candidates who were city workers, or got paid extra money for their political work. After her father won, she remembers sitting in Baltimore's Council meetings watching a council member sleep through the entire proceeding. She saw him set his alarm clock to wake himself when it was time to go home. "I learned about the good and the bad of the legislative process very early," she said.[15]

But Claybrook was not a poor kid from the wrong side of town. She was a member of the Baltimore Junior League—for a while. She went on to graduate from the elite Goucher College. In 1959, after graduating near the top of her class, she went to work for the Social Security Administration. There she was noticed. She was asked to work for President Kennedy's Commission on the Status of Women, headed by the labor leader Esther Peterson, as well as on Social Security issues.

Claybrook's big break came with the American Political Science Association Fellowship and her work for Congressman MacKay. In the course of working with MacKay she met this "extremely shy, introverted young man, named Ralph Nader. He had just written *Unsafe at Any Speed*. He was trying with limited success to fire up Congress about auto safety. Things were not going that well. Then, General Motors changed everything by assigning detectives to tail him."

Claybrook served only four years in the position of NHTSA Administrator (1977 through 1980). But the appointment, surprising as it was, gave her the opportunity to make a series of lasting contributions to motor vehicle safety. As administrator, she convinced Brock Adams and the Carter White House to *reissue* the passive restraint regulation, the one that Bill Haddon had first proposed in 1969 and that President Nixon and his Secretary of Transportation, William Coleman, had just killed.

In 1977, after her appointment, Claybrook says she saw that "Brock Adams, despite his support for the concept of passive restraint systems, was a little bit afraid of the technologically advanced airbag causing physical injury to people in motor vehicles, or not functioning properly. He was not as confident as Bill Haddon had been about forcing the technology."

The automobile industry was vigorously opposed to passive restraints and lobbied Adams, the White House, and Congress for almost any alternative they could think of.[16] Some of the staff of the agency also had concerns about whether the air bag was sufficiently tested to become part of a mandatory safety standard. It ultimately became such a standard— over a decade later.

Claybrook remembers,

> One day Adams said to me, "Joan, maybe we should just issue a mandatory state seat belt rule instead of the federal passive restraint rule." So I went back to my office and wrote him a stinging memo. I still have it. I said, "We don't have the power to do that. That's a state issue not a federal issue." As a lawyer he should have known that. I guess my memo was a little bit insulting. But I also added that the airbag is going to save thousands of lives and that "we cannot pass up this opportunity." At heart he was a Secretary of Transportation who wanted to do the right thing. So . . . he did it.[17]

Before the final decision on reissuing the air bag rule was sent to the White House, General Motors offered Claybrook and Adams a demonstration of how the safety device might work. GM brought a car, outfitted with air bags, to the Department of Transportation in Washington so they could try it out for themselves. At the suggestion of one of the GM engineers, Claybrook sat in the driver's seat of the car. Adams sat in the more vulnerable passenger seat. One of the engineers warned Claybrook that the noise was much louder and the impact greater on the passenger side. She says, "I made a big mistake. I should have switched seats with him. When the airbags went off and the test was completed, Adams emerged from the car limping and in pain. The air bag hit him hard, squarely in the groin. It might have killed the rule right there. I should have switched seats and taken it for the team."

Despite being nervous about issuing the rule, Adams did it anyway. To make it more palatable, Claybrook and Adams added a four-year delay and a phase-in period as well, pushing back full implementation to 1984. By that time, as it turned out, Jimmy Carter was no longer in office. Ronald Reagan was president. Adams and Claybrook were long gone.

The delay in the effective date of the passive restraint rule caused a public fight between Nader and Claybrook. It was all over the newspapers. Her former boss and good friend stormed into her office uninvited. In front of the press corps and a lot of her staff, he demanded to know why she had sacrificed automobile safety through the delay.[18] The leaders of the automobile industry must have been chuckling—or having a good laugh around the water cooler.

Nader said his former aide was a "cowardly defector from the consumer movement. . . . She should quit her job."[19] Nader's attack on Claybrook was based not just on granting the air bag delay, but also on her failure up to then to issue safety standards for vans and pickup trucks and the fact, he said, that she had been too open "in talking about federal program plans" with representatives of the automobile industry. She had been NHTSA administrator for about six months.

Claybrook had no intention of quitting her job. She was pleased with her accomplishments at the time, although she conceded, "We still have a long way to go." In a not-so-subtle dig at her former boss, Claybrook said she was "fully aware of the complexities of running a regulatory agency, an experience he [Nader] has not yet had."[20]

Looking back she says, "To me the four-year delay was a good trade-off. There was no other way to get it through, because Adams was very nervous. He wouldn't do anything more."[21]

About the same time NHTSA issued the results of a national poll on the opinion of American motorists regarding passive restraints versus seat belts. The poll found that 58 percent of those asked supported a federal regulation forcing automakers to include passive restraints in new cars. Only 20 percent of those interviewed said they used their seat belts most of the time.[22]

In addition to her role in issuing the first passive-restraint standard, Claybrook compiled an impressive record in other areas as administrator. One of her major achievements was the creation of the federal New Car Assessment Program (now known as NCAP). Under NCAP the federal government tests dozens of new cars for safety each year. NCAP rates each make and model for safety and assigns gold stars—one through five—to evaluate its performance for the benefit of buyers. It publishes the results of the tests online. Because of a later act of Congress, the gold-star ratings must appear on the window sales stickers of all new cars sold in the United States.

The NCAP program is an example of the former advocate's emphasis on providing useful consumer information in her direction of the federal safety program. The 5-Star program is better known every year as a buying aid in the purchase of automobiles.

NCAP went global. Other countries noted that the United States government was doing motor vehicle crash testing and sharing the results with the public. Consumers in most industrial countries—fifty nations—now have access to public or private organizations that crash-test automobiles based on NCAP, or stronger standards in other countries, and furnish the results to the public. The international NCAP standards are now, in many areas, tougher than the United States versions.[23]

The Insurance Institute for Highway Safety has also established a complementary testing program that rates the safety of selected cars and issues periodic public ratings (also published online) including the IIHS "Top Rated" model designation.[24]

Claybrook says the first NCAP testing made her realize that "this program could be one of the most important efforts we undertook to push manufacturers to pay more attention to safety." The release of the first United States crash tests had caused a lot of commotion in the press and the industry and that had consequences. "We discovered, most importantly, that the 1979 small United States–manufactured cars were significantly safer than the Japanese-made vehicles. We made a point of conveying this to consumers and the U.S. manufacturers."

For the car buyer this was and is important information. In 1979 small, fuel-efficient Japanese cars were extremely popular in the United States, because of gasoline shortages and increasing gas prices. The release of the results, Claybrook says, "helped convey the point that we were not picking on U.S. manufacturers in releasing the test information."

The young administrator was not always critical of the automobile industry's progress on safety issues. In a speech at the Harvard Business School in 1978, she alluded to the challenges they faced. "Historically the domestic automotive manufacturers have had little internal stimulus since the 1920s for the development of motor vehicle innovations, and particularly ones concerned with so-called externalities—that is, health and safety."[25]

One of her victories at NHTSA was in forcing a settlement with Firestone Tire and Rubber, agreeing to the "voluntary" recall of 7.5 million defective Firestone 500 radial tires in 1978. Claybrook used that victory to emphasize that government regulation "is one of the strongest stimuli for safety innovation for the auto industry. . . . It can be done. Far safer, yet attractive and fuel efficient vehicles can be manufactured and can be appealing to the public. This is no safety pin industry. . . . Motor vehicles are an unfinished technology that desperately needs what industry engineering creativity can give it: heavy infusions of engineering progress."[26]

In the decades since, events have proved Claybrook was correct in her prediction of the automobile industry's potential for developing new safety technologies.

Despite her efforts, Claybrook apparently remained a bit of a problem for Secretary Adams and some of his staff. Said one, "She never regards a battle as won until all of her opponents are dead." Another Adams aide said that there was some feeling that Claybrook "pushed the Secretary mightily to back the airbag . . . she is a bit of a fanatic about auto safety." The aide added that they had to "keep a constant eye on her. She comes up with some wacky schemes with politically explosive implications."[27]

Some automobile industry executives praised her as "knowledgeable and courteous" in their dealings, but according to the *Wall Street Journal*, they made it clear to Secretary Adams that they disliked her speeches castigating the industry for not moving fast enough.[28]

The Reagan administration, which followed that of Jimmy Carter, discontinued the publication of the NHTSA testing results in its annual "Car Book," which Claybrook had started to allow NHTSA to publicize its NCAP testing. But "it did not stop the testing program," Claybrook said. "It had gained a very high profile in a very short time and it was strongly supported by Congress."[29] The publication of NHTSA test results was continued in the annual private publication of *The Car Book* by author Jack Gillis and the Center for Auto Safety and by the agency on its Web site.[30]

Despite Nader's charge that she wasn't moving fast enough, the young administrator eventually issued new federal safety standards broadening the scope of many existing safety rules to include vans and pickup trucks, as well as passenger cars. This change brought millions of additional vehicles under federal safety regulation starting in the mid-1980s. NHTSA estimates that about 30 percent of all lives saved by federal safety standards and by voluntary industry actions that they prompted (about 94,000 lives) were saved in light trucks and vans. It was a major expansion of the scope of federal standards.[31]

NHTSA research also found that the new safety standards—mostly seat belts and airbags—saved more than 600,000 lives in the years between 1966 and 2012. After 1968, when vehicles incorporating additional federally mandated technologies replaced older vehicles, the number of deaths avoided rose each year. Since 1988 continued market penetration of seat belt use, air bag installation, and other safety equipment helped drive fatality reductions to over 15,000 lives saved by 2009.[32] The downward trend has continued.

Claybrook issued the first 5 mph "no damage" bumper standard, minimum gasoline mileage (CAFE) rules, tire-quality grading standards, and a rule requiring electronic brakes on large trucks. Pressing the states to enact child seat and safety belt use laws, she traveled to Tennessee to push the first of fifty state laws mandating safety seats for all children under seven and secure anchorages in all new cars. It was a fast pace for the often snail-like federal safety agency.

The years of Claybrook's tenure lasted only from 1977 through 1981. Despite a lot of opposition from an industry such as the automobile makers, which had the political clout to go to the White House and Congress to slow rules down or kill them, things got done. Rules and standards of this scope can often take the government decades. The young administrator's aggressive efforts got them done in record time. She was a four-year shot in the arm for the federal safety program.

After Ronald Reagan defeated Jimmy Carter in 1981, Claybrook resigned from NHTSA and went back to life as a private citizen. On the way out the door she had a message for American car manufacturers. She sent each of them an eleven-page letter itemizing some sixty things they should do in order to better protect the motoring public.[33] Most of her recommendations, such as stronger side impact protection and tire inflation indicators, have since become standard required equipment on American cars.

One reason for her success as a federal administrator appears to have been that she knew how to work with the press and to maneuver on Capitol Hill. "I had a great advantage," she said in an interview. "By the time I came into office television was commonplace, so I decided we had to be a media agency. We took films of our crash tests. We promoted them on television. We had a safety research vehicle that looked like a Porsche that we crashed safely at 50 miles an hour. We took it on the road and showed it to consumers all over the country. We were on the *Today* show and the Phil Donahue television show. We did everything we could to give people a picture of what really happens in a crash, what happens to a person's body."[34]

What surprised a lot of people over the years was, despite her tough exterior, she had an almost gentle management style. Carl Nash, an engineer, was hired to be her special assistant at NHTSA. When she left the agency he stayed on for another twenty years. Nash has served under several NHTSA administrators:

> Joan has a very strong ethical sense about things like auto safety. . . . One thing I liked about working with her is that she knew how to make a good compromise—understood it and realized it was necessary in a lot of cases. She was unwilling to compromise on what she thought were the really crucial things and when she compromised she usually got something back for it. I don't think people realize what a good, astute manager she was. For example, when she called a meeting on a major issue, she wouldn't just invite the people that directly reported to her. They might tell her what they thought she wanted to hear. She would go around and invite the engineers and lawyers and others who had been working on the issue. They participated and spoke up at the meetings. The staff really appreciated that rare opportunity. It improved their morale and their performance.[35]

Media interest in automobile safety, coupled with NHTSA's new initiatives, proved effective. By the early 1980s, after being barraged for four years with real accident images and crash tests produced by the agency, people began to understand the beneficial effects that better-designed vehicles could have.

"No one ever liked accidents," says Claybrook. "But for a long time no one really understood them. It was a matter of people understanding what can happen to your body in a crash. People always were safety conscious. They didn't really change their minds or their attitudes. They just changed their understanding of what it takes to protect you and your children in an automobile crash."[36]

In May 2012 the international safety organization, Global New Car Assessment Program, which has members from fifty countries, gave its first International Safety Award. The recipient was Claybrook. By that time she was serving as president of one of the nation's leading consumer organizations, Public Citizen. She served for twenty-seven years in that position, continuing her efforts for safer automobiles, doubling Public Citizen's staff and increasing its budget.

The Global NCAP award was presented in recognition of her years of service to consumer safety and establishment of the federal automobile crash-testing program. Global NCAP endorsed the United Nations declaration of 2011 through 2020 as the "Vehicle Safety Decade" to honor her.

Automobile safety has gone international. The United States, with its comprehensive safety standards and testing of new models under the New Car Assessment Program, was a primary trigger. For a while, the United States was the leader in international automobile safety.[37]

It may not be now. Other nations have some tougher safety standards and lower death rates in crashes.

Claybrook, called "the Dragon Lady" by some in the automobile industry and a "cowardly defector" by Nader, had become, in the end an international leader.

"Being called 'the Dragon Lady' didn't really bother me. It was actually a big compliment," she said years later. "It showed that the motor vehicle manufacturers were worried about me, about what I could do for automobile safety and for people." She had no comment about Ralph Nader's now forgotten "cowardly defector" remark. They have since worked together once more.

The motor vehicle manufacturers were probably right to worry about Claybrook. For motorists, pedestrians, and taxpayers, her appointment as NHTSA administrator by President Carter was a permanent benefit.

NOTES

1. Hearings before the Senate Commerce Science and Transportation Committee, 95th Congress, 1st Session, March 29, 1977, 1. Cited as "Hearings." The statement was made by senator Wendell Ford, chairman of the Senate Commerce Committee's Consumer Subcommittee.

2. P. L. 92–513 (1974).

3. Larry Kramer, "Driving For Safety," *Washington Post,* June 16, 1978, K-1.

4. Barbara Reynolds, "Auto Safety Chief's Rocky Ride," *Chicago Tribune,* August 27, 1978, A-2.

5. Ernest Holsendolph, "Lobbyist for Nader to Head Safety Unit," *New York Times,* March 19, 1977, 12.

6. *Wall Street Journal,* February 14, 1977, 5.

7. Interview by the author with Joan Claybrook, November 30, 2011, 8–9.

8. Ibid., 8.

9. Ibid.

10. Hearings, Senate Committee on Commerce, Science, and Transportation, First Sess. 95th Cong., March 30, 1977, 47.

11. Ibid., 27.

12. Ibid., 32.

13. Joan Claybrook, "The Airbag Issue: Whether and When," *Washington Post*, September 1, 1976, A-15.

14. Ibid.

15. Interview by the author with Joan Claybrook, 10.

16. Insurance Institute for Highway Safety, *Status Report*, June 25, 1980, Ben Kelley, "GM and the Air Bag: A Decade of Delay," 1.

17. Interview by the author with Joan Claybrook, November 30, 2011, 11.

18. "Nader Calls Former Aide a Cowardly Defector," *Chicago Tribune*, December 1, 1977, 5.

19. Ibid.

20. Ward Sinclair, "A Head-On Collision: Nader Angrily Denounces a Former Ally," *Washington Post*, December 1, 1977, 1.

21. Interview by the author with Joan Claybrook, November 30, 2011, 12.

22. Larry Kramer, "58% Favor Passive Restraints: Seat Belts Ignored by Public," *Washington Post*, August 31, 1978, D-1.

23. Memorandum to the author from Shakireh Ispahani, Administrator, Global NCAP, www.globalncap.org, April 4, 2013.

24. See www.IIHS.org.

25. Larry Kramer, "Claybrook Faults Auto Firms on Safety," *Washington Post*, October, 26, 1978, F-1. The NCAP and Insurance Institute for Highway Safety testing programs appear to have been important in furnishing the stimulus by "changing the safety environment within the automobile companies . . . by giving the safety engineers more of a say, because safety sells" according to Adrian Lund, President, IIHS. Interview by the author, May 8, 2014, 7.

26. Kramer, "Claybrook," *Washington Post*, ibid.

27. Albert R. Karr, "Former Consumerists Now in Agencies Find Jobs Frustrating," *Wall Street Journal*, December 15, 1977, 1.

28. Ibid., 1.

29. Interview with Joan Claybrook by Global NCAP, http://www.globalncap.org/interview-with-joan-claybrook/.

30. Jack Gillis, *The Car Book 2014*, (Washington D.C.: Center for Auto Safety, 2014).

31. There was only a modest affect from federal safety standards before 1980, but a sharp rise in lives saved resulted thereafter, as standards had a greater impact on vehicles. Total crash deaths would have been 57,000 in 2002, rather than 32,000 according to NHTSA. See "Lives Saved by Federal Motor Vehicle Standards and Other Vehicle Safety Technologies 1960–2002," DOT HS 809 833, xii–xv (2004).

32. See NHTSA Report 811 892, "Traffic Safety Facts 2012," table 4. The government now estimates that about 15,000 lives are saved annually by lap and shoulder belts, child seats, and frontal air bags alone.

33. Claybrook's letter is available at http://www.careforcrashvictims.com/assets/claybrook-letter.pdf. Her recommendations included improved roof strength and lap and shoulder belt standards, laminated glass side windows to avoid ejection, improved visibility, improved frontal and side crashworthiness tests with more air bags, adding brake wear and tire pressure indicators, adding high-mounted rear brake lights, upgraded anchors for child seats, and enhanced pedestrian safety by better vehicle body design.

34. Interview by the author with Joan Claybrook, November 16, 2011, 9.

35. Interview by the author with Carl Nash, January 9, 2013, 13–14.

36. Interview by the author with Joan Claybrook, November 16, 2011, 10.

37. The United States has now fallen to eleventh position in international highway safety rankings of deaths per miles driven. England, France, and Sweden, among others, have lower death rates. Tanya Mohn, "Safety First, True Once, But U.S. Now Lags in Road Deaths," *New York Times*, July 22, 2007; World Health Organization Report (Geneva, 2013), table A.2.

NINE

The Birth and Near Death of the Air Bag

On an October evening in 1975, Dr. Arnold Arms was driving along a busy street in Kansas City, Missouri. Arms had spent a long day treating patients and teaching internal medicine at the University of Missouri Medical School. Seated behind the wheel of his new 1974 Oldsmobile Toronado, the doctor was on his way to a nursing home to see one last patient.

He had not buckled his seat belt. Rush hour traffic was heavy as he drove along a busy, four-lane road. Without realizing it, Arms closed his eyes for a moment and dozed off. It was only for a couple of seconds, but in that brief time he lost control of his car and swerved into the oncoming traffic.

A horrific crash ensued. Arms survived. Unknown to the doctor, the car's manufacturer, General Motors, had equipped his Toronado with a new safety device that was not available on any other American car at the time. It was called an air bag.

At a 1977 Senate Commerce Committee hearing,[1] Arms testified about his air bag–crash experience:

> I awakened just an instant or two before I struck a large city passenger bus which was traveling about the same speed I was. That was 35 mph at the moment of impact. It was a very hard collision. It would be comparable to a Volkswagen hitting a Cadillac head-on. The air bag inflated and deflated so fast that I did not see it, feel it, or hear it. I was fully conscious at the moment of collision. I saw that my glasses had been struck from my head.
>
> They were unbroken . . . on the dashboard. I thought I was very badly injured. But in three to four minutes I was able to extricate my foot from under the brake, get out of the car and walk away from the

almost total [wreck] . . . much to the amazement of a nearby policeman. He later told me he expected that I had been killed, or critically injured."[2]

At the same 1977 hearing, Mrs. Jimmie Daniel of Satellite Beach, Florida, told about another near-death experience. Driving with her two young grandchildren in a 1974 Oldsmobile Toronado, her car's air bag was activated after a head-on collision with an oncoming car.

The air bag saved not only my life, but also the lives of my granddaughter Yvonne, and my grandson, Christopher. The abrasions and injuries we received were minor compared to the terrible injuries we would have suffered if I not had an air bag-equipped car. I would not be here giving this testimony today, if I had not had a car equipped with an air bag that day.[3]

The air bags in Dr. Arms's and Mrs. Daniel's Oldsmobiles were part of a demonstration project that, under government pressure, General Motors had authorized. It began with 1974 GM models. The company had agreed to test the performance of up to 10,000 air bag-equipped vehicles that would be sold on the American market. Although GM did not promote the air bag, the demonstration was very successful. There is no record of any air bag seriously malfunctioning. The air bags worked when they were supposed to work. They caused no significant injury or any other problem for their owners.

Despite the positive results, the demonstration project was never expanded to other GM cars, nor adopted at the time by any other manufacturer. GM canceled the pilot project after three years. According to GM, there was a "lack of consumer interest" in paying extra to buy the new safety device.

A later investigation by the Insurance Institute for Highway Safety, reported in the *Chicago Tribune*, found that GM and its dealers failed almost completely to market the safety benefits of the new technology to their customers.[4] Customers could not buy an air bag-equipped car after GM's test ended, until 1988. Even if they asked for it in their new GM car—or from any other American producer.[5]

Today, we know how effective air bags are as a safety device. Since about 1990, when "passive restraints" (another name for air bags) became a government requirement for passenger motor vehicles, frontal air bags alone have saved more than 35,000 lives. In recent years, some 2,500 drivers and passengers each year survive death from collisions in cars equipped with frontal air bags.[6] Tens of thousands more avoided serious often permanent disabilities, such as face, brain, spine, and neck injuries. The numbers of people saved are increasing as more air bags are added in new positions, such as the sides of a car, in the latest models.

Air bags are designed to function automatically, reacting to sensors in the front of the vehicle upon a collision of 30 mph or more into a fixed test barrier (designed to approximate a collision at the same speed into an oncoming vehicle).[7] In other words, air bags are not designed to activate in a minor fender-bender. In a crash of over 30 mph it takes the air bag a split second to inflate and cushion passengers and the driver from impact with the interior of the car. It is designed to avoid or minimize crushing "second collisions" with the dashboard, windshield, steering wheel, side pillars, windows, and other interior parts of a car.

By 2012, General Motors, Ford, Toyota, Volvo, and other companies selling new cars in the United States and worldwide were offering and advertising not only frontal air bags, but side, leg, and rear-seat passenger air bags as well. Lexus boasted eight air bags in its 2013 model ES-350 sedans.

Yet it took more than forty years for air bags to go from invention to deployment in American cars. At many points during those three decades the air bag looked as if it was totally dead.

The concept of using a gas-inflated bag to protect occupants in collisions may seem farfetched. The idea goes back to the early decades of the twentieth century. Many formal U.S. patent applications for different types of automotive air bags were filed, as early as the 1950s. Years later, the Washington Automotive Press Association awarded its prestigious "Golden Gear Award" to John W. Hetrick, who was the original inventor of the automobile air bag, based on his 1952 patent filing.[8] In fact, many other innovators, and automotive suppliers, deserve to share the credit. Some patents were obtained by manufacturers, but air bags were not put into their cars until they were *required* by the federal government thirty years later.

Hetrick started thinking about the idea of passive protection for occupants of cars when, during a Sunday afternoon drive with his family, he was suddenly forced to veer off the road to avoid a large dislodged boulder. The car collided with an embankment with a shuddering impact. It was a lot better than hitting a boulder or a tree would have been. Hetrick and his family escaped serious injury. His wife had somehow managed to physically restrain their daughter from being hurled headfirst into the windshield of the car.

The experience was an epiphany for Hetrick. He could not get the near-disaster out of his mind. He became consumed with the idea that, with a little creative engineering, some design drawings, and some testing, he might be able to develop an "inflatable cushion" that would prevent the type of debilitating injury his wife and daughter had narrowly escaped. His accidental idea became the basis for one of the primary safety systems in use in American cars today.

A bit later, in the early 1960s, Dr. Carl C. Clark further pioneered the development of the air bag. Clark observed that a safety system designed for one transportation system might meet the needs of another. Clark worked as an aircraft engineer at Martin Marietta, which was under contract with the National Aeronautics and Space Administration (NASA) to develop aircraft restraint systems for astronauts. The contract definitely did *not* involve work on automotive issues. Clark saw a connection in his NASA work.

To protect space capsule occupants during landings at high speed, Clark developed and conducted live experiments with an "air-stop" restraint system. Clark was always thinking outside the box. He could see that the government-funded "air-stop" system might be adapted to motor vehicles and could be designed to deploy in relatively moderate collisions.[9]

Using himself as a human guinea pig, Clark proceeded to try out the "air stop." A massive pendulum was set up, aimed at striking Clark while he was seated behind his protective bag system. The pendulum was released, swinging forward with great force and hitting the spot where Clark sat. The air stop inflated. Clark survived the test. He lived to see his idea move toward reality.[10]

Clark was not the first person to consider putting "air cushions" in motor vehicles, although he was the first person to actually test them. He said in 1997,

> The auto companies did some work before my studies [and tests], but their technical work was done in secret. Ours was the first published technical work. They didn't want us stirring the pot. . . . We pushed ourselves right up to the limits. I was knocked unconscious [in the test] perhaps ten times."[11]

Clark's and Hetrick's vision ran into years of opposition from virtually every motor vehicle manufacturer. The initial objections were many. Despite Clark's survival, the "air stop" or "air cushion," or air bag could, it was said, hurt drivers and passengers when it inflated. It might not operate when it was needed. It would cost way too much to build and install in cars.

With automotive manufacturers (as distinguished from aircraft producers) showing little interest in pursuing or developing the air bag as a safety device for automobiles, the momentum shifted to other private companies and to the marketplace. In the mid-1960s, Eaton Yale and Towne, Inc., a Cleveland-based supplier of automotive parts and equipment, started a research center where its engineers were given a free hand to generate ideas for new automotive products. The air bag was one of the most promising of those ideas, both in the view of Eaton's engineers and its chairman, E. M. de Windt.[12] At its facilities in Southfield, Michigan, Eaton spent millions of dollars designing and developing the first experimental air bag system, which it called the "auto-ceptor." Other automotive suppliers such as Allied Chemical Corporation and Olin Corporation were also actively developing early production versions of the air bag. What they needed were customers.

Ford stepped up as the first major automobile manufacturer to show support for the development of the safety device, to test air bags and to consider rapid fleet installation. In 1968 Eaton's engineers and Ford jointly presented a paper to a Society of Automotive Engineers meeting in Detroit describing how an automobile air bag would work in a crash.[13]

Eaton's engineers backed up their SAE paper with a filmed laboratory test showing that baboons protected by air bags had survived front-barrier crashes at much greater speeds than those protected only by seat belts and shoulder harnesses. Eaton produced a film demonstrating the effectiveness of the air bag, which was widely shown by Insurance Institute for Highway Safety and Eaton to lawmakers and the Department of Transportation staff.[14] To the developers of the air bag, it seemed likely that they might be most effective when used in combination with lap belts, which would also help prevent ejection of the occupants from the vehicle.

Eaton projected that the new safety device could be manufactured in a relatively short time and could be standard equipment on all cars by 1971. A similar opinion was voiced by Ford's chief automotive engineer, Robert B. Alexander, who predicted limited real-world use in two years.[15] Economic pressure on Eaton and its desire to quickly recoup its investment and sell the new safety device to motor vehicle manufacturers may have influenced its optimistic projections about when the air bag could be commercialized. Companies like Eaton, Allied Chemical, and Olin deserve major credit for taking a big chance on an untested technology — a technology that could expose manufacturers and developers to major liabilities and investment costs.

The United States government did *not* originate the concept of air bags. Nor did it help develop and refine it for production automobiles. Nonetheless the government played a key role, using a proposed regulation in 1969 to force the new technology on a reluctant industry and on an unaware public. While not actually developing the concept of air bags for passenger automobiles, the government furnished significant help in the early stages. It provided funding and technical support for research at private laboratories, such as Cornell University and the University of Michigan.[16] Without government money and later Haddon's and Claybrook's proposed federal regulations, there would be few passive restraints in automobiles today.

Over the long run, the professional staff of the young National Highway Traffic Safety Administration also played a creative and farsighted role in forcing air bags into general use. The 1966 Safety Act expresses the requirement that all safety standards issued by the agency be "practicable, shall meet the need for motor vehicle safety and shall be stated in objective terms."[17] The legislative history, written primarily by senator Warren Magnuson and his staff, demonstrates a clear preference that standards not be specific as to "design," but rather be "performance standards." The rationale was to set a basic level of protection desired and allow leeway for manufacturers to experiment with different designs that would achieve a specified safety goal, such as a 30 mph or more crash into a fixed barrier, with no significant injury to occupants. Performance standards also encouraged the use of "dynamic" rather than "static" tests, which, while more costly, are more realistic in predicting survival in a real-world crash. The great importance of this approach and its effective incorporation into the new safety law was soon demonstrated.

Passive-restraint technology attracted attention at NHTSA almost immediately. Its first administrator, William Haddon, believed in seat belts. He testified in 1967, just six months after his confirmation: "We would far prefer to adopt only standards that pose no problem to anyone and that do not require any active cooperation on the part of the user. This is the approach that has been used in public health, after all, going back 50 and 100 years, with such programs as pasteurization of milk, chlorinization of water supplies and so forth."[18]

The usage rate of seat belts by the motoring public was then less than 15 percent. It did not help that the belts were poorly designed by manufacturers, in a way that made them uncomfortable to wear and a nuisance to locate and buckle.

Haddon, a doctor who had been Lyndon Johnson's sole choice to start the safety agency, ordered issuance of an advanced notice of rulemaking for a passive standard (FMVSS 208). Published in 1967, proposed standard 208 required, at first, only seat belts and ultimately shoulder belts. But Haddon was impressed with the potential of a *nonactive* safety device (one that did not require any action by the user) and he became a convert to the passive-restraint idea. He and his staff convened a "State of the Air Bag" conference in Washington in 1968, only two years after the enactment of the new federal car-safety law.

Eaton served as the point company in rounding up participants for the air bag conference. A vice president of Eaton wrote to Haddon that they had obtained agreement from most automobile industry companies to participate in a discussion of the future of passive restraints. American Motors, Chrysler, Ford, General Motors, Eaton, and NHTSA's engineers and professional staff attended. Haddon chaired the meeting. Eaton presented a summary paper entitled "Human Factor Elements Requiring Additional Testing," which, according to its representative, listed "a few areas of concern which the company hoped would be discussed at the meeting.[19]

There was vigorous criticism of the idea from all motor vehicle manufacturers. One of GM's engineers, David Martin, called Eaton's (and Ford's) idea "crazy," saying there had not been enough testing done to establish its safety. [20]

In 1969, just after Haddon's meeting with Eaton and the car manufacturers, passive-restraint devices got national attention when senator Warren Magnuson's staff set up a well-publicized hearing. Eaton's engineers testified that technical problems with the air bag had been resolved. Robert Brenner, who was then serving as acting administrator of the federal safety agency, testified that the devices might well be the "key" to occupant safety, at least for small cars. They were then being imported in large numbers from Germany and Japan. Ralph Nader called the air bag "an exciting development." He expressed disappointment that the car manufacturers were not spending enough money on its rapid development and deployment. [21]

General Motors' engineers said that Eaton's claims of reliability and safety were "preposterous." [22] Even at Ford, Eaton's best hope for a real customer, executives were beginning to cool to the idea, citing reliability and cost problems as arguments that could preclude prompt installation of the new technology in passenger vehicles.

In 1969 NHTSA moved forward again, formally issuing an advanced notice for a proposed passive-restraint rule. [23] It was not, at first, a partisan issue. President Richard Nixon, who did not overtly oppose many new consumer protection regulations, had taken office. Thus the safety agency issued its 1969 notice of proposed rulemaking requiring inflatable restraints in all cars, vans, and light trucks by an aggressive effective date of January 1973, during the Nixon administration, under Secretary of Transportation John Volpe and NHSTA administrator Douglas Toms.

In a statement submitted to the NHTSA docket on the proposed rule in 1970 and circulated to members of Congress, General Motors had promised to install air bags as standard or optional equipment on one million of its cars, after a two-year delay it requested for further testing. Despite its president Edward Cole, who was a strong proponent of new technology and of air bags, GM soon reversed course and claimed there were still many technical problems to resolve and opposed any *mandate* by the federal government. [24] The technical problems, the company said, could cause it to request further delays in the now fading timetable for full deployment. Other manufacturers were worried that GM would overpower their air bag technology with its size and financial muscle.

Opposition also arose from the American Seat Belt Council, which feared that its product would be replaced by an "electro-mechanical system which was unreliable."

The depth of the opposition to the air bag became clear when Eaton's early partner, Ford, also reversed its position. In November 1970 it sponsored nationwide television ads attacking air bags and suggesting it had a "better idea." The Ford idea was an alternative device called the "ignition interlock" that was much less expensive to produce. The Ford advertisements said: "Ford Motor Company engineers are researching a new safety device that could actually save up to 6,500 lives a year . . . if everybody used it. But you probably won't even like it. It's a buckle start system that means that either you have to have your seat belts buckled or your key won't start the engine."[25]

All the Detroit companies now joined Ford, saying they preferred to implement the passive-restraint program with Ford's "automatic detachable seat belts" and an "ignition interlock." The reason they gave was that belts would be "less coercive" to consumers. The industry presidents approached President Nixon in force at a White House meeting and urged cancelation of the air bag proposal. White House staff told the Department of Transportation to drop the passive rule—and substitute the ignition interlock.[26] NHTSA, under intense political pressure from the White House, bought Ford's idea. It ordered the "ignition interlock" instead of air bags, to be installed in all new cars by 1973.

But the public did not like Ford's better idea at all. Consumers rebelled when their cars refused to start when, say, the family dog jumped in the front seat or they put a bag of groceries on the passenger seat. So Congress, after receiving a few hundred angry letters from frustrated constituents, ended the "interlock fiasco." In a panic, the legislators repealed the entire passive-restraint rule in 1974.

Haddon's successors at NHTSA in 1970 were President Nixon's Secretary of Transportation, John Volpe, and his new NHTSA administrator Doug Toms. Toms, a traffic safety engineer from Seattle, and Volpe were both solid supporters of air bags. Volpe, a businessman, lifelong Republican, and former governor of Massachusetts, was described as "a decent, kind and compassionate man."[27] He once said of the air bag's potential: "Somebody's got to prove to me it cannot be done."[28]

It turned out that Volpe and Toms were right. It could be done. They were just years ahead of their time.

The opposition of the automobile industry, based on cost and feasibility concerns grew fierce. Henry Ford, appearing on the *Today* show, called the air bag "nothing but baloney."[29] The entire industry, led by company presidents Ford and Lee Iacocca, marched to the White House to persuade President Nixon to overrule Volpe and Toms. Nixon agreed and issued the direction to DOT and NHTSA. It was a major victory for Detroit.

Then, air bags were completely canceled by Congress after consumer complaints about the ignition interlock induced a vote to kill the entire passive-restraint program during the administration of president Gerald Ford, after Nixon's Watergate-forced resignation.

The air bag rule was supposed to be replaced with a large "demonstration" program by the manufacturers in 1976. That never got off the ground.

Momentum for air bags had been almost entirely lost. It looked like air bags and other passive crash protection were on the way out. Only the election in 1976 of president Jimmy Carter saved the idea. He named Brock Adams as Department of Transportation Secretary and Claybrook to head NHTSA. Within a year the passive restraint regulation was jump-started and reissued again. It was made effective for all cars—but not until 1984, with a phase-in period.

Air bags were alive—but only barely. Other factors harmful to air bag implementation were in play. In 1978 both Eaton and Allied Chemical dropped out of the air bag business. Allied said it was doing so "reluctantly" because it believed that the car manufacturers were moving toward an alternative, "detachable" automatic seat belts. Eaton's president, E. M. de Windt, said Eaton had spent $20 million developing air bags and "we have nothing but bruises to show for our efforts."[30]

The tide turned more strongly against air bags when Jimmy Carter lost the 1980 election to Ronald Reagan. President Reagan appointed Raymond A. Peck Jr., a former coal industry lawyer and an advocate of deregulation, as NHTSA administrator. Peck again ordered the rescission of the air bag rule.[31] Peck threw in a proposed voluntary demonstration program by the manufacturers to test the devices. It never got going.

Consumer advocates, including Nader and the Center for Auto Safety, were outraged by Peck's decision. So was the Insurance Institute for Highway Safety, now run by Bill Haddon—and the new senior vice president he brought with him from the Department of Transportation—Ben Kelley.

Congressional leaders such as John Moss (D-California), Tim Wirth (D-Colorado), and senator John Danforth (R-Missouri) tried to block Peck's air bag cancellation decision—the second rescission by proponents of deregulation in a decade (President Nixon's was the first). The motor vehicle manufacturers supported Peck on the grounds that there was no public demand for passive restraints. This, despite at least three polls by GM, Volvo, and NHTSA showing that a majority of the public disliked seat belts and preferred air bags.[32] In addition, the producers claimed that air bags were not yet proven effective and that the added cost for buyers—claimed to be as much as $800 per car—a much higher number than Ford and NHTSA estimates—would be prohibitive. General Motors, in particular, said that "[T]he American public would not accept mandatory seat belt laws or passive restraints."[33]

When Peck told his staff that he had decided to rescind the proposed passive restraint rule, Michael Finkelstein, his associate administrator for rulemaking, says he told Peck "in graphic, profane language, how stupid the decision was."[34] The professional staff of NHTSA was almost unanimous it opposing Peck's decision. Yet there seemed to be no way the decision could be overturned by proponents. Air bags were now on life support. The only thing that kept the idea barely alive in the United States was that some foreign manufacturers, such as Mercedes-Benz, offered optional air bags in some models, as did Ford staring in its 1984 Tempo compacts sold to the government.[35]

But a series of stunning developments in the early 1980s proved air bags were not as dead as they appeared to be. A unanimous Supreme Court ruling in 1983 reviewed the NHTSA cancellation decision and found that the car industry had "waged the regulatory equivalent of war against the airbag." Then a new Reagan appointee, Elizabeth Dole, became the Secretary of Transportation in 1983. Dole brought air bags back from the dead. Together with new mandatory state seat belt laws and federally mandated minimum age state drinking laws, they offered new potential for saving thousands of American lives.

NOTES

1. Hearings before the Subcommittee on Consumers, Committee on Commerce, Science, and Transportation, United States Senate, 95th Congress, September 8, 1977 (Senate Doc. 95–126), 7.

2. Ibid.

3. Ibid., 4.

4. David Young, "Automobile Air Bags: How Much is Highway Safety Worth?" *Chicago Tribune*, September 5, 1976, 14. See Insurance Institute for Highway Safety, "Air Bags: A Chronological History of Delay" (Washington, D.C., 1984), 4–5.

5. In 1984 Mercedes-Benz offered air bags as an option on 5,000 of its high-end models and was prepared to extend it to all its United States sales the next year. In May 1988, pressured by NHTSA, insurers, and consumer groups, Ford and Chrysler became the first American automobile manufacturers to commit to offering driver-side and some front-passenger air bags as standard equipment in many of their models. The Supplemental Restraint System (SRS), as it was called, was already popular in Europe. The price for the SRS system was a steep $800 a car. For some reason Mercedes-Benz never expanded its air bag system as planned, until all companies were forced to by the United States government and the courts by 1990. See, John D. Graham, *Auto Safety: Assessing America's Performance* (Dover, MA: Auburn House Publishing, 1989), 161, cited as *Assessing America's Performance*; Martin Albaum, *Safety Sells*, referred to as "Safety Sells," unpublished manuscript available on the Internet (www.safetysells.org), 143.

6. See DOT HS 811 892 (2012), NHTSA, *Traffic Safety Facts*, March 2014 "Occupant Protection."

7. See FMVSS 208 (NHTSA), 49 CFR 571.208 (July 17, 1984); 49 F.R. 138, 28996.

8. Richard W. Kent, *Airbag Development and Performance: New Perspectives from Industry, Government and Academia*, (Warrendale, PA: Society of Automotive Engineers, Inc., 2003), 4.

9. Ibid., 4.

10. In the late 1960s, the multi-talented Dr. Carl Clark served as a "big data" visionary by designing and testing a new system for the collection of consumer product accident information for the National Commission on Product Safety.

11. Michael Dorsey, "Stirring the Pot," *WPI Journal* (Summer 1997), http://www.wpi.edu/News/Journal/Summer97/pot.html

12. Graham, *Auto Safety*, 37.

13. Ibid., 38.

14. Interview by the author with Ben Kelley, former senior vice president, Insurance Institute for Highway Safety, by email (with attachment), September 18, 2013.

15. Graham, *Assessing America's Performance*, 39.

16. Kent, *Air Bag Development and Performance*, 3.

17. 15 U.S.C. 1392(a) (1976 supp.), 5.

18. Testimony of William Haddon Jr., Administrator, National Highway Safety Agency hearings before the Committee on Commerce, "Implementation of the National Traffic and Motor Vehicle Safety Act of 1966," March 20, 1967, Washington: U.S. Government Printing Office, July 19, 1968; cited in "Air Bags: A Chronological History of Delay" (Washington, D.C: Insurance Institute for Highway Safety, September 1984), 1.

19. Letter from Eaton Yale & Towne, Inc. to Dr. William Haddon, Director, National Highway Traffic Safety Bureau (later the National Highwat Traffic Safety Administration), June 12, 1968.

20. Graham, *Assessing America's Performance*, 40.

21. *New York Times*, April 20, 1969, 92, cited in Graham, *Assessing America's Performance*, 39–40.

22. Ibid., 40.

23. *Federal Register* 34:11, 148 (1969); *New York Times*, July 3, 1969, 12.

24. Insurance Institute for Highway Safety, "Implementation of the National Traffic and Motor Vehicle Safety Act of 1966," 1.

25. "Airbag Briefing Materials," Citizens Legal Clinic, Washington, DC, 1984; Air bags, "Implementation of the National Traffic and Motor Vehicle Safety Act of 1966," IIHS, 3.

26. Ibid.

27. Graham, *Assessing America's Performance*, 41.

28. Ibid., 48.

29. Ibid., 52.

30. Ibid., 124.

31. Albaum, "Safety Sells," 111.

32. Insurance Institute for Highway Safety Status Report, "GM and the Air Bag," June 25, 1980, 10; IIHS Report, 1984, Anne Fleming, ed. "Air Bags: A Chronological History of Delay", 4.

33. Graham, *Assessing America's Performance*, 124–26.

34. Albaum, "Safety Sells," 111.

35. Ibid., 114.

TEN

Elizabeth Dole, State Farm, and How America Got the Air Bag

For many years, the casualty insurance industry favored air bags—and other safety equipment, such as seat belts.

It did not, at first, take an active role in pressing for their mandatory use in automobiles.[1] Beginning about 1970 there was a reversal of the insurance industry's position. Insurance industry executives such as Donald Schaffer of Allstate and Don McHugh of State Farm came to believe that their business, as well as automobile safety in general, would be better off if passive-restraint protection were required by the government in the cars they insured.[2]

The casualty insurance industry's change of position—to one actively supporting federally mandated passive restraints, as well as other federal safety standards—is unprecedented in the annals of industry-regulatory battles. Large industries, such as motor vehicle manufacturers and casualty insurance carriers, usually work out a common position about federal regulations—in private. They do not fight out their differences publicly.

This time it was different. The insurance industry decided to fight it out with the car manufacturers in full view of the press and the public.

It seems likely that insurance industry leaders had developed more than a purely economic commitment to the idea of using the industry's muscle to push a federal air bag standard (and at the same time cut their accident-related costs). But the decision was unique. It does not appear to have been based solely on the bottom line. Of course, competition for customers and state pressure to control ever-rising insurance rates were factors.[3] The high-speed crashes that air bags would mitigate and the lives they would save, however, were not a major cost factor for insurance companies. Millions of less serious car crash injuries actually cost them more total money in claims paid.[4] For the insurance industry, something more than just money was involved in its reversal.

Ben Kelley, formerly senior vice president of the Insurance Institute for Highway Safety (IIHS), recalls that insurance companies and their trade associations "had for years been very frustrated by their inability to get the automobile industry to do the things that they thought would hold down insurance rates and reduce injuries and property damage in automobile crashes. There had been innumerable meetings and seminars, but nothing really changed."[5]

Kelley says that Bill Haddon, then serving as administrator of NHTSA, had been at some of the meetings and seminars.

> The insurance people knew who he was and that he was singularly effective. He was willing to do new things. So as we were exiting the government around 1970, when Richard Nixon was elected president, the insurance industry leaders approached Haddon and asked him to lead a new effort to develop safer cars. Fortunately for me they approached me too.[6]

That is how in 1970 Bill Haddon came to the automobile insurance industry, as president of the Insurance Institute for Highway Safety (IIHS) and its affiliate, the Highway Loss Data Institute (HLDI). He proceeded to lead the industry in a more aggressive safety role, turning the struggle into a political as well as a technological fight. The insurance companies put up the money and muscle. They brought lawsuits, with consumer allies, against the industry opponents of passive restraints. Later they began crash-testing cars to demonstrate passive restraints' effectiveness—and they publicized the results widely.

IIHS and HLDI became major factors in the final adoption of a national passive-restraint requirement. It was a long, bumpy road. And the outcome of the titanic struggle among industry giants, consumer groups, and the United States government was not clear until years later.

The position of the automobile manufacturers on the need for air bags, or some alternative passive-restraint system had not always been the same. General Motors had sold 10,000 air bag–equipped demonstration Oldsmobile vehicles during the 1974–1976 model years. Then it abruptly stopped the experiment. At least twice, Ford broke with other companies and showed a willingness to experiment with air bags. In the 1970s it worked with Eaton and Allied Chemical to develop and use the new air bag technology. In the late 1980s, Ford and Chrysler jumped ahead of GM and announced that driver-side air bags would be standard equipment in some models. Even within companies there were sometimes strong differences of opinion about air bags.

While he was president of GM from 1967 to 1974, Edward N. Cole was a strong supporter of air bags. Cole was an innovative leader. A graduate engineer, he spent his entire professional life at GM. He is credited with the development of the new but ill-fated 1960–1963 Chevy Corvair, made infamous by Ralph Nader's bestseller *Unsafe at Any Speed*. Cole believed and said publically that the Corvair was a safe car.

Cole later led in the development of the small, low-compression engine. It helped wean Americans off leaded gasoline and thus increased automobile fuel efficiency and economy.[7] After he retired from General Motors in 1974, Cole stunned some of his former colleagues by publicly endorsing mandatory air bags. In a letter to Haddon, by then the president of IIHS, Cole wrote in 1977: "The passive restraint . . . technology is available and the need is there. I think the only way passive restraints are going to get to first base is making them mandatory. Another test will prove nothing."[8]

But Cole was reluctant to testify publicly in favor of air bags. He told supporters, "The boys are really pressuring me and I am going to have to say there needs to be [more lead] time."[9]

When Jimmy Carter became president in 1976 he named Brock Adams, a former member of congress from Seattle, as his new Secretary of Transportation. The Carter NHTSA administrator was Joan Claybrook, a dogged supporter of an air bag rule. They promptly reissued the rule, known as Standard 208.[10] However they delayed the effective date for four years, which proved important. Instead of naming a date that would fall within Carter's "first" term, it was set at 1982 for large cars and 1984 for smaller models. Claybrook said it was the only way to get a second air bag proposed standard issued.

There was, of course, no Carter second term. By the time the air bag rule was scheduled to go into effect, Claybrook and Adams would be long gone and Ronald Reagan would be in the White House.

When Reagan won the presidency by a landslide in 1980 the country was in a recession. The automobile industry was suffering a sharp economic downturn, with interest rates rising and sales falling. The new president's platform had been one of shrinking the federal government, deregulating much of American industry and repealing federal regulations. Number one on the automobile industry's wish list was getting rid of the Carter-Adams-Claybrook passive-restraint rule. The industry's blunt message was delivered to the Reagan White House almost immediately: kill it.

To carry out his deregulation policy in transportation, Reagan appointed Drew Lewis as secretary. Lewis named Raymond A. Peck Jr. to be the administrator of the auto safety agency. Peck had worked for many years as an attorney for the coal industry. "I am not a regulatory torpedo," said Peck upon taking up his duties. He added: "This job involves matters of life and death.

Lewis delegated to Peck what turned out to be the most important life-and-death safety decision of the Reagan era. What to do about passive restraints? Peck began a review of the extensive record stretching back to 1967. He held new hearings and talked with the automobile industry, insurance companies, and consumer groups. But ultimately he was under orders from the White House to terminate the rule.[11] He concluded that there was no good evidence that the use of passive restraints (by then defined either as air bags *or* "passive detachable" seat belts) would produce any significant safety benefits to the driving public, over the use of seat belts alone. Peck directed that the air bag rule be rescinded for a second time.[12]

There was still public pressure to keep the rule alive. State Farm, one of the leading insurers supporting passive restraints, thought about suing Reagan, Peck, Lewis, and the department but was reluctant to go to court to directly challenge the administration over the cancellation of the air bag rule. Ultimately, Haddon convinced them it had to be done. So State Farm, the National Association of Independent Insurers, and others brought a lawsuit against Peck and the Department of Transportation to overturn the Reagan-Peck decision. They hired one of the nation's best (and priciest) litigation lawyers, James Fitzpatrick from the law firm Arnold & Porter, to handle the case. The Center for Auto Safety, the Epilepsy Foundation, Mothers Against Drunk Driving, the American Insurance Association, and others joined the case on State Farm's side.

The Motor Vehicle Manufacturers Association joined the Department of Transportation and solicitor general Rex Lee in defending the Reagan rescission. It was indeed a crucial moment for passive restraints and for the driving public.

When the case against Peck and the department reached the courts in 1981, it was believed that the Court of Appeals (the first level of appeal of the Peck/DOT decision)—and then the Supreme Court would affirm the "expert" judgment of the safety agency that air bags would not be effective. In fact, the car manufacturers started dismantling their air bag programs hours after NHTSA and Peck announced the rescission of the rule.

Although the government had reversed course on air bags and seat belts several times over the years, industry leaders and its supporters believed they would finally win this time around. That was because the decision was based on a detailed rule-making record extending back decades.

Most people, including lawyers for the insurance industry and consumer groups fighting to reverse the Reagan/Peck decision, thought the record was probably big and detailed enough to make almost any agency logic not seem totally "arbitrary" to the courts. Most people thought the odds of winning an appeal of the Reagan administration rescission decision were long indeed.[13]

Most people were wrong.

First, the Court of Appeals for the District of Columbia and then, in 1983, the Supreme Court issued decisions overturning the administration's repeal of the passive restraint rule. The opinions were unanimous.

Even consumer advocates and their insurance industry allies were stunned at their own success. Not one of the twelve judges reviewing the Reagan-Lewis-Peck decision approved it. The Supreme Court (and the Court of Appeals) both appeared fed up with the decades of delay and the seemingly endless struggle between the automobile industry and safety proponents over the potentially life-saving passive restraint/air bag rule.

In the Court of Appeals ruling, judge Abner Mikva, a former congressman from Illinois, wrote that the agency's action was "arbitrary and illogical." The agency's "analysis of air bags was nonexistent." Mikva found the Reagan/Peck reversal offered "not one iota of evidence that the standard [which continued to allow passive seat belts as an alternative to air bags] would fail to increase nationwide seat belt use by a significant amount."[14]

The case was immediately appealed to the Supreme Court by the Reagan administration. The Supreme Court's decision said that the rule had "a complex and convoluted history. Over the course of approximately 60 rule-making notices the requirement has been imposed, amended, rescinded, reimposed and now rescinded again."[15]

Then came Supreme Court justice Byron White's articulation of the court's reasoning for the decision. His words echo today: "For nearly a decade, the automobile industry has waged the regulatory equivalent of war against the air bag and lost—the inflatable restraint was proved sufficiently effective. Now the automobile industry has decided to employ a seatbelt system which will not meet the safety objectives of standard 208."[16]

Justice White's opinion must have come as a shock to the motor vehicle industry, which had played a key role in getting the Reagan administration to reverse course. The double-barreled reversal of the administration's action by two appellate courts resulted in the passive-restraint rule being sent back to NHTSA and the Department of Transportation for reconsideration.

The Supreme Court did not specify what the department should do next. It merely held that the existing record did not support cancellation of the rule. That left open the question of whether the agency, and more importantly, the Reagan administration, should revise their reasoning, or improve the supporting record and again try to repeal the rule. Or it could modify and reissue the rule, or start an entirely new proceeding based on new evidence.

The passive-restraint rule had now involved inventors, manufacturers, suppliers, Congress, the Department of Transportation, NHTSA, the Court of Appeals, the White House, and finally, the Supreme Court. It had sucked a large part of American industry and many nonprofit and consumer organizations into the fight. It had, in fact, stimulated the founding of a new safety organization, the National Coalition to Reduce Car Crash Injuries, with a broad-based safety-centered membership. The coalition was funded mostly by the insurance industry, but it was composed of almost every consumer, scientific, insurance, and medical organization with any interest in motor vehicle safety. The result, after Justice White's stinging rebuke to the administration, was to create in 1983, a major hot potato for the new secretary of transportation. Her name was Elizabeth Dole.

The hot potato was dropped squarely on the desk of the new secretary. Named to the post after DOT secretary Drew Lewis resigned, Dole was the wife of senator Bob Dole of Kansas. She had been a surprising appointment by President Reagan, since she had no past experience in the field.

Dole may have been new to transportation safety, but she was not new to government, or to politics. The secretary was an articulate fifty-seven-year-old lawyer with considerable southern charm. Born in Salisbury, a small town in the Piedmont region of North Carolina as Elizabeth Hanford, she was the daughter of a well-off wholesale florist, merchant, and business entrepreneur. She had a comfortable childhood, complete with ballet lessons and vacations at the family's summer home. She was voted "most likely to succeed" when she graduated from Salisbury High School and moved easily on to elite Duke University. There she became a student activist and top scholar. One year she was voted May Queen.

Elizabeth's mother, whom she called her "best friend," was involved in church and community activities. She believed in helping the less fortunate in her small North Carolina community. She was deeply religious all her life.

Dole appears to have followed her mother's example of community service. At Duke, she was active in student affairs and aggressive in promoting women's rights. Her mother had, on the other hand, made it clear that she hoped her daughter would concentrate on home economics and then have a large family.[17]

After graduating from Duke and doing some international travel, Elizabeth Hanford got her master's degree from Harvard, concentrating in both education and political science. She says a "new world opened up" for her. She changed direction and enrolled at Harvard Law School at the suggestion of one of her professors. She says the experience of moving on to Harvard Law School was a painful one. It was a big, impersonal place, filled with intense overachievers. But ultimately, as for so many others, law and Harvard had a major impact on her life.

After law school Dole worked for the United Nations, took an assignment with the Peace Corps and accepted an internship with North Carolina's senator Everett Jordan (a Democrat). She campaigned for the Kennedy-Johnson ticket in 1960 and rode on the Johnson campaign train four years later. And she was noticed. In 1965 she was named a White House Fellow where, she recalled, she and other staff members found President Johnson was a bit stern and frightening.

Nonetheless, Dole wound up getting a job in the Johnson White House. She was given a title, special assistant, and a new cause: consumer affairs. She decided to stay on after President Nixon's Republican victory in 1968. She worked for five years with President Nixon's consumer affairs advisor Virginia Knauer, the third White House consumer advisor, succeeding Betty Furness and Esther Peterson. (The job has not been filled since.)

About that time Elizabeth changed her registration from Democrat to Republican. Then, in a surprise, she was nominated by President Nixon to be a commissioner of the sometimes powerful Federal Trade Commission. She was known around Washington as an independent-minded commissioner, who was sensitive to the interests of consumers.

In 1975 Elizabeth married senator Bob Dole of Kansas, after a friendship lasting several years. When President Reagan was elected in 1980, Dole returned to the White House as assistant for Public Liaison. But she was bound for bigger things. Three years later, in 1983, President Reagan named her secretary of transportation. She later became one of the few women to serve in two cabinet positions, moving on to secretary of labor in 1989.

When she took over as Transportation Secretary, Elizabeth Dole was an unknown quantity in transportation policy. She had never expressed any notable opinions on automobile safety, or specifically about the hot-potato issue of whether or not to require air bags or other passive restraints in all cars. Some people in the Reagan administration found Dole's appointment "particularly irritating." They thought she was a closet Democrat and were sure that, even worse, she was a committed feminist.[18]

As to the air bag decision, the new secretary was pressed by White House staff and the Office of Management and Budget to shelve the passive-restraint rule again after it was sent back to the department by the Supreme Court. The Secretary of Transportation hesitated.

She had several options with regard to handling the Supreme Court's remand of the rule. At stake were billions of dollars in added costs to manufacturers. Automobile prices also would likely rise for consumers if the manufacturers could pass on the cost of passive restraints (along with a profit margin) to their customers. At stake, as well, were the lives of thousands of drivers and passengers and likely long-term economic savings in avoided medical expenses and lost work time, among other potential savings.

The passive-restraint program that the secretary was forced to reconsider in 1983 had narrowly survived a rocky history. Looking back now, when most American cars are equipped with multiple air bags, it is tempting to see the fight as a demonstration of automobile industry stalling and government ineffectiveness. In defense of the combatants, the stakes were very high for motorists, manufacturers, and the government. The ultimate success of the air bag and the lives and dollars it saved can now be viewed as one of the great achievements of federal safety regulation. But it was not clear at first whether the technology would even work effectively.

An antiregulation, antigovernment atmosphere permeated Washington when Elizabeth Dole stepped in as secretary of transportation in 1983. The Reagan-Peck air bag rescission was a key part of the administration's deregulatory policy. Its reversal by the Supreme Court dumped the issue squarely on her.

Dole took over the case personally, as opposed to handing it over to NHTSA. She was encouraged to do so by the White House, which did not trust NHTSA's professionals and engineers. They strongly favored the rule. So did Allstate and other insurance companies. Allstate promptly went on record attacking GM's latest proposal. It was stated in a letter from GM's president Roger Smith to Dole. GM wanted Dole to retain "private consulting firms" to assist in her review of standard 208, which mandated passive restraints—either detachable, passive seat belts—or the hated air bags. This surely would have delayed the decision for years. It might have changed the final outcome.

Allstate's President, Don Schaffer, wrote to Dole that GM's President Smith was an, "avowed opponent" of the passive-restraint rule and "not a credible advisor on this subject." Schaffer was blunt. He wrote that the GM suggestion "should be ignored."[19] The battle lines were drawn—again.

Shortly after her confirmation hearings in April 1983, Dole offered a brief comment on the passive-restraint issue to the *Washington Post*. She did not commit herself on what she might do. But she acknowledged the air bag was "a good safety device."[20] Whether it was good enough remained to be seen.

The new secretary held three more hearings on the issue, promised a prompt decision, and continued to ponder. White House officials attempted to reassure the automobile industry about what Secretary Dole would do. A report in *Ward's Auto World* quoted a "high-ranking aide" to the President, saying: "The Administration plans to fight this challenge all the way. If we lose, the worst the car-makers should expect might be an automatic seat belt requirement some years down the road. Mrs. Dole's marching orders on this one will be cut by the Vice President's task force on regulatory relief."[21]

OMB (Office of Management and Budget) and much of the White House staff opposed reissuing the air bag rule in any form. They stood for minimal regulation, life-saving or otherwise. Reagan's first inaugural address had set national policy firmly: "In this present crisis, government is not the solution to our problem, government is the problem."[22]

The insurance industry, again led by State Farm and Allstate, pushed hard for the new secretary to retain the passive-restraint rule in some form. Consumer leaders like Nader and Claybrook, now president of Public Citizen, who had been fighting since 1969 for a mandatory air bag rule, joined the insurance industry in a coalition. But the safety and insurance side was worried. Dole was an unknown quantity.

The secretary set up a special panel within her office (with no NHTSA professional staff previously involved as members). Diane Steed, the new administrator of NHTSA, was on the panel. The department's general counsel, James Burnley, a solid conservative Republican, was selected by Dole to lead the panel. Dole supervised it closely from day one. The deliberations were secret, causing further concern among consumer advocates.

It was obvious that much of the White House staff and probably President Reagan were opposed to the rule. "It was a Reagan Administration decision to rescind rule 208 of the prior Carter Administration," Jim Burnley recalled. "There was no mystery about what the attitude would be in the Office of Management and Budget. . . . We knew from day one that they would be skeptical and perhaps hostile."[23]

After Peck's resignation he had been replaced by Steed, who had previously worked at the Office of Management and Budget, the prime enforcer of the Reagan policy to "Get the government off our backs."[24] Steed had said publicly that it might very well be possible to make a new case for complete rescission of the air bag rule.[25] Dole's notice of hearings on the issue in early 1983 offered complete rescission of the air bag rule as one option.[26] Would she take this approach?

While she was wrestling with the passive-restraint rule Dole had another major automobile safety issue to deal with: minimum state drinking-age laws. These are state laws, dating back to the Prohibition era, that regulate the age at which young people may consume alcohol. They were and are particularly important to automobile safety, since this age group tends to be involved in more serious and fatal accidents than any other population group. The existence of state laws requiring a twenty-one-year-old minimum drinking age would clearly reduce drunk driving, provided they could be enacted over state's rights objections.

After the repeal of Prohibition in 1933, all states passed laws regulating the legal drinking age. Most fixed the age at twwnty-one. But by the 1970s, twenty-nine states had reduced the legal drinking age to twenty, nineteen, or even eighteen.[27]

Deaths in automobile crashes related to drunk driving began to rise immediately.[28] The Senate and then the House passed the Lautenberg-Lugar bill to withhold 10 percent of federal highway construction money from any state that did not raise the legal drinking age to 21. Depending on the size of the state, as much as $100 million a year in federal highway subsidy funds were at stake.

Under Article X of the United States Constitution, the qualifications of drivers are probably a state issue, as distinguished from the design and construction of motor vehicles. Since the latter are products moving in or affecting commerce, they may be regulated by the federal government under the interstate commerce clause. The Lautenberg-Lugar bill, regulating drinking by individuals, could be seen as something of an indirect expansion of federal authority under the commerce clause. It was for a good cause—reducing highway deaths and injuries among young people—and could also be said to affect interstate commerce. Thus, it was argued such a law, if passed, would be constitutional.

But would the president, a supporter of state, not federal power sign such a law? Dole decided she needed to get involved. She had already cooperated with Frank Lautenberg, a Democrat from New Jersey and Richard Lugar, a Republican from Indiana, and with groups such as Mothers Against Drunk Driving, to push the bill through Congress. Now she met with the president to discuss what she described to him as "blood borders," those between different states with different legal drinking ages and why he should sign the bill.

She remembers the meeting well. "President Reagan said to me, "Elizabeth, are you telling me thousands of kids are losing their lives due to these blood borders?" When she replied with a forceful "absolutely," the president replied, "Then let's support raising the drinking age uniformly to twenty-one." [29]

The Lautenberg-Lugar bill became law. It is now known as the National Minimum Drinking Age Act. [30] Deaths related to drunk driving have gone down from 21,000 a year in 1982 to about 10,000 in 2011, partly in response to the minimum drinking age law. [31] Dole later recalled the fight, along with air bags and state laws requiring mandatory use of lap/shoulder belts, as a safety "triple play." [32]

When the secretary turned to the question of what to do about the air bag regulation, she faced a very "overheated regulatory atmosphere" within the Reagan administration. In addition, the automobile industry was at loggerheads with the insurance industry, Nader, and consumer groups. All were not shy about letting the press and the administration know where they stood.

Before Dole could issue any final decision, she had to convince the president it was the right one. Chris DeMuth, head of the regulatory reform group at OMB, flatly opposed the rule and advised President Reagan that despite the Supreme Court decision, it should be rescinded once again.[33] David Stockman, director of OMB, had already written that the rule should be revoked again.

Jim Burnley, then the Department of Transportation general counsel, ran interference for Elizabeth in advance meetings with White House chief of staff James Baker and attorney general Edwin Meese. Burley's main arguments were that the Supreme Court had signaled it probably would not tolerate further delay and that the effectiveness of air bag technology had been proven. These may have been good lawyer's arguments. But legal experts are very aware that administrative agencies can stall almost forever, or develop endless new reasons for rescinding almost any rule they do not think is justified. The law gives them a lot of leeway in their decisions.

In fact, four justices of the Supreme Court had specifically mapped out a new recission route for Dole in a concurring opinion in the State Farm case. They said a new administration can always change its mind about a policy, provided it can show it is not acting "arbitrarily."[34] That was a very low bar to get over, but it proved a crucial one. The agency had to show it had at least one relevant, logical reason for not requiring air bags. Whether it would try depended on Elizabeth Dole and Ronald Reagan.

Years later Dole said, "I had a strong belief in consumer safety. I never seriously considered terminating the passive restraint proceeding."[35] She may have come to that conclusion, but there was at the time considerable pressure on her to do just the opposite and terminate the rule again.

After spending weeks listening to the combatants at public hearings, and meeting with her special panel, Dole came up with a unique strategy. It turned out to be something of a regulatory masterpiece. She decided, first, despite the clear antiregulatory policy of the Reagan administration, to move ahead with a rule mandating passive restraints in American cars.[36]

But there was a major condition attached to the decision. Perhaps it was her years of Washington-insider experience. Perhaps she was wary of tackling the opponents of the regulation in OMB, the White House, and the automobile industry head-on. In the end it was probably her gut instinct to try to save some lives.

The secretary proposed reissuing the passive-restraint rule. It would be set for full implementation by 1990 (including lead time for the manufacturers). But there was a possible "out" for the rule's opponents. If states totaling two-thirds of the U.S. population passed mandatory seat belt–use laws within five years *and* the state laws met six federally imposed criteria, the air bag rule would be revoked again. At the time only New York had passed a mandatory seat belt law. It was one that probably did not meet Dole's federal standards because it did not include a minimum fine of $25 for not wearing a seat belt. Belt use by consumers was then at a low point of about 13 percent. Passage of state seat belt laws was considered an almost impossible goal politically.

According to James Burnley:

> Elizabeth Dole personally wanted to see air bags out there. If we were going to end up with automatic restraints, she was not happy that we might end up with a fleet of automatic safety belts and no air bags. Of all the alternatives, she did not think that automatic belts were the most attractive. In fact, she felt they were the least attractive because they were so easily disabled. She thought that would be the worst of all safety outcomes. Her desire was to see that air bags were available in significant numbers and see what happened. She personally had a lot to do with that element of this decision. She was quite insistent. [37]

The main federal criteria that the state laws had to meet were:

- Seat belts had to be useable by both the driver and all occupants when the vehicle was moving.
- No occupant waivers could be allowed by the state, except for medical reasons.
- Penalties for non-use of seat belts under state laws would have to be at least $25 for each violation.
- The state laws would have to be in effect no later than September 1, 1989.
- The non-use of belts by consumers could be used as evidence of negligence in a lawsuit arising out of a car accident.

Then Dole went over to the White House to attempt to convince the president to approve her proposed passive-restraint rule, despite his broadly deregulatory views. James Baker, the White House chief of staff, was the only other person in the Oval Office for the meeting. [38]

"The President was actually not very hard to convince," she recalled. "But we did not take any chances. We brought Dr. Paul Meyer, a friend of Nancy Reagan's and a doctor at the spinal cord center at Northwestern Medical School, all the way from Chicago. That was just in case the president needed a medical opinion on how many lives would be saved by enacting the rule. And we had some air bag–equipped demonstration cars sitting in the White House driveway to show the president how well they worked. But we didn't need Dr. Meyer, or the cars. President Reagan, after listening for a while and thinking about it, just plain said he agreed with me." [39]

And a bit of Southern charm and political savvy might have helped too.

Did Dole think that enough states would pass mandatory seat belt–use laws and terminate the federal air bag rule? She has never said. But the bar of getting states with two-thirds of the United States population to pass mandatory all-passenger belt laws was high. The political battles over mandatory state seat belt laws would obviously be fierce. Perhaps Dole understood what would happen in the end.

Dole's decision was at first viewed with great concern by nearly everyone involved. Consumer groups and the insurance industry, the chief advocates of automatic crash protection, were dismayed at the potential for the automobile industry to kill the rule through Elizabeth's "trap door," that is, by getting enough state seat belt laws passed.[40] The motor vehicle manufacturers, who had previously expended virtually no effort to get state seat belt laws passed, now organized and spent millions to try to push through enough mandatory state laws to block the federal air bag rule.[41] The insurance industry–consumer coalition followed them around the country. They battled state by state.

The consumer-insurance coalition strategy was subtle. They did not oppose mandatory state seat belt laws outright. They could not; they wanted both air bags and seat belts. They tried to change the state seat belt laws that passed just enough so they did not meet Dole's six federal criteria. Or they tried for their own "reverse trapdoor" that provided a state law would be repealed if it was counted toward overturning a national passive-restraint rule.

The manufacturers founded an organization called "Traffic Safety Now." They fought in most states for seat belt laws that met all of Dole's federal requirements. They spent millions. By November 1985, still long before the deadline, sixteen states had passed mandatory seat belt laws. It was not clear whether they met Dole's six requirements. Dole never has disclosed how she would have ruled on them, if it had ever come to that.

California was the clincher. After fierce lobbying by the manufacturers against State Farm and consumer groups, the largest state passed a mandatory seat belt law, seemingly putting the anti–air bag forces over the top. The California law, however, included its own "reverse poison pill." California's law, thanks perhaps to a conversation between Ralph Nader and California Assembly speaker Willie Brown, provided that if the federal rule on air bags was ever revoked, California's own mandatory seat belt law would be revoked as well. This would presumably deny the two-thirds population number necessary under Dole's regulation and force, or maintain, the federal air bag rule in effect. It turned out to be an unnecessary club in the closet.

Public opinion began to swing in favor of passive restraints.[42] Air bags were available as an option in some cars. Manufacturers and insurers began receiving "fan mail" from consumers, who had some of the few available, optional air bags in their cars, saying their lives had been saved or serious injuries avoided when the air bags functioned just fine.[43] In part because of Dole's federal prod, state action on seat belt laws and mandatory child-seat restraint laws both increased dramatically. Some automobile companies, such as Volvo, Ford, Chrysler, and Mercedes-

Benz, broke ranks with other car makers and offered optional air bags on selected models.[44] The tide turned. Consumer attitudes toward safety generally, and passive restraints in particular, changed too.

In 1986 an NHTSA survey found that consumers had a more favorable than unfavorable attitude toward air bags in their cars. A total of 90 percent said they had heard about air bags and 76 percent had accurate information on their usefulness. A majority said they were willing to pay as much for air bags as they would for an AM/FM radio/cassette player in their new cars.[45]

Ford dropped the price of its optional air bags to $295. Helen Petrauskas, a Ford vice president for safety, and other members of Ford's management became supporters of air bags. Ford believed they could be a positive selling strategy against other makes. Seat belt usage began to move up from about 13 percent in 1970 to over 40 percent by the mid-1980s and 87 percent in 2013.[46] This was due mostly to the mandatory state seat belt laws, forced by the federal air bag rule.

James Burnley became Secretary of Transportation in 1987 when Dole resigned to work on her husband Bob Dole's campaign for president. Testifying before the Senate Commerce Committee at his own confirmation hearings that year, Burnley said, "It's very clear that while we have a great many (state) seat belt laws, rule 208, the (federal) passive restraint rule is going to be fully implemented."

The insurance companies began to back efforts in Washington and the states with premium reductions for cars that included passive restraints. State Farm announced a 40 percent discount for cars equipped with passive restraints. Nationwide continued its substantial premium discounts for the purchase of air bags. USAA offered a $300 "safety bonus" in 1988.

The end of the passive-restraint battle came in 1989—almost unnoticed. Because a sufficient proportion of states had *not* enacted mandatory seat belt laws that met federal standards, the passive restraint rule went into effect nationally. Automatic occupant crash protection was phased in beginning in 1987, fully effective by September 1989 for 1990 model year passenger cars, and for vans and light trucks by 1998.

Passive-restraint systems, air bags for all front-seating positions, were now required by federal law.[47]

Most states enacted mandatory seat belt laws as well.[48] By 2012 there were forty-nine state mandatory seat belt laws in force. Only New Hampshire (state motto: "Live Free or Die") held out.

Despite the Reagan administration having given every indication that its deregulation policy would prevail and the automobile industry would win its "war" against passive restraints, the final result was just the opposite.

Thanks in large part to Elizabeth Dole's persuasiveness and considerable courage, America ultimately got the designed-in vehicle safety it has now; *both* federally required air bags and state-mandated seat belt use laws.

"I have always had passion for consumer and worker safety," she said in an interview thirty years later. "I had a special fervor for the passive restraint standard."[49]

NOTES

1. Interview by the author with Ben Kelley, formerly senior vice president Insurance Institute for Highway Safety, January 17, 2013, 18.

2. Ibid., 15.

3. Martin Albaum, *Safety Sells*, referred to hereafter as "Safety Sells" (unpublished manuscript available on the internet (http://www.safetysells.org), 61.

4. Interview by the author with Adrian Lund, president, Insurance Institute for Auto Safety, May 8, 2014, 17.

5. Kelley interview, 8.

6. Ibid., 9.

7. "Ed Cole: Father of the Small Block," http://media.gm.com/autoshows/small_block/2011/public/us/en/powertrain/news.detail.html/content/Pages/news/us/en/2011/Nov/100M/1129_100M_Cole.html.

8. David Bollier and Joan Claybrook, *"Freedom From Harm"*(Public Citizen, Washington D.C., 1986), 79.

9. Ibid.

10. Standard 208 (1969) had dealt originally with requirements regarding lap and shoulder belts. The 1977 amendment by Adams and Claybrook proposed adding passive-restraint requirements for front seats. Both safety systems (lap and shoulder belts and frontal air bags) remain the law today.

11. Kelley, interview by email, September 18, 2013.

12. See *Motor Vehicle Manufacturers Association v. State Farm Mutual Insurance Company*, 463 U.S. 29 (1983), 6.

13. Kelley interview, 17.

14. 220 U.S.App.D.C. 170, 680 F.2d 206 (1982), pars. 102, 107, 121.

15. *Motor Vehicle Manufacturers Association v. State Farm Mutual Insurance Company*, 4.

16. Ibid., 11.

17. Bob and Elizabeth Dole, *The Doles: Unlimited Partners* (New York: Simon and Schuster, 1988), 45, 47, 80, 81.

18. See http://politics.salon.com, 2011/11/26.

19. Martin Albaum, "Safety Sells" (IIHS unpublished manuscript), 122.

20. *Washington Post*, April 10, 1983, quoted in Graham, *Assessing America's Performance*, 162.

21. *Ward's Auto World*, August 1983, 45.

22. Quoted in www.Ontheissues.org/celeb/Ronald_Reagan_Government_sourced 6/11/12.

23. Interview with James Burnley, June 8, 1995, quoted in Albaum, "Safety Sells," 121.

24. Ronald Reagan, "Vision for America," election eve address (November 3, 1980), www.presidency.uscb.edu/ws/?pid=85199.

25. Albaum, "Safety Sells," 122.

26. See, Federal Register 48-48622-48641 (October 1983). The notice as approved and issued by Secretary Dole made rescission of the passive-restraint standard again one of several options for the department.

27. See Tracy L. Toomey, Tobin F. Nelson, and Kathleen M. Lenk, "The Age-21 Minimum Legal Drinking Age: A Case Study," *Addiction* (2009): 12, 104; "State Drunk

Driving Laws," Governors Highway Safety Association, http://www.ghsa.org/html./ stateinfo/laws/impaired-lawws.html.

28. NHTSA, "Traffic Safety Facts," (2011) 34, table 13.

29. Memorandum to the author from Elizabeth Dole, April 23, 2014.

30. 23 U.S.C. 158.

31. NHTSA Traffic Safety Facts, (2011) 34, table 13.

32. Interview by the author with Elizabeth Dole, January 19, 2013.

33. Albaum, "Safety Sells," 131.

34. "In particular, I agree that, since the air bag and continuous-spool automatic seatbelts were [both] explicitly approved in the Standard the agency was rescinding, the agency should explain why it declined to leave those requirements intact. In this case the agency gave no explanation at all. . . .The agency's changed view . . . seems related to the election of a new president of a different political party. . . . As long as the agency remains within the bounds established by Congress it is entitled to assess administrative records and evaluate priorities in light of the philosophy of the administration." See 463 U.S.C. 29, 58, Justice Rehnquist, concurring in part, in an opinion with Justices Powell, Burger, and O'Connor.

35. Interview by the author with Elizabeth Dole, January 19, 2013.

36. Occupant Crash Protection, 49 C.F.R. 571.208; 49 F.R. 28, 962 (July 11, 1984); see Graham, *Assessing America's Performance*, 180.

37. Albaum, "Safety Sells," 131.

38. Dole interview with the author, January 19, 2013.

39. Ibid.

40. Kelley interview, 21–22.

41. Interview by the author with Ben Kelley by email 9/18/13. See also, interview by the author with Michael Stanton, president and CEO, Global Automakers, August 28, at 14: "She [Dole] challenged both the government and the industry to elevate the importance of safety belt use . . . we went up from 12% usage to 68%. The industry agreed to put in millions of dollars to educate drivers so that they buckled up . . . we hired lobbyists in every state, the industry put up over $100,000,000, even though we knew we were unlikely to get the required number of states to pass mandatory seat belt laws . . ."

42. Albaum, "Safety Sells," 141.

43. Ibid., 143.

44. "Until recently air bags were available only on a limited number of cars. Now many 1990 models have air bag systems and the number is growing. TV commercials now feature Lee Iacocca, (president of Chrysler) at one time dedicated to squashing any type of passive restraint, actively promoting air bags." "Auto Safety: Assessing America's Performance," in IIHS Status Report, 25, no. 6 (June 30, 1990), 2.

45. Albaum, "Safety Sells," 143. See also, "New Car Dealers Say Quality and Safety Are Top Considerations with Customers," IIHS Status Report, ibid., 1.

46. Observed usage in NHTSA and IIHS surveys.

47. Albaum, "Safety Sells," 134; Graham. *Assessing America's Performance*, 180.

48. About half of the states (thirty-four) now have front seat belt *primary* enforcement laws; twenty-two states have both front and rear seat *primary* enforcement laws. The rest are *secondary* enforcement laws. The former are much more effective because they allow police officers to stop persons not wearing their seat belts, whether or not any other violation is observed. Secondary laws allow a stop only where a separate legal violation is seen.

49. Dole interview with the author, January 19, 2013.

ELEVEN

Rough Road for Recalls

Ford Pinto Gas Tanks to GM Ignition Switches

Americans love cars. We buy more than 15 million of them new, each year.[1] But the joy of motoring is never without risk. As the *Reader's Digest* warned in 1935, "death gets in beside you."[2] There are currently over five million motor vehicle crashes (many involving death or personal injury) each year. It is one of the many results of our love affair with the automobile.[3]

The continuing number of crashes and, more importantly, the deaths and injuries involved are the fallout of that love affair. They are evidence that there are too many poorly designed or defective cars on the roads and too many bad driving decisions.

General Motors' belated recall in 2014 of over 11 million of its cars, including Chevrolet Cobalts, Saturn Ions, and other models is an example of faulty design. The company delayed at least seven years, perhaps longer, in reporting a potentially deadly ignition defect to NHTSA and in recalling the involved cars.[4]

A criminal investigation of General Motors and some of its employees for misstatements to NHTSA under the federal wire-fraud law, being conducted by the Department of Justice, is almost unprecedented in connection with the National Traffic and Motor Vehicle Safety Act. The criminal investigation, which may involve individual GM employees, in addition to General Motors itself, could have a significant impact in the future on compliance by companies with the reporting and recall requirements of the Safety Act.

Over 500 million motor vehicles have been recalled in the United States for "safety-related" defects since the National Traffic and Motor

175

Vehicle Safety Act was signed by president Lyndon Johnson forty-nine years ago.[5] Some of the defects were minor—and many manufacturers voluntarily initiated recalls. But many of the recalls were ordered or were in direct response to government action. Many were and are potentially fatal.

In 1966, when the Motor Vehicle Safety Act was first debated in Congress, the primary goal of its sponsors was the *prevention* of motor vehicle accidents and the resulting deaths and injuries. They wanted to use federal law to develop national safety standards that would require manufacturers to use their immense capability to design and build more crashworthy and crash-avoiding cars. Additions like seat belts, air bags, collapsible steering columns, padded dashboards, and better brakes were what they had in mind. Manufacturers mostly ignored these technological improvements until the threat of federal regulation loomed. Today, they are standard equipment. We take them for granted. We forget the long battle that was fought to put them in place.

Design changes were the basis for the twenty-three initial federal safety standards mandated under the 1966 law. Over the years, they were expanded to more than fifty major government motor vehicle safety standards. Equally important, increased consumer awareness of the dangers of death and injury in car crashes has paralleled the growth of federal safety standards. It has increased the demand by the buying public for safer cars. That has led automobile manufacturers and suppliers to innovate new safety systems. They have good reason for doing so: safety now sells cars.

In writing the original 1966 Safety Act, the Senate did not spend much time considering the recall of and repair of cars *already* on the roads. These were cars that did not meet federal standards, that had some safety-related defect not covered by any standard, or that involved purely manufacturing errors. GM, Ford, and Chrysler trained their political fire on the looming—and what they saw as overly intrusive—federal power to direct the design of their new cars. They focused mostly on blocking or limiting the federal standard-setting power and avoiding the incorporation of criminal penalties in the Safety Act.

They were successful in the effort to avoid the inclusion of criminal penalties *directly* in the Safety Act. In 2014 they were sharply reminded by the Department of Justice's GM and Toyota recall investigations that other criminal laws, such as wire fraud, *did* apply to their conduct.

Meanwhile, nobody focused much on the problem of getting defective cars off the highways and repaired. Almost nobody, that is, except one anonymous Virginia citizen who was mad as hell about some information he learned about his Buick—and a young senator from Minnesota named Walter Mondale.

The Buick owner was incensed about a letter he had received from his local GM dealer. It mentioned offhandedly that a bolt in the braking system of his new car might "prove to be troublesome sometime in the future." "Troublesome" was an understatement. If a plate worked loose and a wheel fell off the car, the defect could prove deadly to everyone in the car.[6] The letter, which came from the dealer after the owner of the Buick had already put 11,000 miles on the car, suggested the owner bring his car in to be repaired. But it did not warn the owner that safety was involved.

Somehow the angry letter the Buick owner wrote wound up on the desk of Walter Mondale, who had only been in the Senate for two years and was a decidedly junior member. While the Senate and industry representatives were concentrating on other parts of the proposed law, he looked into the issue raised by the unhappy Buick owner. Mondale found that while some manufacturers did notify their dealers of possible safety problems in their cars, they normally asked the selling dealer to get in touch with buyers directly. Some dealers did so, some did not. The letters often did not describe the "troublesome" matters in attention-getting, safety-related terms. So even if the dealers did follow up by notifying their customers, buyers were often not responsive to the bland, soothing words. The response rate by consumers could not have exceeded 15 percent at the time. The vast majority of the defective cars stayed unfixed.[7]

Mondale read the letter to the Senate Commerce Committee and then to the entire Senate. It hit home. Ralph Nader added fuel to the fire. He had been told by some conscience-stricken industry insider about the companies' habit of conducting something called "secret recalls." Dealers would repair or replace defective parts during routine maintenance, without telling the owner about the problem—or alerting other owners whose cars potentially had the same defect.[8]

Almost as an afterthought in the original bill, a seemingly minor provision was added without much opposition from manufacturers or dealers. Mondale's little amendment required that "Every manufacturer . . . furnish notification of any defect in any motor vehicle, or motor vehicle equipment, which he determines in good faith relates to motor vehicle safety, to the purchaser . . . within a reasonable time."[9]

Eight years later, in 1974, the section was strengthened to require that the repairs be paid for by the manufacturer, at no cost to the automobile owner, or to the dealer. The industry fought against the amendment—and lost.[10]

Over the succeeding forty-nine years, the notification and recall section has proven to be a major part of the national safety law, proving once again that even one fired-up, concerned citizen can change history.

On average over fifteen million motor vehicles have been recalled each year for the last twenty years, because of section 30118 of the National Traffic and Motor Vehicle Safety Act.[11] In 2013 the number of recalled cars skyrocketed to twenty-seven million. GM's delayed ignition-defect recall and the related criminal investigation and huge recalls by Toyota (sudden acceleration) and Honda (regarding air bag defects) drove the total number of all recalled vehicles to a record number of over sixty million in 2014.[12]

The recall function of the Act reinforces safety standards and may even lead to new standard development. Some of the defects that have triggered recalls have ranged from fire-prone Ford Pinto gasoline tanks, potentially crash-inducing Chevrolet motor mounts, unintended acceleration in over eleven million Toyotas, and defective air bags made by Takata, a major supplier of Honda and eleven other manufacturers. The sheer number of unsafe cars pulled off the roads because of a couple of sentences in the dusty pages of a now-aging federal law boggles the mind. Sometimes it is easier to grasp the scope of a safety revolution of such magnitude through individual experiences, although the events may be painful to read.

THE FORD PINTO FUEL TANK RECALL

The first major recall to test the power of the federal government—and public opinion—to get defective cars off the roads involved Ford Pinto fuel tanks. It happened in 1979—thirteen years after the law was enacted.

Mattie Ulrich received a letter in February 1979 from Ford advising her of a recall of her family's 1973 Ford Pinto. The letter said a faulty rear-mounted fuel tank could cause a gasoline fire in Pintos struck from behind. But the recall had been delayed by years of Washington lobbying by Ford, which had known that the fuel tanks were defective since before the first Pintos were sold in 1971. What could have been a minor fender-bender could ignite the entire car. Eye witnesses had reported that the resulting fires resembled a "napalm bomb."[13] The letter about the defect came too late for the Ulrich family.

In August 1978, Mattie Ulrich's two daughters, eighteen-year-old Julie, seixteen-year-old Lynn, and Mattie's eighteen-year-old niece Donna were burned to death after a minor collision turned into a major fire. After a relatively low speed rear-end collision, their Pinto's doors jammed shut. "A gaping hole" was ripped in the fuel tank, causing the tank to spill gasoline, which then ignited. The car became "a ball of flames," killing the three young women inside. This and hundreds of other deaths were caused by the Pinto's gas tank design.[14] The deaths probably could have been prevented if Ford had elected to include an additional plastic shield behind the fuel tank. The shield would have precluded the tank from being easily punctured during collisions—a fix that would have cost Ford about a dollar a car.[15] The case has become a classic. Business schools use it as an example of how *not* to address a safety problem.

The Pinto fuel tank defect that killed the Ulrich girls resulted in the deaths of more than 500 other drivers and passengers and injured thousands more. Mark Dowie of *Mother Jones* magazine used files obtained by the Center for Auto Safety to publish "Pinto Madness," a Pulitzer Prize–winning investigative series about Ford's decision to manufacture the car. The articles revealed that Ford knew from its own failed production crash tests that Pintos' gas tanks were unsafe.

In an attempt to break into the new "small car" market started by the Volkswagen Beetle in the early 1970s, Ford had rushed the Pinto into production. Within Ford, the Pinto was known as "Lee's car," because it was the brainchild of Lee Iacocca, a Ford engineer turned salesman who became the company's president in 1970. As he oversaw the production of the Pinto, Iacocca enforced what was known within Ford as "the limits of 2000." The car could not weigh over 2,000 pounds, or cost over $2,000.[16] Safety was not a priority for the engineers building the Pinto. Iacocca told them: "Safety doesn't sell."[17]

According to one Ford engineer who worked on the Pinto, if a colleague had raised the issue of safety with Iacocca, "that person would have been fired. Safety wasn't a popular subject around Ford in those days. With Lee it was taboo." Ford, he said, was "run by salesmen, not engineers; so the priority [was] styling, not safety." He acknowledged that there were a few people at Ford who were concerned about safety, "mostly engineers who have to study a lot of accident reports and look at pictures of burned people. But we don't talk about it much. It isn't a popular subject."[18]

In retrospect, the low priority of safety should have been apparent in the Pinto's design. Internal Ford documents obtained in litigation show that the company had crash-tested the car more than forty times. In *every* test where the car was traveling over 25 miles an hour the fuel tank ruptured, spilling gasoline that would ignite if touched by a spark.[19]

According to Dowie's analysis of hundreds of reports and documents about rear-end collisions involving Pintos, the rear bumper was designed to withstand collisions of only five miles per hour. If another car rear-ended a Pinto at over thirty miles per hour, the rear end of the Pinto could buckle all the way to the back seat. The gas line would break. Gas would spill onto the road and around the car. The sharp, protruding bolts on the Pinto's axle would likely rip holes in the tank, spilling even more gas. A spark from the struck Pinto, or scraping metal from the collision, could engulf the vehicle in flames.

Dr. Leslie Ball, who once served as the National Aeronautics and Space Administration's safety chief for the space program and who founded the International Society of Reliability Engineers, called the rush to production of the Pinto "the most reprehensible decision in the history of American engineering." Ball found that more than forty competing models of cars in the Pinto's price and weight range had safer gas tank positioning.[20] An engineering expert, Byron Bloch, called the Pinto fuel system "a catastrophic blunder. . . . Ford made an extremely irresponsible decision when they placed such a weak tank in such a ridiculous location in such a soft rear end. It's almost designed to blow up."[21]

A *Chicago Tribune* article said Ford knew of multiple solutions to the Pinto problem. It owned the patent to a much safer, "saddle-type" tank used in the Ford Capri, which withstood rear-end impacts of up to 60 miles per hour in crash tests. It chose not to use the "saddle-type" tank in the Pinto in an attempt to maximize trunk size—and cut costs.[22] Ford conducted just three crash tests in which the fuel tank did not rupture. Each of these tests included the addition of protective alterations not incorporated in models sold in the United Sates—an additional piece of steel plate between the gas tank and bumper, a rubber bladder lining the fuel tank, and a plastic shield,[23] which stopped the steel bolts from tearing into the tank in the event of an accident.

The total cost of producing and installing rubber fuel bladders in the tanks would have been $5.08 per car. The plastic protector used to stop the bolts from penetrating the tank, another dollar. One Ford engineer said, "The price elasticity on these subcompacts is extremely tight. You can price yourself right out of the market by adding $25 to the production cost of the model. And nobody understands that better than Lee Iacocca."[24]

Ford's attitude is forever memorialized in a company cost-benefit analysis study. It is entitled "Fatalities Associated with Crash-Induced Fuel Leakage and Fires." One prominent claimant's lawyer called the study "possibly the most remarkable document ever produced in an American lawsuit."[25] Ford's cost-benefit analysis calculated that the benefits of preventing burn deaths and injuries (priced at $200,000 per death and $67,000 per injury, or $49.5 million dollars total) were far outweighed by the costs ($11 per vehicle, totaling $137 million). Therefore, Ford concluded that the cost of modifying Pinto gas tanks and preventing their catching fire "was not cost-effective for society."[26]

Several weeks after the publication of "Pinto Madness," a Ford news release challenged the article's claims, stating that the Pinto was never an unsafe vehicle. It used NHTSA data to assert that the Pinto did not cause as many burn deaths or injuries as claimed. Ford did concede that early-model Pintos failed rear-impact tests at 20 miles per hour. But it denied that this made them unsafe—because Ford had "met or surpassed" all NHTSA standards, however weak they were.[27]

What the Ford release did not state was that NHTSA had proposed a new standard (FMVSS 301) to require all vehicles to be able to withstand rear-end crashes at 20 mph without losing fuel.[28] The standard was proposed in 1968, but because Ford did not want to redesign the rear end of the hot-selling Pinto, it targeted standard 301 for delay. Company challenges by Ford were able to delay adoption of the standard until the 1977 model year. NHTSA was thus unable to prevent Ford from producing millions of dangerous Pintos during the intervening six-year period.[29]

An intense public backlash ensued. The flawed Pinto became the target of a *60 Minutes* special, Johnny Carson monologues,[30] and editorial page cartoons.[31] Ford's advertising agency, J. Walter Thompson, dropped a line from a radio spot that read, "Pinto leaves you with that warm feeling."[32] The *American Lawyer* reported that the "Pinto is commonly referred to in automotive engineering circles as the worst American car ever made."[33]

Months after the media began warning the public of the dangers of the Pinto gsa tank, a jury in Orange County, California awarded a Pinto burn victim $125 million in punitive damages for his injuries. The jury's reasoning was that Ford had marketed the car with knowledge that burn injuries and deaths were inevitable. It found that the punitive damages should be more than Ford's profit on the Pinto, which were $124 million.[34]

When the Pinto liability suits began, Ford's initial strategy was to take the cases to juries, hoping that lawyers could "explain" that poor drivers, not design defects, had caused the deaths. The strategy flopped. Al Schlechter, an executive in Ford's Washington office said: "We'll never go to jury again. . . . Not in a fire case. Juries are just too sentimental. They see those charred remains and forget the evidence. No sir, we'll settle."[35]

Taking advantage of the intense public scrutiny that Ford and NHTSA were receiving over Pinto fires, the Center for Auto Safety (which had been recently founded by Ralph Nader and Consumers Union) submitted a petition to NHSTA for a defect investigation and recall of the Pinto. The Center had originally submitted the petition in 1974. But NHTSA sat on it. Finally, in September 1978 Ford "voluntarily" recalled all 1971 through 1976 Pintos (1.5 million cars). It improved their safety by repairing the fuel tanks—installing the $1 plastic shield that prevented the cars' bolts from ripping into the tank, as well as substituting a longer fuel neck, replacing a clamp, installing an additional plastic shield to protect the front of the tank, and upgrading the gas cap.[36]

Years later, in his autobiography, Lee Iacocca said, "We resisted making any changes and that hurt us badly. . . . Whose fault was it? One obvious answer is that it was the fault of Ford's management—including me." But Iacocca added, "There's absolutely no truth to the charge that we tried to save a few bucks and knowingly made a dangerous car. . . . The auto industry has often been arrogant, but it's not that callous. . . . In the end we voluntarily[37] recalled almost a million and a half Pintos. This was in June 1978, the month before I was fired."[38]

The intense publicity involving Ford Pintos and the belated recall contributed to what has been called the "heyday of recalls" during the Carter administration.[39] Major recalls included such problems as faulty carburetor plug clips, weak seat belt anchorages, faulty seat belt buckles, defects in brakes, battery acid leaks, hoods that could fly open, faulty air bags, and spontaneous engine stalls.[40]

Mattie Ulrich said she had purposely bought a Ford Pinto for her family because she believed she could rely on the quality and safety of an American-made car.[41]

CHEVROLET ENGINE MOUNTS

One of the largest recalls occurred just after the law was passed. It was the recall by General Motors of 6.6 million 1965–1970 Chevrolets for defective engine mounts. The mounts, made of steel and rubber, were used to hold the engine in place and to absorb noise, vibration, and torque. In Chevrolet vehicles, including trucks and Nova and Camaro cars, the mounts would break, causing a dangerous "self-perpetuating" sequence.

When the mounts broke, the engine could rise up inside the car, causing a series of problems. The most dangerous of these occurred when the loose motor pulled on the accelerator linkage, which in turn could cause the car's throttle to stick in the open position and result in uncontrolled acceleration. The engine's movement could also pull the power-brake booster hose loose, making it difficult to bring the car to a stop. The faulty motor mounts also caused failures in power steering. They could interfere with the automatic transmission so that the vehicle no longer had a "park" position and could be started in "reverse."

Despite a report to NHTSA by General Motors revealing that it had evidence of at least fourteen cases of motor mount failure in 1968 Chevrolets, NHTSA chose to place its investigation on "inactive status" in June 1970. Six months later, in response to continued consumer complaints and incident reports, NHTSA sent a second information request to GM. This one revealed that there had now been 172 reports of failed motor mounts. These had caused sixty-three accidents and eighteen injuries. NHTSA once again failed to order GM to commence a recall.

Robert Irvin, an automotive writer for the *Detroit Free Press*, described GM's lack of action and NHTSA's limited investigation. Irvin wrote more than seventy articles about the faulty Chevy mounts. The negative publicity that was generated played a large role in forcing NHTSA to order a recall. In October 1971 NHTSA sent out a "consumer protection bulletin" advising of "potential risks" of faulty GM motor mounts. NHTSA administrator Doug Toms was concerned enough to test-drive Chevrolets with the mounts—along with GM president Ed Cole. After more than a year, on December 1, 1971 NHTSA sent GM a letter warning that it was "close" to finding that a safety defect existed.

Three days later, General Motors announced a recall. It refused to concede that the car had a safety problem. Cole, an engineer by training, declared just before the GM announcement that a broken mount was no more dangerous than a "flat tire or a blowout." Cole said that anyone who couldn't control a car with a failed mount at 25 mph "shouldn't be driving."[42]

General Motors did not replace the faulty motor mounts in 95 percent of the vehicles it recalled and fixed. Rather, it wrapped the engine with a cable and bracket to restrict its movement if the mount broke loose. The cable and bracket cost approximately $1 per car, much cheaper for GM than the estimated cost of $50 for installing new mounts. Although the "fix" may have been effective, the resale value of every "wrapped" Chevy was sharply reduced.

Despite delays, NHTSA's belated success in forcing General Motors to repair 6.6 million potentially unsafe vehicles helped to establish the agency's power to force manufacturer repairs. But the agency's hesitation to exert its powers became a major issue again—forty-four years later—in connection with about 11 million General Motors' Cobalts, Saturn Ions, and other models with defective ignition switches. There were reports of many crashed and deaths. NHTSA failed to act on the defect for at least seven years after it received substantial information about the problem from a special investigation by its own staff.[43]

The government has broad authority to issue and enforce safety recalls. That authority was confirmed in two court cases in the 1970s, *United States v. General Motors ("Wheels")*[44] and *United States v. General Motors Corporation ("Pitman Arms")*.[45] The legal victories for NHTSA—despite strenuous industry opposition—led to the agency developing the important *per se* legal theory of safety defects. It has stood the test of time.

The court rulings established that if a critical component of a system designed to control the vehicle, avoid accidents, or mitigate serious injury in the event of a crash is defective, then that defect is safety-related by definition. The court decisions eased NHTSA's burden of proof in recall cases. They allow NHTSA to force a manufacturer to recall its cars in a simplified proceeding: It does not have to show proof of actual crashes and the specific causes of each crash to prove a defect.[46] Whether they stiffened the agency's backbone remains to be seen.

The *per se* theory was developed and memorialized in a memorandum written by NHTSA's first enforcement attorney and chief counsel Frank Berndt.[47] A subsequent decision, *United States v. Ford Motor Co. ("Seatbacks")* confirmed NHTSA's authority to issue recall orders when it determined a defect existed in a "critical component" that made the vehicle unsafe. The case reconfirmed NHTSA's authority to investigate and order recalls of "critical component" safety defects. The court reasoned that the number of lives lost because of a defect is usually unreliable and undercounted, "The causes of many fatal accidents [are] never known, for dead men tell no tales."[48]

Despite the safety agency's early court victories, in 1972 it suffered at least one mixed decision in *Chrysler v. DOT*. It had to do not with a recall, but with the important passive-restraint rule, which had been years in development. After reviewing the rule-making record, a federal appeals court returned the case to the agency. The agency, the court held, had failed to state in the rule the measurements for a test dummy used to establish the standard's effectiveness. This technical omission was quickly fixed by NHTSA. Nonetheless, the ruling in *Chrysler v. DOT* stunned NHTSA. Although the court had clearly affirmed the agency's basic power to set technology-forcing standards, it seemed, against all logic, to conclude that a court should or could review minutely the insignificant technical details of agency safety standards. Whether or not the opinion meant that courts would get into the standards-writing business, the case at least threatened that result. The safety agency became gun-shy over pushing big, expensive rule-making proceedings.[49]

In contrast, in safety-defect cases, the courts have given the agency much more maneuvering room and deferred more to its expertise in deciding what cars are unreasonably dangerous so that they need to be pulled off the roads. Somewhat remarkably, automobile manufacturers have not again seriously challenged the courts' approval of NHTSA's broad recall powers. According to a former senior enforcement attorney for NHTSA, this is because manufacturers "have grudgingly accepted those cases as the law. . . . With hardly any exceptions, when NHTSA and a manufacturer come eyeball-to-eyeball *on a safety defect controversy*, the manufacturer blinks first."[50] That may be true, but there are still many unsettling examples of the government blinking, or delaying, or completely folding, when it challenges a manufacturer over a safety defect.

THE FIRESTONE 500 TIRE RECALL

An example of the tenacity often needed to regulate the automotive industry was Firestone's 1978 and 1980 recall of 14.5 million steel-belted radial tires. It also reveals the Safety Act's sweeping reach, which includes tires (motor vehicle equipment) as well as the vehicles themselves. Many of the tire failures involved Firestone tires used on Ford Explorer SUVs.[51]

In late 1971 and early 1972, Firestone launched an effort to keep up with its rivals Goodyear and Michelin. They had successfully introduced radial tires to the American market in the late 1960s. Firestone rushed to produce "500" radial tires almost two years before it had fully developed the machinery required to produce them safely. Manufacturing problems caused a lack of adhesion between the rubber compounds and the steel wire that was used in the inner belts of the tires. This eventually caused the tires to split, usually while the car was moving at high speed.[52] One Firestone 500 radial tire victim-turned-investigative-journalist wrote that the tires came onto the market "like fast-hatching baby spiders."[53]

Firestone may have known their tires were faulty as early as 1972, but instead of stopping sales and developing a solution to fix the defect, it continued to sell the 500s while attempting to make adjustments to its assembly line.

There were deaths. They included an Alabama state police officer who died in a station wagon accident caused by a Firestone 500 blowout—a 1974 accident that killed four people and orphaned eight children. NHTSA did not investigate Firestone 500 steel-belted radial tires until 1976. Even then, for some reason the investigation was dropped. In the words of one mother of two children whose Firestone-equipped Ford nearly killed the family after a tire blowout, NHTSA's inaction was "turning carpools into games of Russian roulette."[54] In November 1977, after receiving more consumer complaints, the ever-present Center for Auto Safety called on Firestone to recall millions of "500" steel-belted radial tires made up to that time.

A month later NHTSA began to examine all (not just Firestone) radial tires. It conducted a survey of 100,000 car owners. The survey results confirmed that Firestone's tires were significantly less safe than competitors' tires. Firestone sued unsuccessfully in a Cleveland Federal District Court to block the release of the survey results to the public, asserting that the research supporting the survey was unreliable. Firestone then began "unloading" its remaining inventory of tires. In some states, the tires were put on sale and marked down to half-price.[55]

According to one employee, Firestone held a sales meeting at a Holiday Inn in San Jose, California, around this time. The conference room was covered with posters that read "Accentuate the Positive." The salespeople were told, "There was money to be made" in replacing faulty tires. "When you put a car up on the rack to replace a failed tire, what do you do? You do a 'safety inspection.' You recommend shock absorbers, brake jobs, tune-ups. There is $40 to $200 a day to be made on 'add-ons.'"[56]

The Chairman of the House Subcommittee on Oversight and Investigations was then the safety-conscious John Moss. He wanted a lasting record made of Firestone's actions and the agency's delays, as a "message" in future recall cases.[57] Moss also wanted what he saw as "the life-threatening conduct" of Firestone to hit the company in the pocketbook. After extended public hearings, which gained national press attention, the subcommittee issued its report:

The record is clear that Firestone had early knowledge of the serious failure propensities of the 500. Its high adjustment rates in the early years, its unusually brisk activity in settling damage claims, and its energetic efforts to improve on the earlier tires all suggest its early knowledge. These facts lead to but one conclusion. The Firestone Tire and Rubber Company is and has been for some time, in a position to avoid the devastating toll of human destruction which it knew its tires could cause. In the exercise of clear and conscious choice, it nonetheless permitted this destruction to take place.[58]

Faced with intense public and congressional pressure, in November 1978 Firestone agreed to recall all 14.5 million steel-belted radials manufactured before 1977. This was not, however, the end of the saga of Firestone 500 steel-belted radial tires.

In September 1979, in response to "a continuing flood" of consumer complaints and an analysis of internal Firestone documents, the Center for Auto Safety found that tires made and sold by Firestone *after* the 1978 recall *"continued to fail in exactly the same manner, including, tread separations, broken steel belts, and blowouts."* In 1980, after a complete change in top management, Firestone announced that it would recall another 5 million steel-belted radials produced *after* the cutoff date of the earlier recall.[59]

As late as August 1978, Firestone attorney Patrick McCarran said that NHTSA had not thoroughly researched the complaints and that Firestone 500s were "safe, reliable tires." He blamed consumer error such as "improper inflation," not faulty manufacturing, for the rash of blowouts, accidents, and deaths related to the tires.[60]

It is impossible to know the true extent of the damage caused by Firestone's series 500 tires. The Center for Auto Safety reported that failures in Firestone 500s "caused thousands of accidents resulting in hundreds of injuries and over forty known fatalities."[61] It would not be the last time that Firestone tires were involved in a major safety defect recall.[62]

CHRYSLER JEEP FIRES

There have been instances when NHTSA has made questionable compromises with producers. This appears the case with the 2013 recall of 1.7 million Chrysler Jeep Cherokee and Liberty models. In 2011 the Center for Auto Safety petitioned the agency to investigate about 2.7 million Jeeps. It alleged the positioning of the gas tanks, just behind the rear axle and adjacent to the rear bumper, caused a "safety-related" hazard in 1993–2004 Cherokee and 2002–2007 Liberty models.

This was essentially the same fuel tank positioning that caused Ford its historic recall of the poorly designed Pinto forty years earlier. The

Center's director Clarence Ditlow alleged that its investigation, which began in 2009, had found that 201 rear-end fuel tank fires resulted in 285 deaths in Cherokees and 53 deaths in Liberty models. Over the next three years, Ditlow repeatedly asked NHTSA to recall the Jeeps because he said they were twenty times riskier than competing models.[63] In June 2013 NHTSA agreed and ordered a recall.

In the meantime Chrysler, now owned by Fiat, had modified later Jeep models to include protection for the gas tanks. It did nothing about the 2.7 million earlier models, which presumably remained dangers on the roads. At first NHTSA's decision to order a recall looked like a big victory for safety advocates and Jeep owners. But then the company and NHTSA began negotiations over the nature of the fix and the number of Jeeps that would be covered. The agency inexplicably altered its position.

The government and Chrysler agreed to a recall limited to 1.7 million Jeeps. The fix? A trailer hitch—the device a car owner can attach to the rear bumper to pull something. According to Chrysler and NHTSA, this would be a good way to protect the fuel tank from exploding on impact. Ditlow said that the company had not adequately tested the trailer hitches, particularly in off-center, rear-end impacts and that it was putting profits over people's lives.[64] He sounded outraged: "A recall would cost Chrysler around $300 a car. Chrysler would not exist today but for a $10 billion bailout from the United States government."[65]

It seems clear NHTSA should have required public testing of the effectiveness of the trailer-hitch repair *before* accepting Chrysler's offer. But the "fix" remains in effect for Jeep Cherokees and Libertys.

A year later Chrysler had not yet begun repairing the defective Jeeps, even with the doubtful trailer hitches. Four more Jeep owners had died during the year, making a total of 370 Cherokee and Liberty fatal crashes, most involving fires. NHTSA's staff calculated at that rate that it would take Chrysler 4.7 years to finish repairing the recalled Jeeps.[66]

TOYOTA AND UNINTENDED ACCELERATION

In 2009 a recorded 911 call captured the final moments of a Southern California family. It happened just as their Lexus accelerated to speeds of over 120 mph and crashed into an embankment. As the car increased speed uncontrollably, the driver, an off-duty police officer named Mark Saylor, tried to slow it down. A passenger, Chris Lastrella, dialed 911 and told the dispatcher the accelerator was stuck. "We're in trouble," he cried out. "There's no brake!" The police dispatcher advised turning off the ignition. Saylor was apparently unable to do so. The chilling recording ended with a member of the family telling others in the car to pray. Then a woman is heard screaming. All four people in the car died in the ensuing crash.[67]

Sudden Unintended Acceleration (SUA)—the sudden and uncontrollable speeding up of a car—is one of the most perplexing and complex controversies in the annals of automobile safety recalls. From 2002 to 2010 reports of unintended acceleration in several Toyota models—from the company's top-of-the-line Lexus to its more moderately priced Camry—became one of the most deadly examples of a continuing safety problem. During those years consumer groups and plaintiffs' attorneys claimed that "at least 56 people were killed by defects linked to unintended acceleration."[68]

Toyota has consistently denied that any electronic or software problem is the cause of the SUA issue. Other manufacturers have also experienced unintended acceleration incidents; none on the scale of Toyota.

Since 1986, cars made by the top five U.S. manufacturers—Toyota, General Motors, Ford, Honda, and Chrysler—have been recalled for SUA problems, according to NHTSA.[69] Smaller brands have not been immune to the problem either. NHTSA's recall database shows that some Audi, Nissan, BMW, Volkswagen, Mitsubishi, Subaru, Mercedes-Benz, Kia, Mazda, Land Rover, Suzuki, and Volvo models have been recalled because of SUA problems.[70] It is unclear whether the recalls, primarily of Toyota Camrys made from 2007 to 2010, have reached all potentially affected cars, or even more important whether the true cause has ever been determined by NHTSA or manufacturers.

One reason for the persistence of the sudden acceleration problem has been the difficulty in pinpointing the cause. The three most suspected reasons are defective floor mats that can trap the gas pedal in an accelerating position; faulty gas pedal mechanisms that can become stuck; and in newer vehicles, an electronic or software malfunction that uncontrollably speeds up the automobile.[71]

There is a fourth cause that manufacturers have asserted consistently. "Its [the industry's] bugaboo," according to the *Wall Street Journal*, "has been driver error."[72] The reason for leaning on explanation four is simple: If companies can blame driver error (by claiming, for instance, that a driver mistook a gas pedal for a brake pedal) they can avoid paying the cost of recalls (and legal claims) for asserted mechanical or electronic failures.

For years, NHTSA went along with the "blame the driver" explanation. Its mind-set was rooted in a 454-page report issued in January 1989. The report, based on a study conducted after a *60 Minutes* exposé about the acceleration dangers of an earlier Audi 5000 model, said that "the vast majority of sudden acceleration incidents *in which no vehicle malfunction is present* are caused by drivers mistaking the gas pedal for the brake."[73] (emphasis added).

Despite concluding that human error caused the "vast majority" of sudden acceleration cases, the agency report also found that design errors in the Audi 5000's vehicle controls and faulty Audi cruise control systems could have caused sudden acceleration. NHTSA cited three prior Audi 5000 recalls (in which supposedly repaired design errors were involved) as a key factor in its decision to close a broader investigation. Later claims and lawsuits suggest that the repairs may not have eliminated the acceleration problem.[74]

For decades, NHTSA's questionable 1989 Audi report on the causes of SUA had been exhibit A in the "blame the customer" defense. Then, some twenty years later, along came an even larger acceleration problem for Toyota and for a hesitant NHTSA. Cars with newer electronic throttles and microprocessor system accelerators that may be defective have stayed on the roads with the root cause of the problem unresolved. How this happened is a complicated story with plenty of blame to go around—for both Toyota and NHTSA.

For Toyota, the issue began to surface in 2001 when complaints about Camry and Lexus models increased fourfold.[75] Between 2000 and 2010 NHTSA received 2,600 reports of runaway Toyotas, including thirty-four deaths.[76]

Toyota knew unintended acceleration, caused by something then undetermined, was a danger to people who bought and drove its cars. In April 2008 a Michigan woman, Guadalupe Alberto, was killed when her 2005 Camry sped out of control and crashed into a tree. In a court case filed on behalf of Mrs. Alberto, a witness testified that the 76-year-old woman's last moments were spent "standing on the brake while steering."[77]

Before the Alberto case went to court, NHTSA had become aware of the issue. Christopher Santucci, a former NHTSA employee who was hired by Toyota in 2003, testified that Toyota and NHTSA "discussed the scope" of the investigation by the agency. That discussion led to a decision by NHTSA to reduce the extent of its inquiry. "I think it worked out well for both the agency and Toyota," Santucci testified at a 2010 congressional hearing on the issue.

It certainly kept Toyota's recall costs down. In a document obtained by the *Detroit News*, Toyota safety officials said that they had saved more than $100 million by conducting a limited recall in 2007 of only 55,000 floor mats or sticking gas pedals, rather than pursuing a more costly fix of the electrical system.[78] According to former NHTSA administrator Joan Claybrook, "Toyota bamboozled NHTSA" into accepting a limited recall, "or NHTSA was bamboozled by itself."[79]

That was not the end of Toyota's acceleration problem—or of NHTSA's. Neither the manufacturer nor the regulatory agency seemed to be able to get to the bottom of it. Crashes of Toyota cars from SUA continued. The public became alarmed. Eventually Toyota, which originally was dead set against a recall, was forced to recall more than 8 million vehicles worldwide for "floor mat repairs."[80] Jim Lentz, CEO of Toyota Motor Sales USA, testified, "We are confident that no problems exist in our electronic throttle systems in our vehicles . . . we have done extensive testing on this system, and we have never found a malfunction that caused unintended acceleration."[81]

The recall and the storm of related media attention caused Toyota's sales to fall sharply. Its stock price dropped 16 percent. The company stopped producing some models until the defect was addressed.[82] It also settled a class action lawsuit by Toyota car owners and paid more than $1.1 billion in economic loss to the car owners on the grounds that the danger of sudden acceleration caused the resale value of all Toyotas to drop. It was the largest loss-of-value lawsuit ever recorded. The settlement also stipulated that Toyota would install a brake override system, to block SUA based on any cause, in 3.25 million vehicles.[83] The brake override is now standard equipment on many Toyota models.

The safety battle was costly to Toyota. The company lost its position as the leader in vehicles sold in the world and in the United States.[84] The maximum allowable fine and the highest civil penalty in NHTSA history was levied against Toyota for four separate safety violations. They related to delayed or incomplete reporting about SUA to the safety agency. Toyota paid a total of $66.5 million because it "failed to report a safety defect in a timely manner." The Motor Vehicle Safety Act regulations require auto manufacturers to notify NHTSA within five business days of determining a safety-related defect exists and to promptly commence a recall, which the company failed to do.[85]

The delay in reporting the problem also resulted in a much more serious, four-year criminal investigation of Toyota by the Department of Justice. In a settlement agreement with Toyota, the department fined Toyota $1.2 billion in criminal penalties for fraudulent statements concerning the acceleration issue that it made to the government and the public (based on the federal Wire Fraud Act). The sum was the largest criminal penalty ever imposed on an automobile company. Attorney general Eric Holder called Toyota's conduct "shameful" and said Toyota had "internal tests warning of the danger in other, unrecalled models."[86] While the $1.2 billion criminal penalty was the biggest for a motor vehicle manufacturer, it represented only a small fraction of the more than $60 billion that Toyota held in cash reserves.[87]

The Toyota unintended acceleration case is a good example of the important role personal injury lawsuits and personal injury lawyers can play in promoting automobile safety. In a 2013 case in Oklahoma based on alleged unintended acceleration a jury awarded the families of the victims $3 million in damages because of the deaths. The jury was about to continue its deliberations over additional "punitive damages" based on the company's "reckless disregard" of the acceleration problem, when Toyota agreed to settle the case and paid the plaintiffs the $3 million.[88] Toyota then initiated negotiations to settle more than three hundred other personal injury cases involving alleged electronic defects causing unintended acceleration deaths and injuries.[89] Part of the settlements included putting the brake override on most Toyota cars and issuing an apology to consumers by the president of the company for blaming drivers for the crashes.

The Toyota case offers persuasive evidence of the effect that product liability lawsuits based on consumer injury can have on government action and manufacturer design changes.

The General Motors delayed-ignition defect discussed in the next section and the Ford Pinto fuel tank fire recall discussed in this chapter are additional examples of private litigation playing a major role in changing public safety policy. The changes in policy compelled by private litigants and attorneys, together with negative effects of litigation on productivity are ably discussed by four Johns Hopkins University public health professors in an extensive article.[90]

The Hopkins authors consider both survey and analytical data in reaching the conclusion that "Litigation can serve as a powerful tool for prevention. . . . Transferring the costs of injuries through litigation . . . creates a motivation [by manufacturers] to invest in prevention rather than to pay the penalty of neglect."[91]

While there are some economic costs involved in personal injury lawsuits, overall the recent history of automobile safety indicates they have been a decided plus for safety. The Toyota (unintended acceleration), Ford (fuel tank), and General Motors (defective ignition switch) cases all support that conclusion. In each case lawsuits were a significant factor leading to redesign of defective vehicles by manufacturers.

In an attempt to put the damaging publicity behind it, Toyota launched a "brand rehab" advertisement campaign, asserting that the company was spending "$1 million an hour" on safety development and technology.[92] Testifying before the U.S. House Oversight and Government Reform Committee, the grandson of the company's founder and Toyota's current president, Akio Toyoda, told committee members: "I will make sure that we will never, ever blame the customers going forward."[93]

NHTSA came in for its share of criticism for not taking stronger action in the Toyota SUA cases. In 2010 the House Energy and Commerce Committee, which had held hearings on the failure to solve and fix the acceleration problem, reported that NHTSA conducted only one "cursory investigation" into Toyota acceleration incidents. The agency's own lead investigator admitted that he "was not very knowledgeable about the electronic throttle control system in Toyota vehicles." NHTSA told the committee that, shockingly, it had no electrical or software engineers on its staff.

"NHTSA's response to complaints of sudden unintended acceleration in Toyota vehicles appears to have been seriously deficient," the committee wrote in 2010 to Secretary of Transportation Ray LaHood.[94] Even after the Commerce Committee's findings, the NHTSA fines, the civil damage recoveries, and the largest criminal fine ever of a motor vehicle company by the Department Of Justice, the mystery of the real cause or causes of unintended acceleration and the deaths and injuries caused remain just that: an unsolved mystery.

GENERAL MOTORS DELAYED IGNITION RECALL

On December 8, 2010 a NHTSA official wrote to Congressman Barney Frank in response to his inquiry about why a constituent's 2006 Chevrolet Cobalt kept stalling on him. According to the agency official, NHTSA had "reviewed our database in an effort to identify whether a safety defect trend exists with regard to stalling problems in (model year) 2006 Chevrolet Cobalt vehicles. At this time there is insufficient evidence to warrant *opening* a safety defect investigation."[95] (emphasis added).

Four years later, GM announced three sequential recalls involving a total of 2.6 million Chevrolet Cobalt, Saturn Ion, Pontiac Solstice, and other models. The GM recall was for cars with ignition switches similar to the Cobalt, the specific subject of Congressman Frank's letter four years before. NHTSA had received its first complaint about a GM Saturn stalling on a highway in 2004. By the time it brushed off the congressman it had received 174 similar consumer complaints, some involving deaths. There is yet no full public record of how many complaints were made to GM, including injury and death claims during the same period. NHTSA data, which was reviewed by the *New York Times*, was obtained under the Freedom of Information Act. That data indicated that there were 260 complaints and at least thirteen deaths by early 2014 involving similar ignition systems that shut off while the cars were moving. Some put the drivers and passengers in desperate situations.[96] The agency says the death toll will probably go higher. A Reuters analysis of NHTSA data estimated that at least 74 people have died in accidents in GM cars similar to those already made public.[97] The *New York Times* estimated that as of the end of 2014, there were forty-two confirmed deaths.

Some of the submissions received by NHTSA came from drivers with desperate concerns about the safety of their cars:

> "When the vehicle shuts down it gives no warning, it just does it. I drive my car to work praying that it won't shut down on me while I am on the freeway.

> "Engine stops while driving—cannot steer or brake—so controlling the car to a safe stop is very dangerous."

> "This is a safety issue if there ever was one. I don't recall them ever responding."[98]

GM had begun receiving information of an ignition shut-off problem as early as 2003, but did not report the issue to NHTSA as a safety defect. Because GM engineers and lawyers allegedly did not see a connection between the power loss, the crash reports, and the deaths, GM treated the problem as a consumer inconvenience—not as a safety issue—and did not report it. At least five deaths, documented by the *New York Times*, involved air bags being disabled by the power shut down and not inflating in a crash.

Ultimately GM acknowledged that the five deaths were related to the ignition problem, but said many involved speeding or alcohol. It would not reveal the identities of the dead. Mary Ruddy's daughter Kelly was killed in 2010 after being ejected from her Cobalt. Ms. Ruddy wanted to know if her daughter's name was among the five dead. She said she had complained to the safety agency and to GM about the inexplicable stalling four times before the fatal crash.

GM did file abbreviated "Early Warning" death and serious injury reports with NHTSA as mandated by the TREAD Act of 2000. These reports are brief and mostly incomprehensible, because they don't usually identify the failure mode or the likely cause of an accident. They were apparently read by the NHTSA staff and dismissed. Any connection or pattern among the crashes was missed by the agency. The agency's chief counsel was quoted as stating—quite incorrectly—that the safety act requires that an "unreasonable risk to safety" be shown *before* any formal investigation can be started. In fact, no such precondition to an investigation exists in the law.

The Center for Auto Safety issued a statement noting that two of NHTSA's informal death inquiries had resulted in "special investigations" commenced in 2007 in which agency engineers found some evidence that the cause of the accidents was a defective ignition switch. The center claimed that should have resulted in a recall by GM, or one ordered by NHTSA, at least by 2007.[99]

Eventually, a series of in-depth articles by the *New York Times* in 2014 forced GM to initiate the first of several recalls of affected models. GM issued two apologies for its handling of the ignition shut-off case. "We deeply regret the events that led to the recall and this investigation. . . . GM is committed to learning from the past."[100] GM's failure to file prompt and complete reports specifying the probable cause of the crashes appears likely to have been a primary cause of many of the deaths involved. At the time furnishing a probable cause of the crash was optional in a NHTSA Early Warning Report. The reporting requirement was later changed by the agency to be mandatory.

One plausible excuse—other than incompetence—for the agency's long period of inaction on the ignition-switch matter is agency overload. In a statement to the *New York Times*, it claimed that during the extended period of the crashes of Cobalt's, Ions, and other GM cars, it had investigated 929 other recalls, affecting 55 million defective vehicles.

It surely missed this one.

After issuing two apologies, GM started an internal investigation regarding its own actions. So did NHTSA and the Department of Justice. NHTSA then fined GM $35 million, although it had just fined Toyota roughly twice that amount for similar violations.[101]

It is unclear whether the agency will request a change in the EWR reporting law or the Safety Act to give the agency better information, or whether Congress will amend the law's inadequate EWR reporting requirements. Those procedures were mandated by Congress itself after multiple deaths in the Ford-Firestone recall over a decade earlier.

As of now death and serious injury reports under the law are not generally made public. It required Freedom of Information Act requests (and private lawsuit information) for the Center for Auto Safety and the *New York Times* to learn of the GM defective ignition defect in early 2014. The inadequate defect reporting laws remain unchanged by Congress as of this writing.

In June 2014, GM's internal investigation found "a pattern of incompetence and neglect" by GM lawyers and engineers in the long delay in not reporting the defect sooner.[102] After the release of the study, GM fired fifteen employees and disciplined five more.

During the same period, GM's 2014 second-quarter profits reached record levels.[103] Later financial results, however, seemed to indicate that GM was economically damaged by the delayed recalls, brand injury, and settlements with car occupants or owners—or their survivors.

Curing safety defects by issuing recalls *after* vehicles are on the roads, or fines for late or inaccurate reporting are a poor way of assuring consumers that their cars are safe. Many car owners do not receive—or they may disregard—recall notices.[104] As many as 30 percent of all recalled vehicles are never repaired according to the agency. Thus many cars, especially older models, now on the roads contain unrepaired, recalled defects.[105]

In August 2014 NHSTA established a useful online search tool that will allow buyers, owners, and renters of cars to check by vehicle identification (VIN) number, to see if a specific car has been the subject of a recall and whether it has been repaired. The agency expects the new search tool to increase the number of recalled cars that are actually repaired. Manufacturers are required to have similar search engines for their cars, going back fifteen years.[106]

NHTSA would be a more effective safety agency if it had adequate resources and engineering capability to cure safety problems before cars leave the factory by issuing mandatory safety standards to prevent vehicle defects in the first place.

That said, in the absence of new standards, recalling defective vehicles and equipment has played a crucial role in saving lives, preventing injuries, and maintaining car values over five decades. Imperfect (and understaffed) as the recall process may be, the public has benefited greatly from it. The little-noticed Mondale amendment in the very first federal vehicle safety law has proven its worth many times over.

NOTES

1. *Wall Street Journal,* Market Data Center, U.S. Auto Sales, December 3, 2013, accessed December 9. 2013; Jeff Bennett, "U.S. Auto Sales Seen Exceeding 15 Million for Full Year 2013," *Wall Street Journal,* January 2, 2013.

2. J. C. Furnas, "And Sudden Death," *Reader's Digest,* August 1935, 1.

3. NHTSA, "Traffic Safety Facts, 2012," Crashes by Severity, table 1, at 17.

4. Hilary Stout, "As GM Unveils Its Payout Plan, Recalls Expand," *New York Times,* June 30, 2014, A-1; Christopher Jensen, "GM Sent Letter But Didn't Issue Recall," *New York Times,* March 27, 2014; Bill Vlasic, "An Engineer's Eureka Moment With a GM Flaw," *New York Times,* March 28, 2014, 5; Cheryl Jensen, "Safety Agency Says 22 million Vehicles Recalled in 2013," *New York Times,* February 3, 2014.

5. NHTSA Annual Report, "Vehicle Recall Summary By Year," 2013. http://www.careforcrashvictims.com/assets/usrecalls1996-2013.pdf .

6. Congressional Record-Senate (June 24, 1966), 14247.

7. The response rate has generally been low: "I have heard some pretty low compliance numbers over the years—less than 20 percent on some recalls, depending on how serious consumers consider the situation." Keith Crain, "An Easy Solution to Recall Compliance," *Automotive News,* June 30, 2014. http://www.autonews.com/article/20140630/OEM11/306309986/an-easy-solution-to-recall-compliance.   NHTSA claims the current repair rate is now about 70 percent.

8. Mashaw and Harfst, *The Struggle for Auto Safety,* 56–57.

9. 49 USC 30118 (c) 1966. See also S. Rep 1301, 89th Cong., 2d Sess., 4.

10. Motor Vehicle and School Bus Safety Amendments, P.L. 93-492 signed by President Gerald Ford, October 27, 1974.

11. NHTSA, Office of Defects Investigation, 2013 Annual Recall Report, Chart: Quantity of Vehicles Recalled 1993–2013.

12. Cheryl Jensen, "Safety Agency Says 22 million Vehicles Recalled," *New York Times,* February 3, 2014; Jack Linshi, "All the Cars GM Has Recalled This Year Would Wrap the Earth 4 Times," *Time,* July 1, 2014, http://time.com/2945867/gm-recalls-facts/; Bill Vlasic and Hilary Stout, "Auto Industry Galvanized After Record Recall Year," *New York Times,* December 31, 2014, A-1.

13. Lee Strobel, "Pinto Blew Up 'like big napalm bomb': Witness," *Chicago Tribune,* January 18, 1980, 3.

14. Mark Mark Dowie, "Pinto Madness," *Mother Jones,* September 1, 1977, http://www.motherjones.com/politics/1977/09/pinto-madness, accessed May 19, 2013.

15. Lee Strobel, "Dead Girls' Mother Testifies: Pinto Recall Letter Arrived Too Late," *Chicago Tribune,* January 17, 1980. 1.

16. Lee Strobel, "Ford Ignored Pinto Fire Peril, Secret Memos Show," *Chicago Tribune,* October 13, 1979, 1.

17. Mark Dowie, "Pinto Madness," *Mother Jones,* September 1, 1977; *Iacocca: An Autobiography,* see footnote 38 for Lee Iacocca's views of the Pinto, its immediate market success, and its safety problems.

18. Dowie, "Pinto Madness," *Mother Jones,* September 1, 1977.

19. Ibid.

20. Dowie, "Pinto Madness," *Mother Jones*, September 1, 1977.

21. Ibid.

22. Strobel, "Ford Ignored Pinto Fire Peril, Secret Memos Show," *Chicago Tribune*, October 13, 1979, 1.

23. The one-dollar plastic protector was used in Pintos manufactured in Canada, because Canadian safety standards were more stringent than American. *Mother Jones* reported that in a later Pinto crash test which the Pinto surprisingly passed, this part was included. Mysteriously, the car was shipped from Ontario to Phoenix for the test.

24. Mark Dowie, "Pinto Madness," *Mother Jones*, September 1, 1977.

25. W. Michael Hoffman, "Case Study: The Ford Pinto," 1982, http://businessethics. qwriting.qc.cuny.edu/files/2012/01/HoffmanPinto.pdf. The calculation of this cost-benefit analysis was memorialized in the 1999 film *Fight Club*, when the main character describes his job as a "recall coordinator" who uses a formula to calculate when his auto company should conduct a recall. When asked which automobile company he works for, he replies, "a major one."

26. It is important to note that Ford's cost-benefit analysis was for *all* vehicles sold in a typical year (Ford could have produced a breakout of *just* Pintos) and that the analysis included *all* burn deaths and serious injuries, not just those caused by rear-impact crashes. *Mother Jones* also contested Ford's claim that the number of serious burn injuries and burn deaths would be the same each year, claiming the ratio of serious burn injuries to burn deaths could be as high as ten to one. Ford calculated the total *benefits* as 180 burn deaths x $200,000 + 180 serious burn injuries x $67,000 + 21,000 burned vehicles x $700 = $49.5 million. Ford calculated the total *costs* as 11 million cars x $11 + 1.5 million light trucks x $11 = $137 million. A year earlier, NHTSA had also used a "worth per life" figure of $200,000 in a decision to "kill a recall of under-ride bumpers on trucks." See E. S. Grush and C. S. Saunby, "Fatalities Associated with Crash Induced Fuel Leakage and Fires," *The Center for Auto Safety*, http://www.autosafety.org/uploads/phpq3mJ7F_FordMemo.pdf; Gary T. Schwartz, "The Myth of the Ford Pinto Case," *Rutgers Law Review*, 1990–1991, 1022-1024; William Greider, "Your Life May Not Be Worth Saving," *Washington Post*, April 9, 1972. NHTSA currently values a lost life at $9 million; see DOT, NHTSA "Value of a Statistical Life," Departmental Guidance 2013.

27. These claims are endorsed by Gary T. Schwartz, professor at UCLA, who wrote, "The strong claim that the Pinto was a firetrap entails a misconception. To be sure, the Pinto did contain a design problem that was nontrivial and to some extent distinctive. Even so, the number of fatalities that resulted from that design problem is a minor fraction of the fatality estimates relied on by those who present the 'firetrap' characterization." Gary T. Schwartz, "The Myth of the Ford Pinto Case," *Rutgers Law Review*, 1990–1991, 1033; W. Michael Hoffman, "Case Study: The Ford Pinto," 1982, http://businessethics.qwriting.qc.cuny.edu/files/2012/01/HoffmanPinto.pdf.

28. Hoffman, "Case Study," http://businessethics.qwriting.qc.cuny.edu/files/2012/01/HoffmanPinto.pdf.

29. "How Controversial Auto was Developed," *Chicago Tribune*, October 13, 1979; Dowie, "Pinto Madness," *Mother Jones*, September 1, 1977.

30. Schwartz, "The Myth of the Ford Pinto Case," *Rutgers Law Review*, 1990–1991, 1026.

31. One cartoon advised the Carter administration to give Pintos to Iran. Schwartz, "The Myth of the Ford Pinto Case," *Rutgers Law Review*, 1990–1991, 1026.

32. Dowie, "Pinto Madness," *Mother Jones*, September 1, 1977.

33. Schwartz, "The Myth of the Ford Pinto Case," *Rutgers Law Review*, 1990–1991, 1026.

34. "The Ford Pinto Fuel Tank," Center for Auto Safety, http://www.autosafety.org/ford-pinto-fuel-tank. This ruling was later reduced to $3.5 million by the trial judge.

35. Dowie, "Pinto Madness," *Mother Jones*, September 1, 1977.

36. Schwartz, "The Myth of the Ford Pinto Case," *Rutgers Law Review*, 1990–1991, 1026; "The Ford Pinto Fuel Tank," The Center for Auto Safety, http://www.autosafety. org/ford-pinto-fuel-tank.

37. It is debatable whether it is accurate to call the Pinto recall "voluntary." The Center for Auto Safety had already petitioned NHTSA for a recall investigation. The press was reporting on fire deaths in Pintos. And an Indiana grand jury had indicted Ford in 1978 for criminal recklessness. The company was acquitted, but Ford president Lee Iacocca concedes the trial did incalculable damage to Ford's reputation.

38. Lee Iacocca, *Iacocca: An Autobiography*, 35th ed. (New York: Bantam Books, 1985) 171–72.

39. Maslow and Harfst, *The Struggle for Auto Safety*, 164.

40. "Auto Defects," Center for Auto Safety, http://www.autosafety.org/auto-defects, accessed May 19, 2013; Jeffery Skeler, "Why the Alarming Surge of Auto recalls?" *Afro-American*, March 18, 1978; "Carmakers Stung by Rash of Recalls," *United Press International*, April 17, 1983.

41. Strobel, "Dead Girls' Mother Testifies: Pinto Recall Letter Arrived Too Late," *Chicago Tribune*, January 17, 1980.

42. Agis Salpukas, "G.M. Head Denies Engine Mount Peril," *New York Times*, October 29, 1971.

43. Jackie Calmes, "Minding the Minders of GM," *New York Times*, April 5, 2014; see GM Ignition Compensation, Claims Resolution Facility, "Overall Program Statistics" as of September 12, 2014, www.GMIgnitionCompensation.com. Reporting nineteen deceased claimant cases were settled.

44. *United States v. General Motors Corporation ("Wheels")*, 518 F.2d 420 (D.C. Cir. 1975).

45. *United States v. General Motors Corporation ("Pitman Arms")*, 561 F. 2d 923 (D.C. Cir. 1977), cert. denied, 434 1055 (1977).

46. *United States v. Ford Motor Co. ("Seatbacks")*, 421 F. Supp. 1239 (D.D.C. 1976), *aff'd in part, appeal dismissed in part as moot*, 574 F.2d 534 (D.C. Cir. 1978); "NHTSA Safety Defect Investigations." Presentation by Allan J. Kam," American Trial Lawyers Association 2001 Annual Convention, Product Liability Section, Montreal, Canada, July 17, 2001, http://www.htsassociates.com/documents/NHTSA-Safety-Defect-Investigations. pdf, accessed May 19, 2013.

47. A copy of the Frank Berndt's "per se" memo is available at http://www. autosafety.org/sites/default/files/enforcement2.pdf, accessed June 29, 2013.

48. *United States v. Ford Motor Company*, supra.

49. Hearings before the Senate Judiciary Committee, Oversight Subcommittee, http://www.judiciary.senate.gov/meetings/updated-justice-denied-rules-delayed-on-auto-safety-and-mental-health; see testimony of Cary Coglianese, professor of law, University of Pennsylvania, November 7, 2013, for a comprehensive analysis of the impact of the *Chrysler* decision on NHTSA and other possible factors in the agency's shift away from standard setting in favor of recalls as a regulatory strategy.

50. "NHTSA Safety Defect Investigations," Presentation by Allan J. Kam," American Trial Lawyers Association 2001 Annual Convention, Product Liability Section, Montreal, Canada, July 17, 2001, http://www.htsassociates.com/documents/ NHTSA-Safety-Defect-Investigations.pdf.

51. See chapter 12 for a discussion of the greater propensity of SUVs like the Explorer to roll over than other models produced at the time.

52. "Firestone 500 Steel Belted Radials," Center for Auto Safety, http://www. autosafety.org/firestone-500-steel-belted-radials.

53. Moira Johnston, "Hell on Wheels," *New West*, May 9, 1978, 28.

54. Ibid., 29.

55. "Firestone 500 Steel Belted Radials," Center for Auto Safety.

56. Johnston, "Hell on Wheels," *New West*, May 9, 1978, 29.

57. The congressional message may have helped in some cases, but clearly not in all. See Christopher Jensen, "General Motors Recalls, Inaction and a Trail of Fatal Crashes," *New York Times,* March 2, 2014, B-1.

58. "The Safety of Firestone 500 Steel Belted Radial Tires," House Committee on Interstate and Foreign Commerce, 95th Cong., 2nd Sess., August 16, 1978, print 53, 95–60.

59. "Firestone 500 Steel Belted Radials," Center for Auto Safety.

60. "Firestone Defends Radial 500 Tires as Safe, Reliable," *Los Angeles Times,* August 9, 1978.

61. "Firestone 500 Steel Belted Radials," Center for Auto Safety.

62. See chapter 12 for a discussion of another Ford Explorer-Firestone rollover recall.

63. Angela Greiling and Mark Clothier, "Chrysler Gives in on Fixing Jeeps," *Bloomberg,* June 19, 2013; Tom Krisher and Dee-Ann Durbin, "In Rare Rebuff Chrysler Refusing a NHTSA Request for a Recall of 2.7 Million SUVs," *CNN,* June 4, 2013. On the number of deaths involved, see Chris Isidore, "Chrysler refuses to recall 2.7 million Jeep SUVs," *CNN Money,* June 5, 2013, http://money.cnn.com/2013/06/04/autos/chrysler-recall-refusal.

64. Christopher Jensen, "Consumer Group Calls Chrysler's Jeep Fix Inadequate," *New York Times,* June 20, 2013.

65. Clarence Ditlow, "Profits Over People's Lives," *CNN,* June 7, 2013.

66. Center for Auto Safety, Letter to David J. Friedman, Acting NHTSA Administrator, July 2, 2014 at www.autosafety.org and http://www.careforcrashvictims.com/blog-jeepburn.php.

67. "Police Release 911 Tape in Deadly SoCal Crash," *Associated Press,* September 11, 2009; for a further description of the fatal crash, see http://www.nytimes.com/2010/02/01/business/01toyota.html?pagewanted=all

68. Testimony of Clarence Ditlow before the Senate Commerce, Science and Transportation Committee, March 2, 2010.

69. Maggie Mazzetti, "Fact Check: Toyota Not Alone in Acceleration Problems," *CNN,* February 6, 2010.

70. Ibid.

71. Kate Linebaugh and Dionne Searcey, "Cause of Sudden Acceleration Proves Hard to Pinpoint," *Wall Street Journal,* February 25, 2010, http://www.suddenacceleration.com/cause-of-sudden-acceleration-proves-hard-to-pinpoint/.

72. Ibid.

73. See NASA Report to the National Highway Traffic Safety Administration, John Pollard, and E. Donald Sussman, *An Examination of Sudden Acceleration,* DOT HS 807-367, January 1989.

74. Ditlow Testimony, 2010, 1–4, and see "Auto Sudden Acceleration," Center for Auto Safety, http://www.autosafety.org/audi-sudden-acceleration.

75. Ditlow testimony, 2010, 1–4.

76. David Shepardson and Christine Tierney, "Panel Says NHTSA, Toyota Fell Short Investigating Acceleration Complaints," *Detroit News,* February 23, 2010, http://detnews.com?AUTO01/2230357.

77. "Regulators Hired By Toyota Helped Halt Acceleration Probes," Bloomberg.com, New York, February 13, 2010, http://www.bloomberg.com/apps/news?pid=newsarchive&sid=atXvi2msqPOM.

78. *Detroit News,* February 23, 2010, supra.

79. "Regulators Hired by Toyota Helped Halt Acceleration Probes," *Bloomberg,* February 13, 2010, supra.

80. David Shepardson and Christine Tierney, "Panel Says NHTSA, Toyota Fell Short Investigating Acceleration Complaints," *The Detroit News,* February 23, 2010.

81. Phil Baker, "Documents Contradict Testimony in Toyota Unintended Acceleration Case," *San Diego Daily Transcript,* March 25, 2013.

82. "Toyota Shareholders Sue Over Stock Price Drop," *Associated Press,* March 21, 2010; Chris Isidore, "Toyota to Pay Record Safety Fine," *CNN Money,* December 18, 2012.

83. Emily Jane Fox, "Toyota to pay $1.1 billion in recall case," *CNN Money,* December 26, 2012.

84. "Toyota Makes another Global Recall," Zacks Equity Research, November 16, 2012.

85. "Toyota Motor Corp. Will Pay Record $17.35 Million in Civil Penalties for Alleged Violations of Federal Law," National Highway Traffic Safety Administration press release, December 18, 2012.

86. Gail Sullivan, "Toyota Settles with Government for $1.2 Billion in Recall Probe," *Washington Post,* March 19, 2014.

87. Bill Vlasic and Matt Apuzzo, "Toyota Is Fined 1.2 Billion," *New York Times,* March 19, 2014.

88. See *Bookout v. Toyota Motor Corp.* CJ 2008-7969, District Court, Oklahoma County, Oklahoma; http://www.bloomberg.com/news/print/2013-10-24/toyota

89. http://www.safetyresearch.net/blog/articles/toyota-lawsuits-wrapped

90. Jon S. Vernick, Julie Samia Mair, Stephen P. Teret, and Jason W. Sapsin, Johns Hopkins Bloomberg School of Public Health, "Role of Litigation in Preventing Product-Related Injuries," *Epidemiologic Reviews* 25 (2003): 90; http://epirev.oxfordjournals.org/.

91. Ibid. The authors acknowledge, "Litigation is certainly not a perfect tool for product-related injury prevention. . . . It may be associated with potentially harmful societal costs for some industries," 97.

92. Dale Buss, "Toyota Plots Brand Rehab," *Brand Channel,* June 3, 2010. http://www.brandchannel.com/home/post/2010/06/03/Toyota-Brand-Rehab.aspx

93. Linebaugh and Searcey, "Cause of Sudden Acceleration Proves Hard to Pinpoint," *Wall Street Journal,* February 25, 2010.

94. Shepardson and Tierney, "Panel says NHTSA, Toyota Fell Short Investigating Acceleration Complaints," *Detroit News,* February 23, 2010.

95. Hilary Stout, Danielle Ivory, and Mathew L. Wald, "Auto Regulators Dismissed Defect Tied to 13 Deaths," *New York Times,* March 8, 2014, 1.

96. Ibid.

97. http://finance.yahoo.com/news/exclusive-74-dead-crashes-0031008849.html (June 2, 2014)

98. "Dismissed Defect Tied to 13 Deaths," *New York Times,* March 8, 2014, 1.

99. "CAS Reveals Internal NHTSA Files on Cobalt Ignition Airbag Defect," Press Release, March 7. 2014. www.autosafety.org.

100. Jerry Hirsch, "NHTSA Launches Probe Into Cobalt Recall, GM Issues Another Apology," *Los Angeles Times,* February 27, 2014.

101. Bill Vlasic and Matt Apuzzo, "Toyota Is Fined $1.2 Billion for Concealing Safety Defects," *New York Times,* March 19, 2014.

102. The words are those of GM president Mary Barra, commenting on the internal GM report. Bill Vlasic, "G.M. Lawyers Hid Fatal Flaw," *New York Times,* June 6, 2014. The joint responsibility of GM and NHTSA for the failure to report and recall the defective Cobalts and Ions sooner, and the resultant loss of lives and injuries, is discussed in a report by the Majority staff of the House Energy and Commerce Committee, "*Staff Report on the GM Ignition Switch Recall: Review of NHTSA,*" September 16, 2014. Unfortunately, while critical of both GM and NHTSA, the staff report fails to discuss the responsibility of the authorizing and appropriating committees of the Congress for failing to correct gaps in the legal authority of NHTSA to obtain and release potentially life threatening safety-defect information from manufacturers and the lack of staff and funds necessary to permit the agency to implement the TREAD and National Traffic and Motor Vehicle Safety Acts effectively.

103. Reuters Brief: "GM Says: Ahead of Previously Announced Target for 2014 Profit Excluding Recall Costs," June 6, 2014, . . . GM officials: "no meaningful impact [from]

car switch [recall]") on GM sales in North America. http://www.forbes.com/sites/
joannmuller/2014/06/05/how-much-more-will-gms-recall-crisis-cost-shareholders-
only-ken-feinberg-knows/.

104. Mashaw and Harfst, *The Struggle for Auto Safety* (Cambridge, MA: Harvard University Press, 1990), 168; Christopher Jensen, "U.S. Inquiries Over Automobile Safety Dragging On," *New York Times, February* 22, 2013.

105. Ibid.

106. "U.S. Department of Transportation Unveils New, Free, Online Search Tool for Recalls Using VIN Number," www.nhtsa.gov/About+NHTSA/Press+Releases; Cheryl Jensen, "Was a Recalled Car Fixed? Answer Is Now a Click Away," *New York Times,* August 20, 2014.

TWELVE

Forcing New Technology

Safety Standards in the New Century

Motor vehicle safety standards were intended by Congress to be the primary means of saving lives and dollars on the nation's highways.[1] After the National Traffic and Motor Vehicle Safety Act became law in 1966, they worked brilliantly—at least for a while. They triggered a 77 percent drop in the death rate over four-plus decades. They reduced fatalities from approximately 51,000 in 1966 to 34,000 in 2012. They and associated vehicle improvements have saved over 600,000 lives since the Fasety Act was enabled in 1966. They and associated vehicle improvements have saved over 600,000 livessince the Safety Act was enacted n 1966.[2]

The new law and regulations, together with voluntary improvements by manufacturers and federal dollar incentives to the states,[3] now save over $400 billion each year in avoided societal costs, such as loss of life, pain and suffering, medical expenses, lost wages, and production down time.[4] That is over $1,000 a year saved for *each* person in the country—compared with the losses we would have suffered if deaths had continued at a rate of 51,000 people a year. The added cost in a new passenger car sold, in the latest estimate available from NHTSA, for all federal safety standards was $839 per vehicle. Thus the savings to the national economy exceed, at least fifteen times, the cost of all safety standards.[5]

In recent years the development of safety standards by NHTSA has declined.[6] During the past three decades, while motor vehicle safety technology has become more sophisticated, new safety standards have become fewer and farther between. They have been replaced *in part* with something called "regulation by recall"[7]—and also by a dramatic change in the public's attitude toward the value of buying safer cars. Automakers now "sell safety," as well as style, utility, and horsepower.

The falloff in new safety standards may be a result of agency "aging." Regulatory agencies, like people, often lose their fire over time. The causes differ for different regulatory agencies. In the case of NHTSA, continuous political and legal challenges exerted by one of the largest industries in the nation have created immense problems. Court limitations on the rulemaking process, such as the "hard look" doctrine—a more detailed review of agency standards used by many appellate courts—have also imposed burdens on an already burdened NHTSA.[8]

There are other reasons for the federal regulatory slowdown, which extends beyond standard development and upgrading. Foremost of them is inadequate resources. In 2014, a shortage of funds was apparent in the defect investigation process and the agency's inability to recognize and deal promptly with the GM Chevy Cobalt and Ion ignition switch problems that have killed at least twenty-three people. There was in that case, at minimum, a seven-year delay by NHTSA in investigating the GM defect and inaction forcing a vehicle recall.[9]

To be sure, there have been important exceptions to the standards stall at the federal level. The exceptions, many of which were directed by Congress, have made a difference in lives and dollars saved. Three important standard proceedings—the Roof Crush Upgrade (2008), Electronic Stability Control (2012), and Ejection Mitigation (2011)—are good examples. The Roof Crush amendment and the Electronic Stability Control standard offer a sharp contrast in the pace and problems of developing federal vehicle safety standards.[10]

State safety laws and standards, such as mandatory belt use laws, have also played an important role in reducing the rate of motor vehicle deaths and injuries.[11]

DONNA BAILEY AND THE SUV

The introduction of the sport utility vehicle (SUV) in the late 1970s offers an example of the difficulty of relying on recalls rather than new standards to regulate a rapidly changing automobile market. Any rollover crash is a dangerous accident. SUV rollovers became particularly dangerous immediately after SUVs were introduced. SUV rollover deaths rose from about 500 in 1982 to 3,000 in 2006.

The Ford Explorer-Firestone recall of 14 million radial tires in 2000 and the redesign of the Explorer SUV by Ford in order to improve its stability, stand out as a classic case of the tension among standard setting, recalls, and a company's bottom line.

The Ford-Firestone disaster also changed Donna Bailey's life forever.

In March 1999, on a clear, dry day, Bailey was a passenger in a two-door Ford Explorer SUV. The car was heading north with Bailey and two friends on US 181 from Corpus Christi, Texas. She was a forty-three-year-old physical trainer with a husband and two teenage children. She loved outdoor athletic activities and was going to the hills north of Corpus Christi to go rock climbing with two friends.

Bailey describes what happened as the car headed away from the city. She heard the "thudding sound" of a tire coming apart. It happened so fast, she said, that "her friend who was driving was trying real hard to keep control." Bailey remembers yelling. "Then we fell over. They got out. They were fine. But I was hanging upside down from my seatbelt, and I just remembered thinking we were dead. And a man was trying to kick in the windshield to get to me. I don't know if you want to write this, but I died and came back. I saw four angels."[12]

Bailey talked about it from her hospital bed a year later. She said that the best times now are the weekends. Her now ex-husband drives her two teenage children to visit her. It is 200 miles from Corpus Christi to the Houston rehabilitation facility where she resides. Her biggest project was learning to operate an electric wheelchair designed for quadriplegics.

The Explorer SUV Bailey was riding in was equipped with Firestone tires. The key question was what caused accident? The purchase of Firestone tires for use on the Explorer was a compromise decision by Ford's engineers and marketing staff based on cost. Ford had previously used a Goodyear tire that performed better in rollover tests Ford had conducted. Ford engineers recommended that the Explorer be subject to several significant design changes before it was sold, including lowering its engine position and widening the chassis to increase its stability. A previous version of the Explorer, known as the Bronco, had been involved in dozens of rollover crashes that had resulted in deaths and millions of dollars in damage payments by Ford to injured drivers and passengers.

Firestone, as evidenced by its earlier 1978 "500 Radial" recall, had a relatively poor safety history.[13] But Ford had improved the Bronco design with the Explorer. Its management believed that despite the car's cost-conscious design it was adequately resistant to rolling over in a crash. They were wrong.

Bailey's attorney Tab Turner, who specializes in rollover cases, said later, "This was a case of a bad tire on a bad vehicle. Tread separation, which occurred during the accident Bailey was involved in, should not cause a vehicle to roll over."[14]

Still, Ford officials maintained that the Explorer was a safe vehicle that got stuck with a bad tire. They acknowledged that they were slow to spot the problem of the deadly Firestone–Ford combination, because the tire was the only part of the vehicle Ford did not warranty. Thus, they said, Ford had not received accident and damage reports quickly enough.

The Explorer-Firestone case resulted in one of the largest recalls ever. The inter-company battle ultimately resulted in the Firestone tire recall and two separate redesigns of the Explorer in 1995 and 2002. They were intended to make the Explorer more stable and less prone to rollover. But they were too little and too late for Bailey and hundreds of other deceased motorists.[15]

The Ford-Firestone case led to the enactment of a new safety law. The TREAD Act was passed in 2000. The act was a response to the failure of both companies to report defects in the tires and of Ford to report the Explorer's problems to the government as required by the Safety Act. Among other things, the new TREAD Act set up an "Early Warning System" intended to detect emerging safety defects. It directed manufacturers to immediately notify NHTSA of all serious injury and death reports received from car owners.[16] It required new tire-safety standards and the installation of tire pressure monitors in new cars. The new law did not, however, deal with the longstanding issue of the complete absence of any SUV stability standards.

The process of correcting the problems of Explorer rollovers and Firestone blowouts took more than a decade from the first Explorer rollover deaths in 1993 to the Firestone recall of fourteen million tires that began in 2000. It took more years, thousands of deaths and injuries, and several new federal standards to reduce the much bigger SUV stability problem.[17] There is still no federal safety standard regulating vehicle stability directly. The indirect approach that was eventually used involved the loss of many lives.

Even before the Donna Bailey case, Ford had settled 334 rollover cases involving hundreds of deaths, at a cost of at least $113 million.

The Explorer that Bailey was riding in was a new-style SUV that resulted in one of the most spectacular automobile marketing successes since "muscle cars" of the 1960s era. Over 3.6 million Explorer SUVs were sold in the 1990s. Americans fell in love with its style and particularly with the SUV's elevated "command seating." It gave the driver a "king of the road conceit." It was very good for Ford's bottom line, accounting for half of the company's profits in the 1990s.[18]

All makes of SUVs, including the Explorer, by then had a long history of rollovers. They were built on light-truck understructures, thus avoiding passenger car-safety standards. The light-truck chassis also gave the SUVs a higher center of gravity than other passenger cars. That made them many times more likely to roll over during a sharp turn than a station wagon or a sedan. If you fill a sedan with people and suitcases, it becomes *less* likely to roll over in an accident. That is because weight is added below the car's center of gravity. With the SUV, until the relatively recent redesign of many models, the weight of people and baggage was added above the center of gravity, making the vehicle even more likely to tip over.[19] In insurance industry (IIHS) reports based on 1990s data, two-door Explorer SUVs had a significantly higher rollover death rate than other larger SUVs.[20]

NHTSA research in the early 1990s showed that all SUVs were likely to roll over "substantially more often than other designs." The regulatory agency's technical staff forcefully recommended developing a national stability standard based on vehicle height and width. Representative Tim Wirth, chair of the House consumer subcommittee, formally petitioned the agency in 1986 to issue a national stability standard. Despite broad support for the Wirth petition, it was rejected by President Reagan's administrator Diane Steed.[21] No rollover stability standard was ever issued by NHTSA, or anyone else.

SUVs continued to roll over more readily than other models until government standards for increased roof strength, ejection prevention, and Electronic Stability Control, coupled with voluntary redesign by manufacturers, pushed the death and injury rate for SUVs downward to about the same level as other passenger cars between 2000 and 2010.[22] The manufacturers' shift to more popular and smaller "crossover" SUVs, which have better stability, was a big part of the improvement.

It took a long time and many deaths and injuries to force the improvement in SUV design safety. The Ford–Firestone SUV crashes and Donna Bailey's personal tragedy illustrate the need to anticipate new design and mechanical problems through engineering analysis and standards development.

The potential for market-driven safety solutions is demonstrated by the rapid development of new crash-avoidance technologies. These include frontal crash avoidance, lane-change warning, and biomedical systems designed to detect drunk drivers. The new technologies are not yet fully road tested, nor are they required in new cars. There are also no existing federal safety standards for judging their reliability and effectiveness, although NHTSA and the Insurance Institute for Highway Safety (IIHS) do test and evaluate some crash-avoidance systems.[23]

NHTSA's standard development problems in the twenty-first century were enumerated by Clarence Ditlow of the Center for Auto Safety, which has monitored, petitioned, and sometimes sued NHTSA over a period of almost forty years. In testimony before the Senate in 2013, Ditlow found that many of the original standards, such as seat-back strength and head restraints, were woefully out of date. "With rare exception," he said, "revision of the original standards or issuance of major new standards has come from Congressional mandates. Today, standards issued by NHTSA on its own tend to be relatively minor or without significant industry opposition."[24]

ROOF STRENGTH VERSUS ELECTRONIC STABILITY CONTROL

The thirty-five-year history of the battle to upgrade the roof strength standard is a classic story of fierce industry opposition forcing government delay.[25] The standard was proposed in 1971 and rewritten in 1973 in order to protect the heads and necks of drivers and passengers in vehicle crashes, primarily in rollover accidents like Donna Bailey's. In 2012, rollovers of all kinds still accounted for about 7,500 deaths a year.

The original federal roof-strength standard was written by General Motors and Ford for NHTSA in 1972. The new agency did not have the technological ability to do it by itself. It attempted a draft standard, but ultimately had to call on the manufacturers for help. Help was indeed forthcoming. The companies volunteered their expertise and engineers — but not necessarily their political support.[26] It took years of public pressure and consumer-insurance industry lobbying to win an increase in the standard from a requirement that a vehicle withstand 1.5 times its weight on the roof, to three times the vehicle weight in the revised version issued in 2009.

For years the motor vehicle industry argued that roof strength was not the primary cause of rollover deaths and injuries. The manufacturers said that people's heads hit the roof before the collapsing roof hit them. They said the roof standard would not save enough lives to be cost-effective.

An embarrassing dispute over roof strength developed between Volvo and Ford — an argument that came to light in court documents obtained by lawyers for injured parties suing for damages. Volvo, the Swedish company, had always emphasized stronger roofs that it provided in its cars. When Volvo introduced its first sport utility vehicle, the XC90 in 2002, its advertisements boldly proclaimed the roof "exceeds the legal requirements in the U.S.A. by more than 100 percent."[27] Then Volvo was acquired by Ford. Its new owner told the reluctant subsidiary that its advertisements clashed with Ford's official position that there was no proof that a collapsing roof killed many occupants. Ford told Volvo that "close to 110 lawsuits were pending" over deaths and injuries related to roof strength. Ford officials warned Volvo, "The top-most management in the company is impatient" with Volvo advertisements. References to Volvo's increased roof strength soon disappeared from its United States advertising.[28]

In 2006 and again in 2008 industry officials met with NHTSA and the White House staff to urge that the test levels of the proposed upgraded roof standard be weakened. They also argued that testing the strength of a sedan or SUV roof on *both* the passenger and driver sides was not necessary. The manufacturers argued (unsuccessfully) that both sides of the roof collapse in the same manner. Testing one side only, as provided in the original 1973 standard, was enough.[29]

Safety advocates picketed NHTSA over the long delay in upgrading the roof standard and over its weak content. "We have been waiting almost 40 years for an upgraded standard. What has the agency been doing?" asked Jackie Gillan, vice president of the Advocates for Highway and Auto Safety, an insurance industry–consumer safety coalition.[30]

The Alliance of Automobile Manufacturers, representing Detroit's "Big Three" and Toyota, argued that there is "no relationship between a stronger roof and the risk of serious . . . injury for belted occupants." The International Automobile Manufacturers said its members such as Nissan and Suzuki needed, at minimum, a six-year phase-in schedule before they could redesign their SUVs to meet the stronger roof requirements.[31]

Congress got involved. In 2005 it passed a law directing NHTSA to issue a proposed upgraded roof standard by 2008. In an effort to force a strong standard, members of the Senate Commerce Committee held public hearings. Senator Mark Pryor (Arkansas) urged the agency to strengthen the standard and move it promptly to completion. Senator Claire McCaskill (Missouri) questioned why "NHTSA is only nimble enough to update the rules every thirty years."[32]

Republican senator Tom Coburn (Oklahoma) said NHTSA's first proposal was inadequate. "It does not appear that NHTSA is ready to make the leap from the twentieth century to the twenty-first century. NHTSA should back a standard 3 or 3.5 times the car weight." Coburn added that Congress should write its own standard if the agency couldn't get off the dime.[33] NHTSA finally ordered the manufacturers to comply with the upgraded roof standard in some 2012 models; fully effective for all new cars by 2017—eight long years after the revision was first proposed.

The final roof-standard amendment in 2008 was an improvement, but it did not fully please anyone. In addition to the long phase-in period, the industry said that enhanced roof strength was nowhere near as effective as the newly developed Electronic Stability Control in preventing rollovers. The standard would, it said, save only a few hundred lives a year. But public pressure led by consumer groups and the insurance industry convinced NHTSA that a tougher roof standard was necessary.

Safety advocates thought the revised roof-strength standard (which is now set at three times the weight of the vehicle, with required tests on *both* the passenger and driver sides) was still not adequate. According to Laura MacCleery, who worked for Public Citizen in obtaining congressional and agency approval of the higher standard, a "dynamic roof-strength test" (rather than a static test that is less expensive) involving actually rolling over test vehicles, would better replicate real-world conditions.

The Insurance Institute for Highway Safety developed its own test for "Top Rated" roof strength in 2009. It is stronger than the NHTSA standard; at four times the car's weight. But IIHS said the dynamic-testing concept (actually rolling over test cars) needed more study.[34]

When the revised federal standard was issued by the agency, with the static roof-crush test, IIHS in 2012 tested twelve small SUVs. It found that only four had earned its "Top Rated" score for roof strength. They were the Volkswagen Tiguan, the Subaru Forester, the Honda Element, and Chrysler's Jeep Patriot. IIHS said its tougher roof-strength test might ultimately force improved rollover protection in all new cars. It was comparable, IIHS said, to the frontal (corner) offset and side-impact tests that IIHS had developed and publicly tested, well ahead of the government.

Car buyers were thus left with a somewhat confusing situation. Depending on the car's date of manufacture, the buyer needed to consider: 1) whether the car met the existing federal roof-strength standard requiring three times the weight of the vehicle, or 2) the IIHS "Top Rated" standard of four times the car's weight.

ELECTRONIC STABILITY CONTROL

The history of the federal safety standard mandating Electronic Stability Control in new cars, starting with 2012 models, represents a sharp contrast with the checkered thirty-five-year story of the roof-strength standard.[35] ESC is a computer-controlled system building on anti-lock braking system (ABS). ABS has been required in Europe and used in many cars in the United States for years.[36] ESC measures the driver's steering input against the car's yaw (spin) and the traction at the wheels. If differences exist suggesting the imminence of a life-threatening skid, ESC is designed to move the car in the intended direction. If needed, the engine throttle is lowered as well to ease power that may be inducing the skid and to allow the brakes to do their job more effectively. It works faster and more effectively than a driver could to control a skid or slide.[37] Although many drivers had learned to pump their brakes to avoid skidding, the development of electronic and computer technology facilitates much more rapid and effective "brake pumping." Then, of course, drivers needed to unlearn the brake pumping habit and learn to press down firmly and steadily on the brake in a skid.

ESC was developed by Mercedes-Benz in Germany in the mid-1990s. BMW picked up the system shortly thereafter. It took a while for American manufacturers to notice German imports utilizing ESC and its potential appeal to American car buyers. By 2006, 70 percent of American-manufactured sport utility vehicles were equipped with ESC, according to the Alliance of Automobile Manufacturers.[38] At the same time, Ford announced that Electronic Stability Control would be a standard feature on all of its cars and trucks by the 2009 model year. General Motors followed suit by saying that it would have stability control on all vehicles by 2010. Toyota planned to have the system on all models by 2009.

"This is something that everyone can agree on," Ford spokesman Dan Jarvis said.[39] At the time, ESC was found mostly in higher-priced cars. The federal government mandated an expansion of the use of the technology so that it would be included in smaller and lower-priced cars, benefitting less affluent and younger drivers.

"This is one of the best safety features we've seen in a long, long time," said David Champion, then head of automotive testing for *Consumer Reports*, after Consumers Union performed vehicle-handling tests. "Not only will it prevent deaths and injuries, but it also reduces the cost of repairing crashed cars because in many cars you can avoid the accident."[40]

A survey by J.D. Power and Associates, the automotive market-research firm, cited by the *Los Angeles Times*, found that almost two-thirds of all respondents said they would be willing to pay up to $400 to add ESC to their new vehicle.[41]

ESC became a federally mandated standard in record time. The federal rule was proposed in September of 2006. It was finalized in April 2007 less than a year later. It was ordered to be in place for all new models by 2008. NHTSA estimated that when fully implemented, ESC would save between 5,300 and 9,600 lives per year and prevent between 156,000 and 238,000 injuries in all types of crashes.[42]

When the ESC standard was proposed in 2006, president George W. Bush's secretary of transportation Mary Peters predicted that "this technology will save thousands of lives, like air bags and seat belts. Ten years down the road we will look back at the new ESC technology and wonder how we ever drove a car without it."[43]

ESC may have its greatest impact in minimizing rollover deaths and injuries, especially in SUVs. According to IIHS, rollovers are still much more common for SUVs and pickup trucks than for cars and they are more common for SUVs than for pickups.[44]

The percentage of new passenger models with ESC increased after the federal standard was issued, from 9 percent in the 2000 model year to 85 percent in the 2010 model year. Much of that increase was accomplished voluntarily by manufacturers.

There was still some resistance. Car critic Warren Brown of the *Washington Post* commented on, "the congressionally inspired silliness of encouraging the National Highway Traffic Safety Administration to require the installation of electronic stability control systems in all new cars and trucks sold in the United States, beginning in 2009. . . . Such a rule would be nonsensical in Europe where automobile manufacturers . . . have made electronic stability as common as windshield wipers. . . . Exactly what is the point of such a rule?"[45] What may be nonsensical in Europe still appears to be necessary in the United States. Setting the basic rules for what qualifies as ESC, monitoring its effectiveness, and ensuring that all, not some, American cars have it is important.

There is a sad irony involved in this story. Instead of the thirty-five years it took to set federal rules for stronger roofs (a "crashworthiness" standard), it took about a decade for market demand and the government to move the new ESC system from Mercedes cars to a required feature (a "crash-avoidance" standard) on American cars.

The long saga of improving vehicle roof strength compared to the relative cakewalk for ESC raises questions about new automobile safety technologies and safety standards generally. ESC was introduced quickly in American cars through a combination of a marketplace demand and a federal mandate. It was different with the roof-strength upgrade. As we have seen, American manufacturers fought intensely against it. They asserted that it was not necessary or effective. That was disputed by the government, consumer advocates, and the insurance industry.

The reasons for the big difference in the time necessary for the two key safety standards to gain adoption and save lives surely involves several factors. They probably include the interplay between styling, safety, and cost, and the companies' preference for crash-avoidance technology over crashworthiness. Like the reasons for GM's failure to report on the Chevrolet Cobalt ignition defect for up to ten years, we may never know for sure.

What these contrasting safety stories suggest about future safety innovations in American motor vehicles is a mixed message. Consumers now want more vehicle safety. But without an effective government presence, many of the developing safety technologies may be available only as high-end "packages" for those who want them and can afford to pay. The question is whether they should be required and, if so, when. [46]

THE RESEARCH SAFETY VEHICLE

Not all new safety technologies make it to the marketplace. Over forty years ago Robert L. Carter, associate administrator of NHTSA, presented a report to the Second International Conference on Passive Restraints on a promising new safety technology. Carter's report, based on thousands of hours of research by NHTSA engineers and economists, supplemented by testing at Cornell Aeronautical Laboratories, concluded that passive protection of automobile occupants *in 50 mph head-on crashes* was then achievable.

> Inflatable restraint systems and vehicle force structure can be designed to protect occupants in passenger car front collisions of 50 mph barrier equivalent speed. Results show probable savings of more than 75 percent of all fatalities and 60 percent of all injuries now occurring in frontal passenger car collisions below 50 mph. [47]

The federal motor vehicle safety standard for frontal crashes that kill thousands of people each year was 30 mph at that time. The test today is the same 30 mph. NHTSA's 1972 RSV (Research Safety Vehicle) report was produced by a team of government and private engineers at a cost of millions of taxpayer dollars. It was never implemented. In the heady days after the creation of the safety agency in 1966, a 50 mph survival standard seemed quite possible. With the advances in safety technologies since then, engineers believe that it is even more doable than ever.

The 50 mph frontal crash goal was a product of a conscious decision by a pro-active Congress. Its leaders in the 1960s knew that the automobile industry had demonstrated a significant degree of indifference to safety improvements and the technological innovations to support those improvements. It was hoped that the 1966 Safety Act would spur company investment in new safety technologies.[48] So in writing the 1966 Safety Act, the drafters incorporated a prod to force the private market to use its expertise to produce safer cars and to equip NHTSA to evaluate new safety technology and industry claims. The method used by the lawmakers was to mandate that the government buy or build experimental safety vehicles to serve as a technological yardstick in the future.[49]

In response, the Research Safety Vehicle (RSV) program was initiated in 1972 by NHTSA at an initial cost to taxpayers of $30 million. It was designed to prove that an attractive, affordable passenger car could be built with a high degree of safety included. Two different prototype cars were built, one by Minicars, Inc., another by Calspan Corporation, the successor to Cornell Aeronautical Laboratories. The government paid the bill. The safety cars were built. The Minicars' RSV weighed about the same as available small cars (2,500 pounds).

As predicted by associate administrator Carter the RSV, built with a Honda engine, delivered full protection in frontal crashes at speeds up to 50 mph. It also performed up to NHTSA crash specifications in side and rear crashes at 40 to 50 mph. The seventeen test results showed that passengers "Would walk away from a 50 mph crash."[50]

The RSV also delivered an average of 32 miles to the gallon. A 1986 study for NHTSA projected its mass production at about the same price range as smaller cars then available.[51] But without public demand for it or a mandate from the government, automobile manufacturers showed little interest in producing a 50 mph safer car. In 1991 during the administration of president George H. W. Bush, all government-owned RSV test cars were destroyed by the Department of Transportation.[52] This was, arguably, because they had served their purpose. Or perhaps the test cars could be used in lawsuits to demonstrate that safer cars were techniolo possible. The documented proof of their safety potential, however, could not be destroyed.

Another reason for not using the RSV technology may have been that mandatory use of seat belts and air bags subsequently implemented parts

of it. But over the last forty-two years much of the RSV technology—
particularly its body design and use of energy absorbing materials—has
remained on the shelf.

Donald Friedman, the founder and president of Minicars, says,

> Air bags save about 2,500 lives annually, but we still lose about 12,000
> lives a year in frontal crashes, 9,000 in side crashes and over 7,500
> people in rollover crashes. We can do better by simply looking back at
> what the RSV Program achieved.[53]

Friedman, who first worked for eighteen years as a research engineer at
GM, said in 2014, "manufacturers still do not spend much money on
items that they do not think will sell cars. They mostly sell cup holders
and seat heaters. You can get four gold stars from NHTSA for passing the
outdated 30 mph front and side crash tests. It doesn't mean much."[54]

SAFETY PRIORITIES

NHTSA's future planning document is its annual "Priority Plan." It is an
enlightening, if troubling, document. Some of the safety projects on the
priority list have been on the drawing boards for years, without much
progress toward getting them completed. Some examples are: forward-
collision warning, lane-departure warning, distracted-driver sensors,
drunk driver ignition interlocks, improved child restraints, and rear-visibility cameras.[55]

There is a second, lower priority list in the NHTSA plan, "Other Significant Projects." This part of the Priority Plan is even further from implementation. It includes blind-spot detection, pedestrian protection, seat
belt restraint effectiveness (to prevent ejection), and dynamic rollover
testing. In all, out of eleven pending Priority Projects, only two (including
one for rear-visibility cameras) have been proposed as final rules. In
seven of the projects, NHTSA's Plan says that "staffing limitations"
caused postponement of the work.

Testifying in November 2013, Professor Thomas O. McGarity of the
University of Texas Law School, summarized the status of safety standards at NHTSA:

> For rules that really matter and as to which regulatees are prepared to
> devote substantial [opposition] resources . . . the existing rulemaking
> model is not working . . . Under the pressure of constant opposition
> from the regulated industries and with only sporadic countervailing
> pressure from beneficiaries of the regulated programs, statutory dead-
> lines are missed, ambitious policy goals remain unachieved, and the
> protections envisioned by the authors of the statute gradually erode
> away. . . . The current rulemaking process is not merely ossified, it is
> broken.[56]

Ditlow, of the Center for Auto Safety, agreed. He listed seven examples of safety problems where only congressional intervention—when the votes were there—made it possible to enact new safety standards:

1. The 1974 Motor Vehicle Safety Amendments. Required recall repairs to be paid for by the manufacturer. Mandated fuel system rear impact standards and school bus safety standards.[57]
2. The 1991 ISTEA ACT.[58] Required full frontal air bags for all seating positions, revised the existing head injury standard.
3. The 1998 TEA 21.[59] Required an improved air bag rule, designed to better protect children and small occupants.
4. The TREAD Act (2000).[60] Required a revised tire safety standard, tire pressure monitoring gauges, and the Early Warning defect reporting system.
5. Anton's Law (2002).[61] Required child booster seat and improved lap and shoulder belt standards.
6. SAFETEA-LU (2009).[62] Required rollover protection through Electronic Stability Control (ESC) by 2009, upgraded side impact regulations, the roof-crush standard, improved occupant ejection protection, power window locking switches, better crashworthiness data ratings, and large passenger van-safety proceedings.
7. Cameron Gulbransen Act (2007).[63] Required commencement of backup camera, power window safety lock, and brake shift interlock rules.

The Center for Auto Safety noted that NHTSA was studying the use and potential dangers inherent in the use of increased electronics and computers in vehicles in the mid-1970s. It has never issued a electronics-computer standard. The average new car includes over fifty microcomputers to operate its engine and safety systems. The Center called for the development of a standard for electronic controls and computer units that are used in current models. The Toyota sudden acceleration recalls could have involved the computer software systems in those vehicles. A minimum safety standard, including a warning of malfunctions in the car's software, would be a major step forward in detecting and reporting defects to the government and the public.

Adrian Lund, president of the Insurance Institute for Highway Safety, takes a somewhat different view on the effectiveness of the regulatory process. He has been involved in vehicle safety for 30 years. Lund describes some recent changes in the motor vehicle industry's approach to new-car technology:

> The adoption of new safety technologies has been a slow-starting evolution that is finally coming of age. Progress came slowly at first, because safety technology was something new. Automakers had to be

convinced that there was a market for this kind of technology, and then we had to convince the public that they should buy it."[64]

A series of shocks within the industry also pushed the evolution, Lund pointed out. The first came in the 1960s and 1970s when automakers, with their years of experience and technical expertise in producing cars, were told by government and "a bunch of consumer advocates" how to make cars. "That was certainly a big cultural change." Today, he added, there are still "issues with developing new regulations, but it is no longer warfare. It is more of a vigorous discussion."[65]

Within the companies, Lund said another important change has taken place. Where marketing officials, with their eye on style and horsepower, had once carried the major weight on production issues, "The safety engineers within the automobile companies have more of a say now. And so they get heard."[66]

THE FUTURE

In evaluating the future of the federal automobile safety program, including the development of new safety standards and the effectiveness of safety recalls, several factors are in play.

NHTSA has always had fewer resources than it needed. It has fallen even further behind in recent decades, receiving only about one percent of the Department of Transportation budget to police the entire United States motor vehicle fleet.[67] And the fleet is changing fast. Only about 18 percent of NHTSA's $248 million annual budget is used for vehicle safety. Highway safety grants to the states account for about 66 percent; research on driver behavior about 14 percent.

In 1980, there were 161 million vehicles on the road and 119 NHTSA people working on safety enforcement. In 2012, there were 266 million vehicles on the roads, but the number of people working on investigating and correcting possible defects had shrunk to fifty-seven. It has remained at that number for about ten years.

NHTSA's current budget for vehicle safety enforcement is less than eight cents per registered vehicle. NHTSA has never had its own testing facility. It leases space from Honda.[68]

The safety agency currently is authorized to have a total of just over six hundred full-time positions to oversee one of the largest industries in the world.[69] It lost more than three hundred engineers and other staff in budget cutbacks made in the Reagan administration years.[70] It never got them back, despite the skyrocketing number of vehicles on the roads.

It has often been proven politically impossible to obtain the funding and legislative authorization for NHTSA to hire the skilled engineering and investigatory staff necessary to keep up with the increasingly complex problems of vehicle safety. The gap becomes most obvious in the development of new standards. It is also evident in the defect investigation process as evidenced by the agency's inability to deal effectively with the Toyota sudden unintended acceleration and GM Chevy Cobalt ignition recalls.[71]

The nation's only vehicle safety "cop" was sharply criticized, by the usually supportive members of the Senate Commerce Committee in the fall of 2014, for delay and "incompetence" in its investigations of automobile safety defects, including the General Motors ignition investigation.[72] Consumer groups testifying at the hearing said that NHTSA is "grossly underfunded" and understaffed to do its "daunting task" of assuring the safety of the 266 million motor vehicles currently used by Americans.[73]

NHTSA's acting administrator David J. Friedman, replied that agency personnel were inadequate to keep up with vehicle technology and "firewall" defensive tactics of companies with much greater resources, such as GM and others.[74]

According to a former administrator who has followed the agency closely since its inception, "The industry repeatedly lobbies the House and Senate Appropriations committees to cut NHTSA's budget and keep it that way. They are usually quite successful."[75]

NHTSA has also demonstrated an unfortunate inclination toward secrecy. The 2000 TREAD Act required the Early Warning Reporting (EWR) system. Manufacturers are required to promptly report evidence of deaths or serious injuries to the agency. NHTSA has opened hundreds of investigations using this system. But unlike "formal" NHTSA investigations, these indicators of possibly dangerous vehicles on the roads are not regularly made public, nor are they as informative as to the causation of the incidents as they should be. NHTSA has the power to remove much of the secrecy in the Early Warning system by regulation, without the need for intervention by Congress.

The EWR data appears to be the type of federal information that President Obama's Open Data Initiative of December 2009 directed federal agencies to make public. The directive says agencies must "publish information online in an open format that can be retrieved, downloaded, indexed, and searched by commonly used web search applications."[76] Instead, important EWR safety information is now hidden within the files of NHTSA and labeled "business secret." It is available to the public only through the slow and often expensive process of Freedom of Information Act requests to the agency, or the courts.

Keeping safety information from the public, regardless of how it is labeled by manufacturers, prevents consumers from obtaining data on real-world performance and safety. It limits public analysis of safety reports. Posting NHTSA Early Warning reports and other defect information in digital form would allow its examination by the public, outside experts, and the press. It could reduce some of NHTSA's person-power shortage, by allowing individuals outside of government to review and comment on possible safety defects.

THE ROLE OF CONGRESS

Since 1966, federal motor vehicle safety standards and federally subsidized state highway safety standards have performed an invaluable service to Americans. They have saved *hundreds of thousands* of lives. They could do much more.[77]

Congress can, if it chooses, foster more effective vehicle safety progress. It can end off-the-record political interference with the government safety agency. It can limit the "revolving door" of personnel to and from industry to NHTSA. It can limit the degree of secrecy of potentially life-threatening defect information submitted by manufacturers to NHTSA. It can substantially increase civil penalties for failure to provide timely and accurate safety reports to the government and add criminal penalties for persons and corporations intentionally violating the Safety Act. Whether Congress will accomplish these things and whether the safety agency implements them will only be determined by their actions in the future. The payoff would be saving many of the nearly 100 lives, 400 serious injuries, and two billion taxpayer dollars lost *every* day in motor vehicle crashes.

NOTES

1. 49 USC 30101—Purpose and Policy. "The purpose of this chapter is to reduce traffic accidents and deaths and injuries resulting from traffic accidents. Therefore it is necessary (1) to prescribe motor vehicle safety standards for motor vehicles and motor vehicle equipment in interstate commerce."

2. *Traffic Safety Facts, 2012*, NHTSA, inside cover; DOT HS 812 069 (2015), "Lives Saved by Federal Motor Vehicle Standards, 1960–2012."

3. "2013 Safety Overview," Advocates for Highway and Auto Safety, Washington D.C., January 2014, Review of State Highway Safety Laws.

4. DOT, NHTSA, "*The Economic and Societal Impact of Motor Vehicle Crashes—2010*, DOT HS 812 013 (May 2014). See also, NHTSA Report, http://www-nrd.nhtsa.dot.gov/Pubs/812032.pdf (2014).

5. The basis of our cost-benefit estimate is as follows: The cost off all federal safety standards was estimated by DOT/NHSTA to be $839 per car in 2001 (see DOT HS 809 834). Adjusting for inflation through 2014 and 33 percent and adding 50 percent per car to account for new standards adopted since 2001 (such as roof strength, ejection prevention, and stability control), we estimate the added safety cost in 2014 dollars to be $1,700. Since about 16.5 million new vehicles were sold in 2014, the total cost to buyers was $28 billion. The economic and societal costs to society were estimated by DOT/NHSTA to be $871 billion in 2010 (see DOT/HS 812 013, "The Economic and Societal Impact of Motor Vehicle Crashes, 2010"), including avoided loss of life, injuries, medical costs, industrial down time, and property damage. The ratio of costs to society each year of $871 billion divided by estimated annual costs of vehicle safety technologies of $28 billion is a cost-benefit ratio of approximately 30 to 1.

Alternatively, if the number of crash deaths in 2010, which were 33,000, were at the 1966 level of 51,000 per year, we would be experiencing 18,000 more crash deaths per year today. The societal costs of $871 billion in 2010 would have increased to $1,346 billion associated with 51,000 crash deaths. The $1,346 billion would be an increase of $475 billion over the $871 billion in 2010. Thus the ratio of annual savings due to the laws and regulations by 2010 over the costs of safety standards would have been the additional costs to society of $475 billion divided by the estimated vehicle costs of $28 billion. This would be a benefit to society ratio of more than 15 to 1.

6. A summary of fifty-four current major Federal Motor Vehicle Safety Standards, applicable to passenger vehicles is found in appendix A.

7. Mashaw and Harfst, *The Struggle for Auto Safety*, 147. The authors question whether the Congress that passed the tough 1974 amendments to the Act, reinforcing the agency's recall powers, was about to "multiply the agency's regulatory budget by a factor that would make it a match for the industry's full court press (against) rule-making proceedings."

8. See testimony of Cary Coglianese, professor of law, University of Pennsylvania, before the Senate Committee on the Judiciary, November 7, 2013 at 2–4, furnishing a summary of judicial intervention in NHTSA rulemaking, even under the limited review authority provided by Congress in the Administrative Procedure Act. Coglianese suggests other reasons for the NHTSA slowdown, such as recent complicating amendments to the Administrative Procedure Act's supposedly "informal" processes, as well as the industry's superior technical capability and greater resources; see also, *Chrysler v. DOT*, 472 F.2d 659 (6th Cir. 1972) at 676 remanding the passive restraint rule to NHTSA because the specifications of a test dummy were not included in the rule; see testimony of professor Thomas O. McGarity before the Senate Judiciary Committee, November 7, 2013: "Overly Aggressive Judicial Review," 9, referring to the "hard look" doctrine most courts now apply to NHTSA rules.

9. See chapter 11 for a discussion of the 2014 GM Cobalt ignition defect recall.

10. Roof Crush standard: issued 38 F.R. 21930 (August 14, 1973), amended 74 F.R. 22384 (2009), FMVSS 216a; Electronic Stability Control standard: proposed rule issued 72 F.R. 17310 (April 6, 2007), final rule effective 77 F.R. 760 (January 6, 2012) FMVSS 126; Ejection Mitigation standard, final rule effective 78 F.R. 55138 (September 6, 2011), FMVSS 226.

11. The decline of alcohol-related deaths, and related costs from 21,000 deaths in 1981 to 10,000 in 2011, must be attributed to tougher state laws (triggered by federal actions) relating to: 1) the minimum legal drinking age, and 2) drunk driving prevention through court-imposed sanctions and driver education. The National Minimum Age Drinking Act sponsored in 1984 by senators Frank Lautenberg and Richard Lugar and signed by President Reagan, makes 21 the minimum drinking age in all 50 states. All states also have driving laws limiting the lawful blood-alcohol level of drivers to 0.08 percent, based on NHTSA guidelines and federal funding incentives. See 23 U.S.C. 158; *Governors Highway Safety Association* (2014). In contrast, after mandatory motorcycle helmet laws were repealed in Texas, Arkansas, Kentucky, Florida, Pennsylvania, and Michigan between 1993 and 2012, deaths of motorcyclists not wearing helmets increased sharply. Alastair Dant and Hannah Fairfield, "Fewer Helmets, More Deaths," *New York Times*, March 31, 2014.

12. Michael Winerip, "What's Tab Turner Got Against Ford?" *New York Times*, December 17, 2000, SM 49, 87.

13. See chapter 11 for a discussion of the earlier Firestone "500" tire recall.

14. Interview by the author with Tab Turner, May 30, 2012; Michael Winerip, "What's Tab Turner Got Against Ford?" *New York Times*, December 17, 2000, SM 49, 87; Adam L. Penenberg, *Tragic Indifference: One Man's Battle with the Auto Industry over the Dangers of SUVs* (New York: HarperCollins, 2003) 12, 14–18.

15. Winerip, "What's Tab Turner Got Against Ford?" *New York Times*, December 17, 2000, 49; Penenberg, *Tragic Indifference*, 12.

16. The Transportation Recall Enhancement, Accountability and Documentation (TREAD) Act, 49 USC 30101–30170 (2000). The implementation of the TREAD Act has been criticized because of NHTSA's failure to make all consumer complaints about safety-related defects involving deaths and serious injuries available to the public. See, testimony of Joan Claybrook, President, Public Citizen, before the Senate Committee on Competition, Foreign Commerce and Infrastructure, June 3, 2004.

17. NHTSA data show that since 1978 there have been more than 350,000 rollover deaths in all types of vehicles, including SUVs, sedans, vans, and light trucks of all makes and models. Since 2002 there have been more than 50,000 deaths in SUV rollovers. NHTSA data cited in *Care For Crash Victims* (December 2013), http://www.careforcrashvictims.com/assets/MRDec-AmericanVictims.pdf. See also NHTSA, Traffic Safety Facts 2012, DOT HS 813 032, 2014, table 23, 60.

18. Winerip, "What's Tab Turner Got Against Ford?" *New York Times*, December 17, 2000, SM 49.

19. Keith Bradsher, "Explorer Model Raises Doubts About Safety," *New York Times*, April 26, 2001.

20. Ibid.

21. "Rollover: The Hidden History of the SUV," *Frontline* (original airdate February 21, 2002, #2013) by Marc Shaffer and Barak Goodman, https://vimeo.com/59514384

22. Memorandum to the author from Adrian Lund, President, Insurance Institute for Highway Safety (May 27, 2014): "It is likely this decline in rollover deaths reflected the increasing inclusion of occupant protection features like ESC and frontal air bags, coupled with the advantage that SUVs on average weigh more (than other passenger vehicles)."

23. See appendix B for a listing of sources of consumer information on crash avoidance and other safety technologies.

24. Statement of Clarence Ditlow, Executive Director, Center for Auto Safety, "Delays in NHTSA Rulemaking," before the Senate Judiciary Committee, Subcommittee on Oversight, November 7, 2013

25. For a summary of the thirty-five-year struggle to upgrade the Roof Strength standard, see paper by Laura MacCleary, director of Congress Watch, Public Citizen, www.citizen.org/Roof Crush, "Roof Crush Update."

26. David Shepardson, "NHTSA Roof Crush Rules Will Cost Up to $1.4 Billion Annually," *Detroit News*, May 5, 2009.

27. Danny Hakim, "Ford and Volvo at Odds Over Roof Strength," *New York Times*, May 14, 2005.

28. Ibid.

29. David Shepardson, "Senators Press NHTSA on Roof-Crush Rules," *Detroit News*, June 5, 2008. See also, Justin Hyde, "SUVs Need Stronger Roofs, Group Says," *Detroit Free Press*, March 12, 2008.

30. Cindy Skrzycki, "Stricter Roof Crush Rule Hits a Road Block," *Washington Post*, June 17, 2008.

31. Ibid.

32. David Shepardson, "Senators Press NHTSA on Roof-Crush Rules," *Detroit News*, June 5, 2008. See also Hearings Before Senate Commerce Committee, June 5, 2008.

33. Ibid.; see Statement of Public Citizen by Lena Pons (April 30, 2009), "New Roof Crush Standard Falls Short," http://www.nhtsa.gov/About+NHTSA/Press+Release2009/U.S.+DOT+Doubles+Roof+Strength+Standard+for+Light+Vehicles,+Announces+First+Ever+Standards+for+Heavier+Vehicles.

34. Statement of Adrian Lund, President, Insurance Institute for Highway Safety, "Roof Strength is Focus of New Rating System," Insurance Institute for Highway Safety, News Release, March 24, 2009; http://www.iihs.org/iihs/news/desktopnews/roof-strength-is-focus-of-new-rating-system-4-of-12-small-suvs-evaluated-earn-top-marks

35. Electronic Stability Control, FMVSS 126, 72 Fed. Reg.17310 (April 6, 2007).

36. NHTSA has evaluated, but has never mandated, ABS braking systems. It concluded that "When used properly ABS is a safe and effective braking system." See NHTSA, "Questions and Answers Regarding Antilock Brake Systems," www.nhtsa.gov/cars/problems/equipment/absbrakes.html.

37. "Understanding Electronic Stability Control," J.D. Power, February 24, 2012; http://autos.jdpower.com/content/consumer-interest/VXn50Sx/understanding-electronic-stability-control.htm

38. Martin Zimmerman, "Car Stability Rule is Proposed," *Los Angeles Times*, September 15, 2006, 19; http://articles.latimes.com/2006/sep/15/business/fi-stability15.

39. Ibid.

40. Ibid.

41. Ibid.

42. http://www.nhtsa.gov/Laws+&+Regulations/Electronic+Stability+Control+%28ESC%29.

43. David Shepardson, "Officials Mandate Anti-Rollover Rule," *Detroit News*, April 6, 2007, http://faculty.wwu.edu/dunnc3/rprnts.antirolloverregulation.pdf; David Shepardson, "Officials Mandate Anti-Rollover Rule," *Detroit News*, April 6, 2007, http://faculty.wwu.edu/dunnc3/rprnts.antirolloverregulation.pdf.

44. Insurance Institute for Highway Safety (cited in *"Care for Crash Victims"*), www.careforcrashvictims.com (February 2013); see NHTSA, Traffic Safety Facts 2012, table 23, p. 60 at http://www-nrd.nhtsa.dot.gov/Pubs/812032.pdf.

45. Warren Brown, "A Rule to Require What We're Already Buying," *Washington Post*, Sept. 24, 2006, http://www.washingtonpost.com/wp-dyn/content/article/2006/09/22/AR2006092200577.html

46. Interview by the author with Edward B. Cohen, vice president, Honda Motor Cars, Inc. by telephone, April 25, 2014, formerly Seante Commerce Committee staff counsel.

47. Robert L. Carter, associate administrator, Motor Vehicle Programs (National Highway Traffic Safety Administration 1972), paper presented before the Second International Conference on Passive Restraints, May 22–25, 1972, 37.

48. David Bollier and Joan Claybrook, *Freedom from Harm* (Public Citizen and the Democracy Project, Washington, DC, 1986), 83–84.

49. National Traffic and Motor Vehicle Safety Act, 49 U.S. Code, Section 30168 (a)(1)(B), "The Secretary of Transportation shall conduct research, testing, development and training (which) shall include obtaining experimental and other motor vehicles . . . for research or testing."

50. Rob Cirincione, "Innovation and Stagnation in Automotive Safety and Fuel Economy," Center for Study of Responsive Law, Washington D.C., 2006, 64.

51. "The Safe Fuel Efficient Car, A Report on its Producibility and Marketing," National Highway Traffic Safety Administration, October 1980, 33–34; and see, Donald E. Struble, Vice President of Engineering, Minicars Inc., "Highlights of the Minicars' RSV Program," June 6, 1979, https://www.dropbox.com/sh/gglmy)rifwaoj11/tp9_fwRq, 3.

52. GM and at least one contractor, KARCO, may still own two restored RSVs. http://www.autosafety.org/destruction-research-safety-vehicle-rsvhttp://www.autosafety.org/category/categories/video-archive/research-safety-vehicle-rsv.

53. Donald Friedman, Center for Injury Research, "The Mini Cars RSV—Still a Car for the Future," (paper # 09-0480, 2009) before the Enhanced Safety of Vehicles Conference, June 15–18, 2009 Stuttgart, Germany. http://www-nrd.nhtsa.dot.gov/pdf/esv/esv21/09-0480.pdf

54. Interview by the author with Donald Friedman, March 14, 2014, 11. To earn "Five Stars" from the New Car Assessment Program (NHTSA's NCAP testing program) cars must crash safely at 35 miles per hour.

55. National Highway Traffic Safety Administration, "Vehicle Safety and Fuel Economy Rulemaking and Researching Priority Plan" (2011–2013), published March 2011, www.nhtsa.gov.

56. Thomas O. McGarity, professor of Administrative Law, University of Texas Law School, "Justice Denied: Rules Delayed on Auto Safety," Testimony before the Senate Judiciary Committee, November 7, 2013, 2–3.

57. P.L. 93-492.

58. P.L. 102-240.

59. P.L. 105-178.

60. P.L. 106-414.

61. P.L. 107-318.

62. P.L. 109-59.

63. P.L. 110-189.

64. Interview by the author with Adrian Lund, president, Insurance Institute for Highway Safety, May 8, 2014, 5–7.

65. Ibid.

66. Ibid.

67. $77 billion was requested by the agency for 2014; $53 billion of it for "highway, transit and highway safety programs." U. S. Department of Transportation, Budget Highlights, Fiscal Year 2014, 2, http://www.dot.gov/budget/dot-budget-highlights-fiscal-year-2014.

68. Statement of Clarence M. Ditlow, Executive Director, Center for Auto Safety, "Toyota Sudden Unintended Acceleration," before the Senate Commerce, Science, and Transportation Committee, March 2, 2010.

69. National Highway Traffic Safety Administration, *Fiscal Year 2014 Budget Overview*, http://www.nhtsa.gov/staticfiles/administration/pdf/Budgets/NHTSA-FY2014_Budget_Overview-041013.pdf, accessed June 24, 2013.

70. On the reduction in NHTSA staff from 1980 to 2012, see Martin Albaum, "Safety Sells" (unpublished manuscript), http://safetysells.org/chapter5.pdf, 103 and compare NHTSA 2014 Budget Overview, 20.

71. See chapter 11, for an analysis of the Toyota and GM Cobalt proceedings.

72. Hearings, Senate Commerce Committee, Subcommittee on Consumer Protection, Product Safety and Insurance, September 16, 2014.

73. Testimony of Jackie Gillan before the Senate Commerce Committee, Subcommittee on Consumer Protection, Product Safety and Insurance, September 16, 2014.

74. Ibid. See also Hiroko Tabuchi, "Air Bag Flaw, Long Known to Honda and Takata, Led to Recalls," *New York Times*, September 11, 2014; Hilary Stout, Danielle Ivory, Rebecca R. Ruiz, "Regulator Slow to Respond to Deadly Vehicle Defects, *New York Times*, September 14, 2014; Center for Auto Safety, "NHTSA and Takata Strike Deadly Deal To Limit Air Bag Inflator Recall," June 25, 2014, www.autosafety.org, (criticizing NHTSA's judgment in agreeing to a "regional recall" only of defective Honda air bags allegedly due to high humidity conditions); Karl Brauer, contributor, "Takata Airbag Recall Could Dwarf GM and Toyota Recalls," *Forbes*, September 15, 2014. http://onforb.es/1qDWKd6.

75. Telephone interview by the author with Joan Claybrook, November, 15, 2013.

76. "Open Government Directive," December 8, 2009, 2. http://www.whitehouse.gov/open/documents/open-government-directive, accessed May 19, 2013.

77. Volvo and the Swedish government have set a "Vision Zero" goal for no automobile deaths or serious injuries in their cars by 2020. They are pursuing it with new crash-avoidance technologies. See, Paul A. Eisenstein, "Death-Free Highways Have Become A real Possibility," *The Detroit Bureau*, August 22, 2014 http://www.thedetroitbureau.com/2014/08/death-free-highways-have-become-a-real-possibility/. According to Adrian Lund, president of the Insurance Institute for Highway Safety, Vision Zero is "an attainable goal." Interview by the author with Adrian Lund, May 8, 2014.

Epilogue

A Hard Road to Travel

The nation has lived through over one hundred years of the equivalent of war between the automobile industry, safety advocates, and the government. It was long. It was painful. It cost a lot of lives and dollars along the way. It has not ended yet.

What have we learned about ourselves and our country from the bloody struggle for safer motor vehicles and highways? That is the question raised by this book and the history of the past century.

One cannot read that history without concluding that effective safety regulation, forged among public advocates, government, and, finally, the automobile industry has worked. It has saved not thousands but millions of American people from death and injury. It has saved billions of taxpayer's and individual's dollars. Effective safety regulation in cooperation with citizens and the automobile industry can do much more in the future.

It is often hard to get big things done in this country. It is even harder to remember how they were done. But some basic facts about automobile safety are now clear:

Automobiles and driving are safer today than they were at the dawn of the car culture and throughout much of the twentieth century. The rates of deaths and injuries, down 77 percent from 1966 and the overall cost to our society, now $871 billion a year according to the Department of Transportation, have both *decreased* sharply from what they would have been without safety regulation and programs. Over 600,000 lives have been saved by federal safety standards and related action since 1966.

Yet the United States has fallen behind other nations in national fatality rate rankings. Australia, England, France, Sweden, and six other nations have death rates that are lower than the United States.

Despite our progress in vehicle safety, until the revolutionary decade of the 1960s, a blind eye was often turned on the mounting epidemic of automobile accident victims. That earlier era remains an indelible blot on our history.

By any measure, the big leap in motor vehicle and highway safety came with the enactment of the National Traffic and Motor Vehicle Safety Act and the Highway Safety Act in 1966. It came over the determined opposition of much of the automotive industry. And it ultimately caused a major shift in public attitudes favoring safety and the value of buying a safer car. That shift has continued, sometimes sporadically, to the present day. It has changed the collective minds of the automobile industry toward engineering and selling safety.[1]

The progress is by no means complete. Vehicles and driving are nowhere near as safe as they could be. Beyond the now-proven methods of building more crashworthy vehicles and recalling unsafe ones, there still are new and old safety threats confronting the nation's drivers, passengers, and pedestrians.

Younger drivers tend to speed and drive more recklessly. Crashes involving teenage drivers resulted in over 4,600 deaths in 2012. Stronger state laws requiring graduated licensing, supervised driver training, mandatory driver education, and a reduction of the legally permissible blood-alcohol level would reduce that toll.[2]

Although the rates are lower in recent years, drunk driving continues to claim about 10,000 lives a year. On average a person convicted of drunk driving has driven drunk eighty-seven times before being convicted.[3] Engine interlock systems that prevent a car from starting when a driver's blood-alcohol level exceeds the legal limit are now technologically proven, but are required *after* a DUI conviction in only twenty states.[4] The National Transportation Safety Board has called for the states to lower the maximum legal blood-alcohol level from 0.08 to 0.05 percent. Thirty other nations have already done this. Why not the United States? It might not solve the massive drinking-and-driving problem, but it would surely help reduce it.

A new threat to safety on the roadways is caused by distracted driving. This is a growing challenge for safety advocates, the automobile industry, the states, and NHTSA. It may have been one of the causes of a surprising and worrisome reversal in the long downward trend of automobile deaths in 2012. They rose over 5 percent to about 33,000 deaths that year. Texting while driving has become a deadly habit. Ironically, the same new electronic and computer technologies that can be designed to protect drivers and passengers (through systems like crash avoidance and lane-change warning) may be causing drivers to become too focused on complex electronic entertainment and communication systems, rather than on careful driving. NHTSA has expressed alarm over the dangers of distracted driving and issued nonenforceable guidelines. But so far that is about all it has done.

The public has shown year after year that it wants and will pay for safer cars and safety technology. The cost will be more than paid back in the annual savings from avoided and less deadly crashes. Just a glance at current automobile advertising proves manufacturers now believe that safety sells cars.

We have come a long way in automobile and highway safety in the decades from 1966 to the present. From 5.5 deaths for each 100 million miles driven, down to 1.13 deaths. That is a dramatic improvement. The 33,500 deaths in 2012 are still way too many, but that is a big change from the 51,000 lives lost in 1966, a reduction achieved despite many more cars on the roads and miles driven today.

While still incomplete, automotive safety today represents a major national achievement. It is a success story for federal and state safety laws and for the public, which has supported them. It is a success story for the unsung heroes who made it happen. It is a success story for a long-ago Congress and the public and private advocates who led in the enactment of the first federal motor vehicle and highway safety laws, and for the Supreme Court of thirty years ago, whose opinion in 1983 in the State Farm case blocked President Ronald Reagan's attempt to terminate the federal air bag rule. That court's words live on: "For nearly a decade," the Justices said, "the automobile industry has waged the equivalent of a war against passive restraints and lost."

Much of the last six decades of progress might not have occurred absent a stunning policy decision by casualty-insurance industry leaders. They turned on a dime and formed a safety alliance with Ralph Nader and consumer–public health organizations. They took the automobile industry and the Reagan administration to the Supreme Court over the cancellation of the air bag rule—and amazingly they won.

Looking back over a century of an often bitter struggle, how did this progress happen? How was a public safety victory snatched from the jaws of half a century of endless defeat? What aroused the American public and changed the automobile industry's collective mind?

At least four things triggered the creation and successes of federal (and state) motor vehicle and highway safety programs and the turnaround in public opinion about safety.

- The public learned what happens inside a car in a crash and the reasons why people die in preventable crashes and "second collisions," inside their own vehicles. That understanding fueled a new public attitude and a demand for safer cars.
- The media got involved; automobile safety issues stayed alive long enough for the public to react and for the political process to work.
- A continuing public advocacy presence, led by consumer and insurance organizations over many years, avoided total capture of the regulatory process by economically and politically powerful interests. In the words of the safety law's chief sponsor, senator Warren Magnuson, they "kept the big boys honest."
- The Congress, at least for a while, adequately funded and supported NHTSA.

All of these things, together with some startling blunders by General Motors and its private detectives in trailing young Nader, played the major role in forcing action at the national level. State action in most states followed, often triggered by federal mandates and money. These forces have continued over the years to mandate and promote safer cars and roads. This kind of progress, while still incomplete, does not happen easily under a political system like ours. It does not happen without crushing defeats along the way.

We are reminded of the words of Union soldiers in the midst of the seemingly endless, bloody Civil War. They sang the now-forgotten ballad, "Richmond is a Hard Road to Travel I Believe. . . ." as they marched wearily on toward victory. So too is democracy a hard road to travel. In time it can be traveled, just as it was in the successful, but still incomplete, fight to save lives in automobiles and on our highways.

NOTES

1. See Interviews by the author with Michael Stanton, president, Global Automakers; Adrian Lund, president, Insurance Institute for Highway Safety, supra.
2. Advocates for Highway and Auto Safety, "Annual Roadmap of State Highway Safety Laws," Washington, D.C., 2014, 24.
3. Ibid., 27.
4. Ibid., 6.

Appendix A

Major Federal Motor Vehicle Safety Standards (As of February 2011)

SUMMARY[1]

All vehicle safety standards (FMVSS) are written in terms of minimum performance requirements. The 100 series of standards are for prevention and mitigation of crashes. The 200 series are for prevention and mitigation of death injury in crashes. The 300 series are for prevention and mitigation of injuries after a crash occurs. The system was created by NHTSA using Dr. William Haddon's initial [1964] safety matrix designed to address the prevention and mitigation of injuries before, during, and after a crash.

Standard 101 — Controls and Displays

Performance requirements for location, identification, color and illumination of motor vehicle controls and indicators to assure accessibility, visibility, and recognition by drivers under both day and night conditions.

Standard 102 — Transmission Shift Sequence

Requirements for transmission shift sequence (P, R, N, D) starter interlock and braking effect of automatic transmissions to reduce likelihood of shifting errors and prevent starting when transmission is in drive position.

Standard 103 — Windshield Defrosting and Defogging

Requirements for windshield defrosting and defogging, to provide visibility for the driver.

Standard 104 — Windshield Wiping and Washing Systems

Requirements for windshield washing and wiping systems to ensure they cover a specified area of the windshield with at least two speeds.

Standard 105 — Hydraulic and Electric Brake Systems

Requirements to assure safe braking performance in all vehicles under normal conditions and emergency conditions.

Standard 106 — Brake Hoses

Establishes performance and labeling requirements for brake hoses, assemblies, and brake hose fittings for motor vehicles in order to reduce brake system failure.

Standard 108 — Lamps and Reflective Devices

Requirements for original and replacement headlights, lamps, and reflectors to reduce traffic accidents by providing adequate roadway illumination and conspicuity of motor vehicles on roads in daylight and darkness and conditions of reduced visibility.

Standard 110 — Tire Selection and Rims

Requirements for original equipment and replacement tire selection to prevent overloading.

Standard 111 — Rear View Mirrors

Requirements for performance and location of rear view mirrors to ensure a clear and reasonably unobstructed view to the rear for the driver.

Standard 113 — Hood Latch System

Requires all passenger motor vehicles to provide a safety hood latch system to prevent hood opening while the vehicle is in motion.

Standard 114 — Theft Protection

Specifies vehicle performance requirements to reduce theft and accidental rollaway of motor vehicles.

Standard 116 — Motor Vehicle Brake Fluids

Sets requirements for brake fluids for use in hydraulic brake systems to reduce failures in braking system.

Standard 117 — Retreaded Pneumatic Tires

Sets performance, labeling, and certification requirements for re-treaded passenger car tires to meet safety criteria similar to new passenger car tires.

Standard 118 — Power Operated Windows and Roofs

Specifies requirements for power-operated windows, partitions, and roof panels to minimize likelihood of death or injury from accidental operation.

Standard 121 — Air Brake Systems

The standard establishes performance requirements for trucks, buses, and trailers using air brake systems to ensure safe braking under normal and emergency conditions.

Standard 122 — Motorcycle Brake Systems

Specifies equipment and performance for braking systems of motorcycles to ensure safe braking performance under normal and emergency conditions.

Standard 123 — Motorcycle Controls and Displays

Specifies location, operation, identification, and illumination of motorcycle controls and displays to minimize accidents caused by operator error.

Standard 124 — Accelerator Control Systems

Sets requirements for the return of a vehicle's throttle to the idle position when driver removes his or her foot from the accelerator pedal.

Standard 125 — Warning Devices

Establishes requirements for separate emergency warning signals used to warn approaching traffic of a stopped vehicle. Applies to trucks and buses over 10,000 lbs.

Standard 126 — Electronic Stability Control (ESC)

Establishes requirements for newly required electronic stability control systems to reduce loss of directional control in crashes and rollover crashes.

Standard 131—School Bus Pedestrian Safety Devices

Requirements for devices that can be installed on school buses to improve safety of children and other pedestrians in the vicinity of stopped school buses.

Standard 135—Light Vehicle Brake Systems

Specifies requirements for service and parking brake systems to ensure safe braking performance under normal and emergency driving conditions.

Standard 138—Tire Pressure Monitoring Systems

This newly adopted standard sets performance requirements for tire pressure monitoring systems to warn drivers of under-inflation of tires and resulting safety problems.

Standard 139—Radial Tires

Specifies tire dimensions, test requirements, label requirements, and defines tire load ratings for radial tires for use on passenger vehicles and light trucks.

Standard 201—Occupant Protection in Interior Impact

Performance requirements for padding and other interior protection to minimize injury to occupants upon impact.

Standard 202—Head Restraints

Requirements for design and performance of head restraints to reduce frequency and severity of neck injury in rear-end and other collisions.

Standard 203—Impact Protection for Driver from Steering Control System

Requirements for performance of steering control systems to minimize chest, neck, and facial injuries to the driver as a result of crash impact.

Standard 204—Steering Control Rearward Displacement

Specifies requirements limiting rearward displacement of steering column and controls into passenger compartment to reduce likelihood of chest, neck, or head injury.

Standard 205 — Glazing Materials

Specifies requirements for glazing materials used in motor vehicles to reduce injuries from impact with the windshield and other glazed surfaces, to ensure necessary transparency for driver visibility, and to minimize the possibility of occupants being ejected through vehicle windows.

Standard 206 — Door Locks and Door Retention

Specifies requirements for passenger car door locks, latches, and hinges to minimize likelihood of doors opening and passengers being ejected as a result of impact.

Standard 207 — Seating Systems

Sets requirements for seats, their attachment assemblies, and installation to minimize possibility of failure as the result of vehicle impact.

Standard 208 — Occupant Crash Protection (Active and Passive Restraints)

Sets performance crashworthiness requirements for protection of vehicle occupants in crashes. Specifies vehicle crashworthiness limits in terms of forces measured on crash test dummies. Applies to cars and other passenger motor vehicles.

Standard 209 — Seat Belt Assemblies

Sets requirements for seat belt assemblies such as straps, buckles, and hardware designed to secure occupants of motor vehicles in order to mitigate the results of crashes. Applies to passenger motor vehicles, trucks, and buses.

Standard 210 — Seat Belt Assembly Anchorages

Establishes requirements for seat belt anchorages to ensure their proper location for effective occupant restraint in the event of crashes. Applies to passenger motor vehicles, trucks, buses, and school buses.

Standard 212 — Windshield Mounting

Establishes windshield retention requirements for windshields of passenger and other motor vehicles in crashes, to reduce ejection from the vehicle.

Standard 213 — Child Restraint Systems

Sets requirements for child restraint systems used in most motor vehicles and aircraft to reduce the number of children killed or injured in crashes.

Standard 214 — Side Impact Protection

Sets performance requirements for protection of vehicle occupants in side impacts with another vehicle or object. The purpose is to reduce serious and fatal injury in side impacts by specifying strength requirements for side doors and other vehicle structures, and limiting forces, as measured on crash test dummies, by other means such as air bags.

Standard 216 — Roof Crush Resistance

Establishes strength requirements, now 3.5 times the vehicle weight for passenger compartment roofs, to reduce deaths and injuries due to the crushing of the roof into the occupant compartment in rollover crashes. Applies to passenger cars (except convertibles), trucks, and buses (except school buses) of 10,000 lbs. or less.

Standard 217 — Bus Emergency Exits and Window Retention

Establishes requirements for window retention and opening dimensions, operating forces, and markings for emergency exits. Applies to buses (including school buses).

Standard 218 — Motor Cycle Helmets

The standard establishes minimum performance requirements for motorcycle helmets to reduce death and injury resulting from head impacts. Applies to all helmets designed for use by motorcycle users.

Standard 220 — School Bus Rollover Protection

Establishes performance requirements for bus structure to reduce likelihood of death and injury in school bus rollover crashes.

Standard 221 — School Bus Body Strength

Establishes requirements for strength of body panel joints in school buses to reduce likelihood of death and injury resulting from structural collapse during crashes.

Standard 222 — School Bus Passenger Seating and Crash Protection

Establishes occupant protection requirements for school bus passenger seating and restraining barriers to reduce likelihood of death and injury from impact with bus interior during crashes and sudden driving maneuvers.

Standards 223 and 224 — Truck and Trailer Rear Impact Guards and Protection

Set requirements for rear impact guards for trailers and semi-trailers and required installation to reduce likelihood of death and injury from rear-end collisions by passenger and light vehicles with trailers.

Standard 225 — Child Restraint Anchorage Systems

Requirements for anchorage systems for child restraints to ensure proper location, installation, and strength in crashes. Applies to cars, trucks, multipurpose passenger vehicles, and school buses with a weight rating of 10,000 lbs. or less.

Standard 226 — Ejection Mitigation

Establishes requirements for ejection mitigation to reduce the likelihood of ejection of occupants through side windows during rollovers or side impact crashes.

Standard 301 — Fuel System Integrity

Specifies requirements for integrity of motor vehicle fuel systems to reduce death and injury from fires resulting from fuel spillage during and after motor vehicle crashes. Applies to passenger vehicles, light trucks, and buses (10,000 lbs. or less).

Standard 302 — Flammability of Interior Materials

Specifies burn resistance requirements for materials used in occupant compartments of passenger vehicles in order to reduce death and injury caused by vehicle fires, including fires caused by matches or cigarettes. Applies to cars, multipurpose passenger vehicles, trucks, and buses.

Standard 401 — Interior Trunk Release

Establishes a requirement for providing an emergency release mechanism inside the trunk compartment of passenger cars, to permit persons trapped to escape the compartment. Applies to passenger cars with trunk compartment.

NOTE

1. The summarized standards apply to passenger motor vehicles, SUVs, passenger vans, and pickup trucks, unless otherwise specified in the text. See the complete summary in DOT HS 811 439 (February 2011) and the full text at 49 C.F.R. Part 571. Other regulations, such as manufacturer certification of compliance, vehicle indentation (VIN) numbers, and compliance labeling of vehicles are found in 49 C.F.R. Parts 523–595.

Appendix B

Sources for Passenger Motor Vehicle Safety Information

The following is a partial list of easy-to-access places (usually on the Internet) where a car owner or prospective buyer can obtain information on a vehicle's safety rating and comparisons with similar vehicle makes and models. There is a great deal of comparative rating and testing information at your fingertips.

1. **National Highway Traffic Safety Administration.** NHTSA, through its studies and documents, publishes vast amounts of safety materials. Its authoritative website lists government safety standards for all motor vehicles, current and past recall information, as well as comparative test information. NHTSA, the U.S. government's safety and testing agency, under its New Car Assessment Program (NCAP), rates the safety performance of most currently available makes and models and compliance with all existing federal safety standards. See http://wwwsafercar.gov.

2. **Insurance Institute for Highway Safety (IIHS).** IIHS is the nonprofit safety testing and analysis organization funded by the U.S. insurance industry. It tests many currently available vehicles for crashworthiness, crash-avoidance, and crash-mitigation performance. For crashworthiness IIHS rates tested vehicles as "good, acceptable, marginal, or poor" based on five crash tests. The tests are: 1) moderate front overlap, 2) small front overlap, 3) side impact, 4) roof strength, and 5) head restraints. Some of these tests supplement and expand on the government required tests for vehicle safety crashworthiness.

   - In the area of crash avoidance and mitigation, IIHS tests and rates vehicles with available front crash prevention systems. The crash-avoidance ratings are: "basic, advanced, or superior."
   - IIHS issues two safety awards: the "Top Safety Pick" and the "Top Safety Pick+" based on its tests of crashworthiness and crash-avoidance safety features.
   - In 2014, IIHS awarded "Top Safety Pick" ratings to vehicles that earned good or acceptable ratings in all crashworthiness tests. "Top Safety Pick+" ratings were awarded to vehicles

that, in addition to earning a "Top Safety Pick" rating for crashworthiness results, also earned a basic, advanced, or superior rating for frontal crash prevention. See http://www. iihs.org/iihs/ratings.

3. *Consumer Reports* **magazine and Consumers Union**. This outstanding consumer publication periodically reports on its own and other organizations' testing of the safety performance of a broad range of U.S. passenger vehicles, including such considerations as NHTSA and IIHS crash tests and predicted reliability of the vehicle (based on annual reader surveys). In rating vehicles for safety and other performance factors, *Consumer Reports* uses symbols representing "excellent, very good, good, fair, or poor." Potential purchasers can find most currently available cars rated and can compare the safety and performance of different models. The website includes buying recommendations and ratings for both new and used cars. See http://www.consumerreports.org.

4. **The Center for Auto Safety**. The Center was founded by Consumers Union and Ralph Nader in 1970. It is currently headed by Clarence Ditlow. Its magazine and website offer information on major safety issues, current safety recalls, state lemon laws, and manufacturer service campaigns, including many major safety-defect investigations by NHTSA. The Center has been at the forefront of motor vehicle–consumer safety issues, both in government agencies and in the courts for decades. See http://www.autosafety. org.

5. *The Car Book*. This annual volume offers a wealth of safety, fuel economy, warranty, and maintenance information regarding vehicle ownership and purchasing. *The Car Book* also rates currently available makes and models using independent and government crash testing (including frontal, side, and side pole crashes). It furnishes its own combined crash test rating system. *The Car Book* can be obtained through the Center for Auto Safety, 1825 Connecticut Ave., N.W., Washington, D.C. 20009-5708. It is written by safety expert Jack Gillis in cooperation with the Center.

Interviews by the Author

Interview with Isaac D. Benkin Esq., National Transportation Safety Board/Federal Highway Administration legal staff (1967–1974), May 22–June 3, 2013, by email.

Interviews with Joan Claybrook, former administrator, National Highway Traffic Safety Administration, November 16 and 30, 2011.

Interview with Edward B. Cohen, former staff counsel, Senate Commerce Committee, Vice President, Honda Motor Cars, Inc., April 25, 2014.

Interviews with Clarence Ditlow, executive director, Center for Auto Safety, June 4 and 25, 2013.

Interview with Elizabeth H. Dole, former Secretary of Transportation, January 19, 2013.

Interview with Donald Friedman, president, Minicars, Inc., March 14, 2014.

Interview with Henry Hamburger, professor emeritus and chair, Department of Computer Science, George Mason University. Confirmed by memorandum to author, May 11, 2012.

Interview with Gene Haddon, January 14, 2015.

Interview with Ben Kelley, former senior vice president, IIHS, January 17 and September 15, 2013.

Interview with Louis Lombardo, January 2, 2013, former Research Scientist, National Highway Traffic Safety Administration.

Interview with Adrian Lund, President, IIHS, May 8, 2014.

Interview with Morton Mintz, formerly *Washington Post*, February 12, 2012.

Interviews with Ralph Nader, October 1, 2012 and December 12, 2013.

Interview with Carl E. Nash, former senior staff, National Highway Traffic Safety Administration, adjunct professor, George Washington University, January 9, 2013.

Interview with Joseph A. Page, professor of law, Georgetown University Law School, May 26, 2014.

Interview with Donald A. Randall, formerly counsel Senate Judiciary Committee, January 3, 2013.

Interview with Allison Sinrod, February 8, 2012.

Interview with Michael Stanton, President, Association of Global Automakers, August 28, 2013.

Interview with litigation attorney Tab Turner Esq., May 30, 2012.

Interview with Sergeant Timothy Whelan, Massachusetts State Police, Yarmouth Barracks, June 7, 2012.

Bibliography

Albaum, Martin. "Safety Sells." Unpublished manuscript available on the Internet at http://www.safetysells.org.
"Annual Roadmap of State Highway Safety Laws." Advocates for Highway and Auto Safety, Washington, D.C., 2014.
Armaghan, Sarah, and Ehab Zahriyeh. "Cape Cod Car Crash Kills Recent Yale University Graduate." *New York Daily News*, May 27, 2012.
"Auto Defects." Center for Auto Safety. http://www.autosafety.org/auto-defects, accessed May 19, 2013.
"Congress Studies Automotive Industry, Related Issues." *Congressional Quarterly Almanac* (1968): 682.
"Auto Makers Sue on Safety Rules." *United Press International*, April 1, 1967.
"Auto Safety." *Congress and the Nation*, Vol. II, Congressional Quarterly (1970): 804.
"Auto Safety Code Row Looms," *Associated Press*, January 2, 1967.
"Auto Safety Official Has Kick Coming," *Associated Press*, November 27, 1966.
Ayres Jr., Drummond. "Haddon at the Wheel." *New York Times*, April 2, 1967.
————. "Nader Charges Safety Agency Shows Timidity." *New York Times*, March 22, 1967.
Baker, Phil. "Documents Contradict Testimony in Toyota Unintended Acceleration Case." *San Diego Daily Transcript*, March 25, 2013.
Bollier, David, and Joan Claybrook. *Freedom From Harm: The Civilizing Influence of Health, Safety and Environmental Regulation*. Public Citizen and the Democracy Project, Washington, D.C., 1986.
Buckhorn, Robert F. "Motorists Beset Haddon with All Kinds of Gripes." *United Press International*, June 12, 1967.
Bradsher, Keith. "Explorer Model Raises Doubts About Safety." *New York Times*, April 26, 2001.
Brandon, Henry. "One Man Who Mattered." *Science Magazine* (May 28, 1966): 9.
Brown, Warren. "A Rule to Require What We're Already Buying." *Washington Post*, September 24, 2006.
"Business Leaders Back Car Makers on Safety Issue." *New York Times*, May 14, 1966.
Buss, Dale. "Toyota Plots Brand Rehab." *Brand Channel*, June 3, 2010.
Calmes, Jackie. "Minding the Minders of GM." *New York Times*, April 5, 2014.
Cantor, Eric, Paul Ryan, and Kevin McCarthy. *Young Guns*. New York: Simon & Schuster, 2010, 113.
"Car Industry Consent to Federal Standards for Vehicle Safety Causes Mixed Response." *Wall Street Journal* (April 27, 1966): 5.
"Car Makers Blamed in Highway Deaths." *New York Times*, October 3, 1958, 56.
"Carmakers Stung by Rash of Recalls." *United Press International*, April 17, 1983.
Carter, Susan B., Scott Sigmund Gartner, and Michael R. Haines, et al., eds. *Historical Statistics of the United States*, millennial ed., vol. 4. Cambridge, UK: Cambridge University Press, 2006.
"CAS Reveals Internal NHTSA Files on Cobalt Ignition Airbag Defect." Press Release, March 7, 2014. www.autosafety.org, accessed March 11, 2014.
Cirincione, Robert. "Innovation and Stagnation in Automotive Safety and Fuel Economy." Center for Study of Responsive Law, Washington, D.C., 2006.
Claybrook, Joan. "The Airbag Issue: Whether and When." *Washington Post*, September 1, 1976.

Claybrook, Joan, and the Staff of Public Citizen. *Retreat from Safety: Reagan's Attack on America's Health.* New York: Pantheon Books, 1984.

"Congress Acts on Traffic and Auto Safety." *Congressional Quarterly Almanac* (1966): 266.

Cordtz, Dan. "The Face in the Mirror at General Motors." *Fortune,* August 1966, 117, 210.

"Cornell Gets Grant of $150,000 to Study Auto Crash Injuries." *New York Times,* September 15, 1958, 23.

Corrigan, Richard. "Behind the 'Chrome Curtain.'" *Washington Post-Times Herald,* February 21, 1966.

Crain, Keith, ed. "An Easy Solution to Recall Compliance." *Automotive News,* June 30, 2014. http://www.autonews.com/article/20140630/OEM11/306309986/an-easy-solution-to-recall-compliance.

Dant, Alastair, and Hannah Fairfield. "Fewer Helmets, More Deaths." *New York Times,* March 31, 2014, 12.

"Death on the Highways." *Journal of the American Medical Association* 163, no. 4 (January 26, 1957).

DeHaven, Hugh. "Mechanical Analysis of Survival in Falls." *War Medicine* 2 (July 1942): 586–96.

Ditlow, Clarence; quoted in *Huffington Post,* May 29, 2012, http://www.huffingtonpost.com/2012/05/28/yale-student-marina-keegan-dies-dead-graduation_n_1550673.html.

"Doctor Wages War on Traffic Deaths." *United Press International,* November 24, 1977.

Dole, Bob, and Elizabeth Dole. *The Doles: Unlimited Partners.* New York: Simon and Schuster, 1988.

"Dole Touts Air Bags As U.S. Fights Them." *Washington Post,* April 10, 1983, quoted in Graham, *Assessing America's Performance,* 162.

Dorsey, Michael "Stirring the Pot." *WPI Journal* (Summer 1997). http://www.wpi.edu/News/Journal/Summer97/pot.html

DOT, HS 809 833. "Lives Saved by the Federal Motor Vehicle Safety Standards and Other Vehicle Safety Technologies, 1960–2002." National Highway Traffic Safety Administration, Washington, D.C., 2004.

DOT HS 809 834. "Cost and Weight Added by the Federal Motor Vehicle Safety Standards, 1968–2001." National Highway Traffic Safety Administration, Washington, D.C., December 2004.

DOT, NHTSA. "The Safe, Fuel-Efficient Car: A Report on Its Producibility and Marketing." National Highway Traffic Safety Administration Report, October 1980.

Dowie, Mark. "Pinto Madness." *Mother Jones,* September 1, 1977. http://www.motherjones.com/politics/1977/09/pinto-madness, accessed May 19, 2013.

"Dr. Haddon Under Fire." *New York Times,* February 5, 1967.

Drew, Elizabeth. "The Politics of Auto Safety." *The Atlantic* (October 1966): 95.

Eastman, Joel W. *Styling Versus Safety: The American Automobile Industry and the Development of Automotive Safety, 1900–1966.* Lanham, MD: University Press of America, 1984.

Eberstadt, Nicholas N. "Daniel Patrick Moynihan, Epidemiologist." In *An Intellectual in Public Life.* Washington, D.C.: Woodrow Wilson Center Press, 44, 47.

"Evolving Public Narrative of Unintended Acceleration." Quality Control Systems Corp. Accessed 4/17/13, http://www.quality-control.us/evolving_narrative.html.

"Federal Program on Traffic Safety to Curb Deaths Seen." *Washington Post,* September 26, 1962, A-1.

"Firestone Defends Radial 500 Tire as Safe, Reliable." *Los Angeles Times,* August 9, 1978.

Flink, James J. *The Automobile Age.* Cambridge, MA: MIT Press, 1988.

———. *The Car Culture.* Cambridge, MA: MIT Press, 1976.

"For Federal Auto Registration." *New York Times,* December 6, 1908. ProQuest Historical Newspapers.

"The Ford Pinto Fuel Tank." Center for Auto Safety. http://www.autosafety.org/ford-pinto-fuel-tank, accessed 5/19/2013.

"47 New Safety Proposals for Motor Vehicles Listed." *Associated Press,* October 13, 1967.

Frisbee, John L. "The Track to Survival." *Air Force Magazine,* May 1983, 54.

Furnas, J. C. "And Sudden Death." *Reader's Digest,* August 1935.

GAO Report CED-76-121, p. ii, cited in House Subcommittee on Oversight and Investigations of the Committee on Interstate and Foreign Commerce, U.S. Government Accountability Office, *Federal Regulation and Regulatory Reform,* 94th Cong., 2nd Sess. October, 1976, 169.

Gawande, Atul. "Slow Ideas." *The New Yorker,* July 29, 2013, 36. http://www.newyorker.com/reporting/2013/07/29/130729fa_fact_gawande.

General Motors. "Ed Cole: Father of the Small Block." *100 Millionth Small Block,* General Motors media, http://media.gm.com/content/autoshows/smallblock/2011/public/us.

Gikas, Paul W. "Crashworthiness as a Cultural Ideal." In *The Automobile and American Culture,* edited by David L. Lewis and Lawrence Goldstein. Ann Arbor: University of Michigan Press, 1983.

Gillis, Jack. *The Car Book 2014.* Washington D.C.: Center for Auto Safety, 2014.

Gladwell, Malcolm. "Wrong Turn: How the Fight to Make America's Highways Safer Went Off Course." *New Yorker,* June 11, 2001, 60.

"GM Says Ahead of Previously Announced Target for 2014 Profit, Excluding Recall Costs." www.reuters.com/assets/print?aid=USWEN00DFC20140605.

"GM Says It Spent $193 million in 1964 on Automobile Safety." *Wall Street Journal* (July 19, 1965): 5.

Graham, John D. *Auto Safety: Assessing America's Performance.* Dover, MA: Auburn House Publishing Co., 1989.

Greider, William. "Your Life May Not Be Worth Saving." *Washington Post,* April 9, 1972.

Greiling, Angela, and Mark Clothier. "Chrysler Gives in on Fixing Jeeps." *Bloomberg,* June 19, 2013.

Grush, E. S. and C. S. Saunby. "Fatalities Associated with Crash Induced Fuel Leakage and Fires." *The Center for Auto Safety,* http://www.autosafety.org/uploads/phpq3mJ7F_FordMemo.pdf

"Haddon is Sworn in Capital as Traffic Safety Director." *Associated Press,* October 21, 1966.

Haeusler, Roy. "The Automotive Safety Engineer and Company Policies." *Journal of the Society of Automotive Engineers* (September 1956): 44.

Hakim, Danny. "Ford and Volvo at Odds Over Roof Strength." *New York Times,* May 14, 2005.

Hearings before the Senate Commerce Science and Transportation Committee, 95th Congress, 1st Sess., March 29, 1977.

Hirsch, Jerry. "NHTSA Launches Probe Into Cobalt Recall, GM Issues Another Apology." *Los Angeles Times,* February 27, 2014.

Hoffman, W. Michael. "Case Study: The Ford Pinto." 1982. http://businessethics.qwriting.qc.cuny.edu/files/2012/01/HoffmanPinto.pdf, accessed May 19, 2013.

Holsendolph, Ernest. "Lobbyist for Nader to Head Safety Unit." *New York Times,* March 19, 1977.

"House Passage of Automobile Safety Bill Near." *Chicago Daily Defender,* July 27, 1966, 6.

House Subcommittee on Oversight and Investigations, Committee on Interstate and Foreign Commerce, *Federal Regulation and Regulatory Reform,* 94th Cong., 2nd Sess. October, 1976.

"House Unit Urges U.S. Highway Code." *Christian Science Monitor,* January 7, 1957, 5.

"How Controversial Auto was Developed." *Chicago Tribune,* October 13, 1979.

Iacocca, Lee. *Iacocca: An Autobiography.* New York: Bantam Books, 1988.

Ingrassia, Paul. *Crash Course: The American Automobile Industry's Road from Glory to Disaster*. New York: Random House, 2010.

Insurance Institute for Highway Safety. "Air Bags: A Chronological History of Delay." Washington, D.C., 1984.

———. "Auto Safety: Assessing America's Performance." IIHS Status Report 25, no. 6. June 30, 1990.

———. "Implementation of the National Traffic and Motor Vehicle Safety Act of 1966."

———. "Is a Recall by Any Other name still a Recall?" *New York Times*, October 22, 2003.

Isidore, Chris. "Chrysler refuses to recall 2.7 million Jeep SUVs." *CNN Money*, June 5, 2013, http://money.cnn.com/2013/06/04/autos/chrysler-recall-refusal.

Israel, Fred L. *State of the Union Messages of the Presidents: 1790–1966*. New York: Chelsea House Publishers, 1967.

Jensen, Cheryl. "Safety Agency Says 22 million Vehicles Recalled in 2013." *New York Times*, February 3, 2014.

Jensen, Christopher. "Consumer Group Calls Chrysler's Jeep Fix Inadequate." *New York Times*, June 20, 2013.

———. "General Motors Recalls, Inaction and a Trail of Fatal Crashes." *New York Times*, March 2, 2014.

———. "U.S. Inquiries Over Automobile Safety Dragging On." *New York Times*, February 22, 2013.

Johnson, Steven. *The Ghost Map: The Story of London's Most Terrifying Epidemic and How It Changed Science, Cities, and the Modern World*. New York: Penguin Group, 2006.

Johnston, Moira. "Hell on Wheels." *New West*, May 9, 1978, 29.

Kam, Allan J. "NHTSA Safety Defect Investigations." Presentation at the Association of Trial Lawyers of America 2001 Annual Convention, Product Liability Section, Montreal, Canada, July 17, 2001. http://www.htsassociates.com/NHTSA_safety_defect_investigations.shtml, accessed May 19, 2013.

Karr, Albert R. "Former Consumerists Now in Agencies Find Jobs Frustrating." *Wall Street Journal*, December 15, 1977.

Katz, Harold A. "Liability of Automobile Manufacturers for Unsafe Design of Passenger Cars." *Harvard Law Review* 69 (1956): 863.

Keegan, Marina. *The Opposite of Loneliness: Essays and Stories*. New York: Scribner, 2012.

Kelley, Ben. "GM and the Air Bag: A Decade of Delay." Insurance Institute for Highway Safety, Status Report, June 25, 1980.

Kent, Richard W. *Air Bag Development and Performance: New Perspectives from Industry, Government, and Academia*. Warrendale, PA: Society of Automotive Engineers, Inc., 2003.

Koerth-Baker, Maggie. "How to Move a Mind." *New York Times Magazine*, August 19, 2012.

Kowalke, Ron. *Old Car Wrecks*. Iola, WI: Krause Publications, 1997.

Kramer, Larry. "Claybrook Faults Auto Firms on Safety." *Washington Post* , October, 26, 1978.

———. "Driving For Safety." *Washington Post*, June 16, 1978.

———. "58% Favor Passive Restraints: Seat Belts Ignored by Public." *Washington Post*, August 31, 1978.

Kurylko, Diane. "Ford Had A Better Idea in 1956, But it Found That Safety Didn't Sell." *Automotive News*, June 26, 1996. http://www.autonews.com/article/19960626/ANA/606260836/ford-had-a-better-idea-in-1956-but-it-found-that-safety-didnt-sell, accessed May 7, 2014.

Lemov, Michael R. *People's Warrior: John Moss and the Fight for Freedom of Information and Consumer Rights* (Madison, NJ: Fairleigh Dickinson University Press/Lanham, MD: Rowman & Littlefield Publishing Group, Inc., 2011).

Linebaugh, Kate, and Dionne Searcey. "Cause of Sudden Acceleration Proves Hard to Pinpoint." *Wall Street Journal*, February 25, 2010.

Linshi, Jack. "All the Cars GM Has Recalled This Year Would Wrap the Earth 4 Times." *Time*, July 1, 2014, http://time.com/2945867/gm-recalls-facts/

"List of Motor Vehicle Safety Hazards." *New York Times*, November 23, 1966.

Lombardo, Louis. "Vision of a Safer America." (12-18-08). http://www.careforcrashvictims.com, accessed 5/23/2012.

MacLennan, Carol A. "From Accident to Crash: The Auto Industry and the Politics of Injury," *Medical Anthropology Quarterly* 2, no. 3 (September 1988): 233–37.

Macness, James. "Auto Safety Plan Offered." *Baltimore Sun*, May 13, 1966, 6.

Mantle, Jonathan. *Car Wars: Fifty Years of Greed, Treachery, and Skulduggery in the Global Marketplace*. New York: Arcade Publishing, 1995.

Martin, Justin. *Nader: Crusader, Spoiler, Icon*. New York: Perseus Books, 2002.

Mashaw, Jerry L., and David L. Harfst. *The Struggle for Auto Safety*. Cambridge, MA: Harvard University Press, 1990.

Mintz, Morton. "Capitol Reading." *Washington Post*, March 29, 1966, A14.

———. "GM's Goliath Bows to David." *Washington Post*, March 27, 1966, A-7. ProQuest Historical Newspapers.

———. Nader Sees Signs of Auto Safety Lag, Suspects Intimidation of U.S. Agency." *Washington Post*, January 24, 1967.

———. "Nader Raps GM, Ford on Faulty Seatbelts," *Washington Post*, April 26, 1966, A-1.

———."Stieglitz Quits Auto Safety Job After Reading Standards for '68." *Washington Post*, February 3, 1967.

Mohn, Tanya. "Safety First, True Once, But U.S. Now Lags in Road Deaths." *New York Times*, July 22, 2007.

Morris, Crawford. "Motor Vehicle Safety Regulation: Genesis," *Law and Contemporary Problems* (Summer 1968): 542.

Morris, John D. "Car Makers Said to Delay Safety." *New York Times*, June 4, 1966, 1.

———. "Nader Sees Signs of Auto Safety Lag, Suspects Intimidation of U.S. Agency." *Washington Post*, January 24, 1967.

———. "Safety Chief Has Pedal Trouble; He and Ford Agree It's a 'Freak.'" *New York Times*, November 26, 1966.

———. "U.S. Will Relax Standards for Auto Safety Padding." *New York Times*, May 26, 1967.

Moynihan, Daniel P. *Coping: Essays on the Practice of Government*. New York: Random House, 1974.

———. "Epidemic on the Highways." *The Reporter*, April 30, 1959, 17.

———."The War Against the Automobile." *In the Public Interest* 3 (Spring 1966): 13.

"Nader Calls Former Aide a Cowardly Defector." *Chicago Tribune*, December 1, 1977.

Nader, Ralph. "Detroit Makes Your Choice: Fashion or Safety." *Nation*, October 12, 1963, 214.

———. "The Safe Car You Can't Buy," *The Nation*, April 11, 1959, 214.

———. "Safer Cars: Time for Decision." *Consumer Reports*, April 1966, 195.

———. *Unsafe at Any Speed: The Designed-In Dangers of the American Automobile*. New York: Bantam Books/Grossman, 1972.

"New Car Dealers Say Quality and Safety Are Top Considerations with Customers." IIHS Status Report 1, June 30, 1990.

"1967 Passenger-Car Engineering Trends." *Journal of the Society of Automotive Engineers* 44, no. 11 (1967): 33.

NHTSA, Office of Defects Investigation. "2013 Annual Recall Report. Chart: Quantity of Vehicles Recalled 1993–2013."

———. "Questions and Answers Regarding Antilock Brake Systems." www.nhtsa.gov/cars/problems/equipment/absbrakes.html, accessed March 21, 2014.

———. *The Economic and Societal Impact of Motor Vehicle Crashes—2010*. DOT HS 812 013 (May 2014).

———. Technical Report, "Lives Saved by the Federal Motor Vehicle Safety Standards and Other Vehicle Safety Technologies, 1960–2002." DOT HS 809 833, October, 2004.

———. *Traffic Safety Facts, 2010.* "Crashes by Severity, 1988–2010," table 1, at 16.

———. *Traffic Safety Facts, 2012.*

———."Vehicle Safety and Fuel Economy Rulemaking and Research Priority Plan for 2011–2013." Published March 2011. www.nhtsa.com.

O'Connell, Jeffrey, and Arthur Myers. *Safety Last: An Indictment of the Auto Industry.* New York: Random House, 1966.

O'Neill, Brian. "Accidents: Highway Safety and William Haddon, Jr." *Contingencies,* January/February 2002, 30.

Ostrow, Ronald J. "Some Details of Eased Auto Safety Rules Told." *Los Angeles Times,* February 1, 1967.

Pearson, Drew. "Auto Safety Pressure Rises." *Las Angeles Times,* January 24, 1967.

Pearson, Drew, and Jack Anderson. "Heat Put on Auto Safety Boss." *Washington Post,* January 24, 1967.

Penenberg, Adam L. *Tragic Indifference: One Man's Battle with the Auto Industry over the Dangers of SUVs.* New York: HarperCollins, 2003.

Pertschuk, Michael. *Revolt Against Regulation: The Rise and Pause of the Consumer Movement.* Berkeley: University of California Press, 1982.

"Police Release 911 Tape in Deadly SoCal Crash." *Associated Press,* September 11, 2009.

Pryne, Eric. "Maggie's Legacy Is More than Money." *Seattle Times,* May 22, 1989.

"Regulators Hired by Toyota Helped Halt Acceleration Probes." *Bloomberg,* March 13, 2010.

Reynolds, Barbara. "Auto Safety Chief's Rocky Ride." *Chicago Tribune,* August 27, 1978.

Ridgeway, James. "The Dick." *New Republic,* March 12, 1966.

Robertson, L. S. "Groundless Attack on an Uncommon Man: William Haddon Jr., MD," *Injury Prevention* (2001): 7:261.

"Roof Strength is Focus of New Rating System." Insurance Institute for Highway Safety, News Release. March 24, 2009.

Rose, Michael. "The Birth of the Muscle Car: The Pontiac GTO at 50." *The Detroit Bureau,* May 13, 2013. www.thedetroitbureau.com.

Rugaber, Walter. "Defect Publicity Angers Industry." *New York Times,* November 23, 1966.

———. "3 Car Makers Say They Can't Meet Safety Deadline." *New York Times,* January 4, 1967.

"Safety Group Asks Limit on Power of Automobile Engines." *The Christian Science Monitor,* February 19, 1937, 2.

"Safety Standard on '68 Cars Eased." *Associated Press,* August 13, 1967.

Salpukas, Agis. "G.M. Head Denies Engine Mount Peril." *New York Times,* October 29, 1971.

Scates, Shelby. *Warren G. Magnuson and the Shaping of Twentieth-Century America.* Seattle: University of Washington Press, 1998.

Schwartz, Gary T. "The Myth of the Ford Pinto Case." *Rutgers Law Review* 43 (1990–1991): 1013.

"See Safety Over Cars Easing." *Associated Press,* February 12, 1967.

"Senate Confirms Haddon as Road Safety Director." *Associated Press,* October 15, 1966.

Shephardson, David. "Officials Mandate Anti-Rollover Rule." *Detroit News,* April 6, 2007.

———. "Senators Press NHTSA on Roof-Crush Rules." *Detroit News,* June 5, 2008.

Shepardson, David, and Christine Tierney. "Panel Says NHTSA, Toyota Fell Short Investigating Acceleration Complaints." *Detroit News,* February 23, 2010. http://detnews.com?AUTO01/2230357.

Shidle, Norman G., ed. "Looking at the Future of Car Design." *Journal of the Society of Automotive Engineers* (January 1937): 13–14.

Simon, Bernard, and Jonathan Sable. "Toyota Recovers after Accelerator Remedy." *Financial Times,* February 3, 2010.

Sinclair, Ward. "A Head-On Collision: Nader Angrily Denounces a Former Ally." *Washington Post,* December 1, 1977.

"16 Safety Rules Endorsed by G.M." *Associated Press,* January 1, 1967.

"'68–'69 Cars Flunk Six Tests." *Associated Press,* November 11, 1969.

Skeler, Jeffery . "Why the Alarming Surge of Auto recalls?" *Afro-American,* March 18, 1978.

Sky, Theodore. *The National Road and the Difficult Path to Sustainable National Investment.* Newark: University of Delaware Press, 2011.

Skrzycki, Cindy. "Stricter Roof Crush Rule Hits a Road Block." *Washington Post,* June 17, 2008.

"State Drunk Driving Laws." Governors Highway Safety Association. http://www.ghsa.org/html/stateinfo/laws/impaired_laws.html.

Stetson, Damon. "High-Power Cars Defended By GM." *New York Times,* August 28, 1956, 29.

Stevens, Arthur W. *Highway Safety and Automobile Styling.* Boston, MA: Christopher Publishing House, 1941.

Stieglitz, W. I. "A Note on Crashworthiness." Sherman Fairchild Publication Fund Preprint No. 266, *Institute of the Aeronautical Sciences,* January, 1950.

Stout, Hilary. "As GM Unveils Its Payout Plan, Recalls Expand." *New York Times,* July 1, 2014.

Stout, Hilary, Danielle Ivory, and Matthew L. Wald, "Auto Regulators Dismissed Defect Tied to 13 Deaths." *New York Times,* March 8, 2014, 1.

Straith, Claire L., M.D. "Guest Passenger Injuries." *Journal of the American Medical Association* (May 22, 1948): 348.

Strobel, Lee. "Dead Girls' Mother Testifies: Pinto Recall Letter Arrived Too Late." *Chicago Tribune,* January 17, 1980.

———. "Ford Ignored Pinto Fire Peril, Secret Memos Show." *Chicago Tribune,* October 13, 1979.

———. "Pinto Blew Up 'like big napalm bomb': Witness." *Chicago Tribune,* January 18, 1980.

Sullivan, Gail. "Toyota Settles with Government for $1.2 Billion in Recall Probe." *Washington Post,* March 19, 2014.

Struble, Donald E. "Highlights of the Minicars' RSV Program," June 6, 1979, https://www.dropbox.com/sh/gglmy)rifwaoj11/tp9_fwRq, 36.

"Text of Speech by Head of National Traffic Safety Agency at Auto Industry Dinner." *New York Times,* November 30, 1966.

Thomas, Bob. "Safety Standards Author Denies Being Impractical." *Los Angeles Times,* February 19, 1967.

Toomey, Tracy L., Tobin F. Nelson, and Kathleen M. Lenk. "The Age-21 Minimum Legal Drinking Age: A Case Study." *Addiction,* 2009.

"Toyota Makes another Global Recall." Zacks Equity Research, November 16, 2012.

"Toyota Motor Corp. Will Pay Record $17.35 Million in Civil Penalties for Alleged Violations of Federal Law." National Highway Traffic Safety Administration press release, December 18, 2012.

"Toyota Shareholders Sue Over Stock Price Drop." *Associated Press,* March 21, 2010.

"Traffic Danger Factors Listed by House Group." *New York Times,* January 8, 1957, 18.

"Traffic Safety Head: William Haddon Jr.; Man in the News Pays for Own Safety Long Service with State" *New York Times,* September 10, 1966.

"Understanding Electronic Stability Control." J.D. Power, McGraw Hill Financial. http://autos.jdpower.com, February 24, 2012.

U.S. Department of Transportation National Highway Traffic Safety Administration. "An Analysis of the Significant Decline in Motor Vehicle Traffic Fatalities in 2008." June 2010, DOT HS 811 346, 27.

U.S. Department of Transportation National Highway Traffic Safety Administration. *Federal Motor Vehicle Safety Standards and Regulations* http://www.nhtsa.gov/cars/rules/import/fmvss/index.html#SN101, accessed February 5, 2013.

"U.S. Law on Safe Car Construction Seen." *New York Times*, August 4, 1956, 14.

U.S. Senate Committee on Commerce, *The Implementation of the National Traffic and Motor Vehicle Safety Act of 1966*, 90th Cong., 1st Sess., March 20–21, 1967, 154–57.

Vernick, Jon S., Julie Samia Mair, Stephen P. Teret, and Jason W. Sapsin, Johns Hopkins Bloomberg School of Public Health. "Role of Litigation in Preventing Product-Related Injuries," *Epidemiologic Reviews* 25 (2003): 90, http://epirev.oxfordjournals.org/.

Vlasic, Bill. "An Engineer's Eureka Moment With a GM Flaw," *New York Times*, March 28, 2014.

Vlasic, Bill, and Matt Apuzzo. "Toyota Is Fined 1.2 Billion for Concealing Safety Defects." *New York Times*, March 19, 2014.

Vlasic, Bill and Hilary Stout. "Auto Industry Galvanized After Record Recall Year." *New York Times*, December 31, 2014, A-1.

Wall Street Journal, Market Data Center, U.S. Auto Sales, December 3, 2013 (accessed December 12, 2013) http://wap.wsj.com/mdc/public/page/2_3022-autosales.html.

"Wayland Woman Dies in Dennis Car Crash." *Boston Globe*, May 26, 2012.

Weber, Naomi. "The Doctor's Prescription for Motoring." *Saturday Review*, March 2, 1957, http://www.unz.org/Pub/SaturdayRev-1957mar02-00048.

"What Future for Auto Safety?" *New York Times*, February 8, 1969.

White, Lawrence J. *The Automobile Industry Since 1945*. Cambridge, MA: Harvard University Press, 1971.

Whitman, Marina von Neumann. *The Martian's Daughter: A Memoir*. Ann Arbor: The University of Michigan Press, 2012.

Wilson, Timothy D. *Redirect: The Surprising New Science of Psychological Change*. New York: Little Brown and Co., 2011.

Winerip, Michael. "What's Tab Turner Got Against Ford?" *New York Times*. December 17, 2000, SM 49.

Young, David. "Automobile Air Bags: How Much is Highway Safety Worth?" *Chicago Tribune*, September 5, 1976.

Zimmerman, Mark. "Car Stability Rule is Proposed." *Los Angeles Times*, September 15, 2006, 9.

Index

About the Author

During his career with the Congress, **Michael R. Lemov** served as counsel to the subcommittees on Commerce and Finance, and Oversight and Investigations of the House Commerce Committee. As counsel to the House Commerce Committee, he participated in writing the Motor Vehicle Safety Act Amendments of 1964. He was chief counsel to the Oversight subcommittee in its evaluation, under chairman John E. Moss of California, of the motor vehicle safety laws and the performance of the National Highway Traffic Safety Administration.

Prior to his service on the House Commerce Committee, Mr. Lemov was counsel to the House Banking and Currency Committee under its chairman Wright Patman of Texas. He was appointed by president Lyndon Johnson as general counsel of the National Commission on Product Safety and was a trial attorney with the U.S. Department of Justice.

Subsequent to his government service, Mr. Lemov practiced law in the private sector, representing private and public clients, primarily in product safety and motor vehicle safety matters.

Mike Lemov is also the author of *People's Warrior: John Moss and the Fight for Freedom of Information and Consumer Rights* (2011) and the *Consumer Product Safety Commission Regulatory Manual* (1983).

He was appointed to the Maryland Consumer Advisory Council by governor Martin O'Malley in 2009 and served for five years. Mike is a graduate of the Harvard Law School and Colgate University. He resides with his wife, journalist Penelope Lemov in Bethesda, Maryland. His children, Rebecca and Douglas, are both authors.